An APEC Trade Agenda?

The **APEC Business Advisory Council (ABAC)** was created by the APEC Leaders in 1995 to advise APEC on the implementation of its agenda and provide the business perspective on specific areas of cooperation. ABAC comprises of up to three members from each of APEC's 21 member economies representing a range of business sectors. ABAC holds an annual dialogue with the APEC Leaders and regular discussions with APEC ministers in charge of trade, finance and other economic matters. For more details visit http://www.abaconline.org.

The **Pacific Economic Cooperation Council (PECC)** is one of the Asia-Pacific's most influential organizations. Since its foundation in 1980 it has been a policy innovator in trade, finance, information technology and capacity-building, among others. PECC brings together leading thinkers and decision-makers from government and business in an informal setting to discuss and formulate ideas on the most significant issues facing the Asia-Pacific. PECC is the only non-government official observer in APEC.

The **Institute of Southeast Asian Studies (ISEAS)** was established as an autonomous organization in 1968. It is a regional centre dedicated to the study of socio-political, security and economic trends and developments in Southeast Asia and its wider geostrategic and economic environment. The Institute's research programmes are the Regional Economic Studies (RES, including ASEAN and APEC), Regional Strategic and Political Studies (RSPS), and Regional Social and Cultural Studies (RSCS).

ISEAS Publishing, an established academic press, has issued almost 2,000 books and journals. It is the largest scholarly publisher of research about Southeast Asia from within the region. ISEAS Publishing works with many other academic and trade publishers and distributors to disseminate important research and analyses from and about Southeast Asia to the rest of the world.

An APEC Trade Agenda?

The Political Economy of a Free Trade Area of the Asia-Pacific

EDITED BY

Charles E. Morrison
and **Eduardo Pedrosa**

ABAC pecc

A Joint Study by the Pacific Economic
Cooperation Council and the APEC
Business Advisory Council

ISEAS

INSTITUTE OF SOUTHEAST ASIAN STUDIES
SINGAPORE

First published in Singapore in 2007 by ISEAS Publishing
Institute of Southeast Asian Studies
30 Heng Mui Keng Terrace
Pasir Panjang
Singapore 119614

E-mail: publish@iseas.edu.sg
Website: http://bookshop.iseas.edu.sg

ISEAS Library Cataloguing-in-Publication Data

An APEC trade agenda? : the political economy of a free trade area of the Asia-Pacific / edited by Charles E. Morrison and Eduardo Pedrosa.
  1. Free trade—Asia.
  2. Free trade—Pacific Area.
  3. Asia—Commercial policy.
  4. Pacific Area—Commercial policy.
  I. Morrison, Charles E. (Charles Edward), 1944–
  II. Pedrosa, Eduardo.
  II. Title: Free trade area of the Asia-Pacific

HF1733 A8A83   2007
ISBN 978-981-230-460-5 (soft cover)
ISBN 978-981-230-461-2 (PDF)

Typeset by Superskill Graphics Pte Ltd
Printed in Singapore by Seng Lee Press Pte Ltd

Contents

List of Tables

List of Figures

1

An APEC Trade Agenda

Charles E. Morrison

I. INTRODUCTION

The papers in this report are the results of a study undertaken through the
PECC with sponsorship from the APEC Business Advisory Committee
(ABAC). As the result of agreement between the ABAC and the PECC, it
was agreed that the study should look at the political feasibility of a
proposal to establish a Free Trade Area of the Asia-Pacific (FTAAP) as well
as alternatives that APEC could take to promote greater regional trade and
investment. The authors were selected by the two parties, and since
proponents and opponents of the FTAAP were included there was no
unanimous consensus within the study group regarding the FTAAP issue.
This overview reviews the current economic context, reviews the arguments
both for and against an FTAAP, makes an evaluation regarding its political
feasibility, and sketches out an outline for an APEC 2010 Trade Agenda
that the author regards as a more realistic and still ambitious approach to
trade liberalization, but not inconsistent with the FTAAP as a possible
longer-term objective.

II. THE ECONOMIC CONTEXT

By standards of any other region of the world, the Asia-Pacific region is doing very well. A number of its economies, especially China and Vietnam, are achieving extraordinary growth. The performance of the U.S. economy has continued to confound pessimists, and Japan, for long the weak performer of the region, is now experiencing solidly based growth. Moreover, inflation remains low, despite commodity and fuel price spikes. Trade and investment continues to boom around the region. Since the 1994 Bogor Goals were set, trade barriers have continued to go down, with average tariffs lower in all of the sub-regions of the Asia-Pacific.[1] Moreover, despite some protectionist sentiments in some parts of the region, the APEC economies adhere to their World Trade Organization (WTO) obligations. The WTO system enjoys high favour and continues to attract additional membership by Asia Pacific Economic Cooperation process (APEC) economies. China became a WTO member in 2001, Vietnam joined in 2006, and Russia is also seeking WTO membership.

Despite these successes, the APEC economies face numerous challenges to continued strong performances. Virtually all the member economies are experiencing a backlash against globalization and trade liberalization from weak or non-competitive sectors. The backlash, which is not just in the APEC region but global, has increased the difficulties of negotiating a mutually beneficial Doha Development Agenda (DDA) liberalization package, forcing suspension of active DDA negotiations in July 2006. Many observers believe that this suspension will result in an even more frenetic pace of negotiating bilateral and mini-lateral PTAs (preferential trade agreements, frequently mislabelled "free trade agreements" by their supporters).

Projections of the world economy suggest a global slowing of growth, and some pessimists are extremely worried about a possible "train wreck" as the result of the huge macroeconomic imbalances between the United States and other countries, particularly East Asia. Two of the most important drivers of contemporary global growth are the American consumers and investors in China. There are concerns about both. The United States interest rates have been creeping up, cooling the bubble-like American housing market. This in turn affects the perceived wealth of households and curtails consumer spending. On the other side of the Pacific, Chinese economic growth is highly leveraged on exports (especially to the United States).[2] A U.S. slowdown will be felt through the global economy, but especially in China. In the meantime, China's high investment rate continues to build export capacity that may become idle if there is a serious recession in the United States. Unfortunately, with growth rates in Europe also declining, that continent will not be in a position to pick up the slack if there is a significant medium-term decline in U.S. consumer spending.

APEC should be a vehicle through which the major economies in the region review economic analysis and policy options and potentially undertake reinforcing policies that could help ensure a "soft landing" and a restored, healthier growth trajectory. Such policies could include measured currency realignments and further trade liberalization. However, it was the sense of many members of the study team that APEC is not fulfilling this role, in part because a decline in government and public interest in the APEC process and in part because governmental attention has been diverted to other issues, especially terrorism. While never carefully defined, APEC's 1994 Bogor Goal of "free trade and investment in the region" by 2010 for developed economies and 2020 for all economies, seems very unlikely to be met, and APEC trade liberalization and facilitation initiatives seem more designed to take advantage of trends already occurring through market activity rather than proactively stepping up the pace.

In sum, while not necessarily accepting the most pessimistic prognoses of the regional and global economies, there are reasons for serious concern. The ABAC-PECC study team sees as among the most urgent challenges a need to restart the DDA, a need to contain the further proliferation of preferential trading arrangements (PTAs) while developing compatibilities among existing PTAs, the need to manage trans-Pacific macroeconomic imbalances in both their economic and political dimensions, and a need to revitalize and give new meaning to the APEC.

The combination of concerns about APEC, the DDA, and the health of the region economy led the ABAC in 2004 to ask the governments to study the FTAAP proposal.[3] When the governments failed to act on a study, the ABAC moved forward on its own to make the study, asking PECC to join in this effort.

III. EVALUATING THE FTAAP

Arguments For and Against

The proposal for a regional free trade agreement (FTA) is one of the oldest ideas for promoting mutually beneficial Asia-Pacific regional co-operation.

Japanese economist Kiyoshi Kojima is usually credited with first Pacific Free Trade Agreement proposal in 1966.[4] While that proposal was clearly premature and unrealistic, it enhanced awareness of regional interdependencies and potentials for increased benefit through co-operation, and eventually led to the establishment of both the Pacific Economic Cooperation Council (PECC) and to the APEC process.[5]

In more recent times, American economist C. Fred Bergsten has been the foremost advocate of the FTAAP. His paper, prepared as part of this study, provides a most comprehensive and forceful statement in favour of an FTAAP. In Dr Bergsten's view, if the FTAAP could be realized, it would provide the largest single liberalization in history. Moreover, its benefits would extend beyond the APEC economies because it would effectively force the Europeans to sit up and take notice, probably restarting the WTO's multilateral trade negotiations. Even if it did not, it is the best "Plan B" available, since its own benefits would be so great. It would also sweep up the extending smaller PTAs with their proliferation of unwieldy rules of origins into a larger framework, thus dampening the "noodle bowl" effect. It would also prevent competitive liberalizations in the Americas and Asia, which Dr Bergsten believes threaten to "draw a line down the Pacific".[6] The FTAAP would provide a framework for the United States and China to head off trade tensions and revitalize APEC. Dr Bergsten believes that because the economic logic of the FTAAP is so compelling, it is also politically feasible, although he acknowledges the difficulty of getting governments to recognize their longer-term interests and overcome protectionist pressures.

Some of the other papers in this volume critique Bergsten's FTAAP proposal. Most of the study team are sceptical of the political feasibility of the FTAAP concept. The most direct and comprehensive rebuttal to the proposal comes from American political scientist, Vinod K. Aggarwal. Based on an analysis of the American political economy, Dr Aggarwal argues that the FTAAP is neither politically feasible nor desirable. In his view, selective liberalization through sector and bilateral trade agreements has rewarded freer trade interests, but left trade policy dominated by protectionist interests. Thus the free trade coalition needed to push an FTAAP through Congress is no longer there. Moreover, the politically charged massive trade deficit with China makes any FTA effectively "dead on arrival" in Congress. Dr Aggarwal also argues that APEC does not have the institutional basis to negotiate an accord and, from an American perspective, dismisses the FTAAP as a good "Plan B", noting that it would not accomplish the agricultural and industrial market objectives the United States is seeking through the Doha Round.

Evaluation Factors

How do we evaluate the political viability of the FTAAP proposal in light of these differing assessments? In my mind, a logical way to proceed was to make as the working hypothesis the proposition that the FTAAP is politically feasible, and see if this could stand up during a review of various important factors that would affect its viability. These factors are: (1) the magnitude of the undertaking, (2) the requirements for political leadership and will to successfully negotiate an FTAAP, (3) the scope of changes required in APEC and the likely political support for those changes, and (4) the political desirability of pursuing the FTAAP. An assessment of the last has to consider the potentially positive and negative political impacts of an FTAAP on the WTO and the current DDA round, the risks for economies and their leaders of trying to achieve an FTAAP but failing, and the potential risks of failing to attempt an FTAAP.

Magnitude: Dr Bergsten notes that an FTAAP would be a historically significant liberalization, especially when set against the objectives of the current DDA. This is no doubt correct since, in fact, an FTAAP would be a much more ambitious undertaking. The APEC ministers themselves insist that free trade agreements must be of "high quality", and WTO rules (GATT Article 24) require that they cover substantially all trade. This combination means that an FTAAP must cover between 80 and 95 per cent of trade among member economies and address behind-the-border issues such as finance, telecommunications, national treatment for foreign direct investment, and intellectual property protection. Even mild forms of proposed liberalization in some of these areas were enough to sink the 2002 Cancun WTO ministerial meeting. Based on the experience of the Free Trade Area of the Americas (FTAA) proposal, which had much less internal variation in levels of economic development, legal development, current and financial regimes, and political and international relations issues, an FTAAP would require at least five, and probably more, years of negotiation. As suggested by Sherry Stephenson in her chapter on the lessons of the FTAA experience, a successful FTAAP negotiation would also require the participating partners to make it their central trade negotiating activity. Dr Stephenson, in fact, suggests that there be a standstill agreement at the outset for negotiating other regional trade agreements.

Political Will and Leadership: Obviously, an undertaking of the magnitude just outlined will require a huge investment in leadership time and bargaining chips in the major APEC economies. Lukewarm support will not be enough. Again, Dr Stephenson makes this point very clearly, based on the FTAA experience. Without the required support, sustained over the entire period of the negotiations, the FTAAP is unlikely to succeed. She suggests that a "unity of vision" is needed among China, Japan, and the United States. We believe that to be politically viable, the FTAAP would need at least one of the major APEC economies to become its very committed champion and remain so throughout the negotiation.

Changes in APEC: APEC was designed as a community-building institution for general socio-economic co-operation, not as an institution for trade negotiations. However, strengthening trade flows has always been an important part of its agenda. In 1994, the APEC economies adopted the Bogor Vision, to be achieved through a voluntary and concerted process of liberalization rather than on the basis of binding commitments. To this day, this continues to be the accepted basis of APEC co-operation in trade liberalization. At Busan in 2005, the APEC ministers committed themselves again to the principle that "APEC must not be an inward-looking trade bloc that diverts from the pursuit of global free trade".[7]

An FTAAP negotiation would obviously require a different kind of APEC process, one involving formal negotiations and binding rather than voluntary commitments. An FTAAP would also require rules of origin, discriminating against those outside the FTAAP. Moreover, a different kind of secretariat and base of funding support would be needed to sustain the negotiating process over a several year period of time. Thus, the political feasibility of the FTAAP requires an assessment of how likely it is that such significant changes in APEC can be achieved.

Political Desirability of an FTAAP: Desirability and feasibility are very closely linked because if something is highly desirable to political leaders, it will obviously become much more politically feasible than otherwise. For example, will an FTAAP help achieve a successful conclusion of the

DDA, to which all the leaders of APEC are committed? Dr Bergsten argues that if the FTAAP is launched — or even just seriously studied by the governments — it would have a powerful impact on outsiders, possibly reviving the DDA. Dr Aggarwal argues that even if an attempt is made to use the FTAAP only as a tactic to advance the WTO agenda, it is likely to backfire.

Another powerful political argument that advocates of FTAAP make is that the proposal will revitalize APEC itself. Clearly, APEC has lost much of its political lustre after 1997–98, and almost every year the issue of its relevance is raised, even by Asia-Pacific community-building advocates.[8] On the other hand, it can be argued that an effort that is doomed to failure from the start would only add to the woes of the world and regional trade system and further discredit APEC. It could also result in "community-destroying" rather than community-building activities if the result were a blame game by the economies involved. Given the tremendous time and political commitments that the APEC economies would have to make to conclude a successful FTAAP, and considering the implications of success or failure of the FTAAP proposal to perceptions of APEC's importance and success, a central question has to be whether the FTAAP would be a good investment, either for the individual governments or for the institution.

One should also consider whether there may be an unacceptable risk of not undertaking the FTAAP. Dr Bergsten argues that there would be a continued proliferation of PTAs that are likely to take an East Asian versus American character, creating two competing blocs and drawing a line down the Pacific. Is this a serious prospect, and if so, is an FTAAP the best way to check it? This issue also requires consideration.

The Net Political Assessment: An FTAAP Is Not Politically Viable

Taking these factors into consideration, and consulting with many others, my net assessment is that a successful negotiation of a high-quality FTAAP is not politically feasible at present or in the near term. Most of the study team shares this basic assessment.

The main reason for this assessment is that the political challenges of negotiating a high-quality, comprehensive FTAAP are so massive when placed against any likely political will. Even before any negotiations could begin, they would require major and controversial changes in APEC's "social contract", which our studies indicate is likely to be resisted by a number of important member economies. Even if this high entry barrier could be surmounted, an FTA compatible with the WTO and with APEC's own enunciated standards for "high quality", must cover highly controversial sectors, such as agriculture and complicated behind-the-border issues. There are powerful political interest groups in the APEC economies that will oppose concessions in these areas. Even if there were "a unity of vision" among China, Japan, and the United States, the negotiations will take a likely minimum of five years. The FTAAP, requiring almost exclusive attention from trade ministries during this period, would cause postponement of other negotiations that are of high priority to some of the key APEC economies. Many regional trade negotiators are unenthusiastic because they see little likelihood of success given that less ambitious projects — such as the FTAA and the DDA — have floundered.

An implicit assumption underlying the FTAAP proposal — and particularly the notion that of the FTAAP as a "Plan B" in the event of an unsuccessful DDA — is that the constellation of political and economic interests in the Asia-Pacific venue makes trade liberalization politically more attractive for economies in the region than is the case globally. While some of the economies that have complicated the WTO negotiations (for example, EU, India, Brazil) are left out of an FTAAP negotiation, the FTAAP is so large and diverse, it still encompasses many protectionist interests. And the goal of the FTAAP — free trade — is much more politically demanding than the much less ambitious DDA goals. This would be true even if the standards were somewhat relaxed and a full FTA is not fully achieved. Therefore, as the gains from smaller size are cancelled out by a much more politically demanding agenda, there is no particular political advantage to the FTAAP venue.

For these reasons, sufficient political champions and political will for an FTAAP are not visible now. Could this change? It might if governments or publics become convinced that there is compelling urgency to negotiate such a regional agreement. But in fact, regional trade and economic growth is continuing without an FTAAP. A crisis (or perceived opportunities) of the scale needed to change political calculations so much that an FTAAP would be politically attractive to government leaders and their publics, would undoubtedly also make politically possible the DDA. The DDA remains the region's "Plan A".

The papers prepared for this study underscore some specific problems for APEC economies that reinforce the main points above.

In the case of China, Sheng Bin's study suggests that the priority interest for China's leaders is an East Asia Free Trade Agreement (EAFTA). Moreover, China is strongly committed to APEC as an institution based on open and voluntary regional co-operation. According to Sheng Bin, the membership of Chinese Taipei in APEC may also introduce political complications.

In the case of Japan, Shujiro Urata's chapter shows that agriculture liberalization remains a very difficult domestic political issue. Agricultural interests have also strongly opposed even bilateral free trade agreements in the case of Korea. Moreover, Japan's government also may have a stronger interest in East Asian regionalism, as highlighted by the 2006 proposal of Minister for Economy, Trade and Industry Toshihiro Nikai for an East Asia free trade agreement based on the membership of the sixteen-member East Asia Summit.

In the case of ASEAN, the chapter by Chia Siow Yue and Hadi Soesastro indicates that some ASEAN economies are not at all prepared politically or otherwise to enter an undertaking of the magnitude of the FTAAP. Dr Stephenson points out that this was also the case of the FTAA, which resulted in a deliberate decision to stretch the FTAA negotiations over a ten-year time-frame while capacity was being built. As it turned out, the time-frame was too long for sustained political commitment.

Very importantly, the Trade Promotion Authority (TPA) of the United States expires in July 2007. No viable negotiations involving the United States can take place without an extension of the TPA. This looks increasingly doubtful because of growing protectionist tendencies, which could be further reinforced by the outcome of the November 2006 Congressional elections. Moreover, as pointed out above, because of the already highly controversial American trade deficit with China, it seems very unlikely that a TPA extension could be achieved for a project involving free trade with China.

Yet other problems should be mentioned.

• The underlying purpose of APEC is to bring the economies together to recognize and act on common interests. Trade negotiations, however, are an inherently adversarial process. There may be a basic incompatibility between the APEC's community-building mission and an effort to transform it into a trade negotiating body.

- APEC economies have different approaches to FTAs. As pointed out by Sheng Bin, China (and some other Asian economies) prefer a "piecemeal" approach. However, a comprehensive template is preferred in North America. Because of these differences in approach, and the preference of some Asian economies to move forward on an East Asian agreement based on Asian approaches, it has been suggested that an effort to push forward an FTAAP in a serious way by some governments would be more likely to "draw a line down the Pacific" than the current PTA noodle bowl (which includes quite a few trans-Pacific noodles).
- Finally, with respect to the impact on the WTO and APEC's own credibility, the FTAAP carries high side risks of diverting rather than galvanizing the DDA and of further jeopardizing APEC's credibility. Given the political unreality of the FTAAP proposal, a formal study of an FTAAP is unlikely to be taken so seriously by outsiders to result in changes in bargaining positions on the DDA. However, it could help reinforce a further sense of erosion of the world trading system into competing blocs. In hoping to erase a potential line down the Pacific, the FTAAP proposal could create other lines, ones down the Atlantic or across the Eurasian land mass.

In sum, FTAAP is not currently politically viable, and this affects its political desirability. However, the proposal has attractive elements, particularly if it could be an avenue towards global freer trade. For this reason, it will continue to have advocates and should continue to be studied. We believe, however, these studies should continue to be with the non-governmental sector, rather than official and governmental.

There are certainly risks to doing nothing or completely ignoring trade liberalization in favour of trade facilitation. The spectre of a continued unruly proliferation of free trade agreements and an erosion of the global trade order remains a real one, particularly as protectionist pressures continue to grow with globalization. The APEC economies need and can take more immediate and politically realistic steps towards achieving the Bogor vision. These steps do not preclude a future FTAAP as a long-range objective. If crafted properly, they can create the conditions in which an FTAAP could become more politically realistic as well as more economically desirable.

IV. A CREDIBLE APEC 2010 TRADE AGENDA

As pointed out by FTAAP advocates and others, APEC needs a credible trade agenda. The suspension of the WTO negotiations and the proliferation of PTAs are regarded by the entire study team as undesirable. The Bogor vision of free trade and investment in the region, although not clearly defined, remains highly relevant. Trade liberalization and facilitation are an essential part of the APEC community-building process. The dilemma, however, is that APEC itself does not have a mechanism for achieving the Bogor vision. The APEC mechanism of concerted, voluntary liberalization may have helped economies who understand the value of liberalizing to do so, but even the most dedicated advocates of the voluntary process understand that at the end of the day some kind of negotiations based on binding commitments and reciprocity will be needed to achieve the objectives set out at Bogor. For this reason, achievement of the Bogor vision is dependent on successful WTO negotiations.

To strengthen its own credibility as a mechanism for trade liberalization and facilitation, APEC needs to set realistic objectives and achieve these. This entails reviewing and being willing to discard old and increasingly unrealistic goals that it cannot achieve through APEC's own processes. While many others would disagree, I believe this means dropping or revising the Bogor 2010 and 2020 goals even while maintaining the Bogor vision.

Positive steps include developing a more coherent, focused and strategic approach based on mid-term, multi-year building blocks and a strong effort to steer PTAs in a positive direction, making use of the energy behind the proliferation of PTAs. APEC also needs to broaden its stakeholder base beyond the relative narrow bureaucratic, business, and academic groups currently involved in the APEC processes.

This is an excellent time for launching a three-year APEC trade agenda to wind up in 2010, Japan's year to chair APEC, as a first phase. An APEC 2010 Trade Agenda project, led by all the host economies from Vietnam through Japan, and with specific goals to be achieved over this period, would provide an ambitious but doable trade agenda for APEC. The Busan Road Map, while quite general, provides some important principles, and the ideas and principles need to be linked to specific tasks.

An APEC 2010 Trade Agenda might consist of four broad elements: deepening the WTO, aligning regional PTAs, enhancing outreach, and undertaking APEC reform.

Deepening the WTO: APEC has already been successful in deepening knowledge of and strengthening adherence to WTO disciplines among the APEC economies. Even without entailing new obligations, more effective implementation of existing obligations constitutes a major contribution to the international trading system. This contribution can be more consciously pursued and publicized.

It would be a significant achievement if the APEC process could help restart the stalemated DDA. This would require dialogue with non-APEC negotiators, especially with the EU and among the emerging developing economies, as well as greater initiative among some APEC economies, who have held back making offers in the DDA while awaiting the outcome of American-European negotiations.

Aligning PTAs: Even while contributing to the so-called "noodle bowl", the PTAs in the region reflect a desire to deepen economic co-operation and integration and lock-in domestic reforms. They also can provide economies with the opportunity to test the waters in breaking through protectionist barriers that are too difficult to address at the global or broad regional scale. As part of its APEC 2010 Trade Agenda, APEC can encourage the outward orientation of PTAs through the focus, sophisticated efforts to develop model measures, which it has begun, and a credible review process of existing PTAs and those under negotiation. It is particularly important that larger PTAs, such as those being negotiated around the ASEAN group and the proposed U.S.-Korea PTA, achieve the highest possible standards. The chapter by Robert Scollay provides some practical and realistic means for APEC to move ahead on PTAs, fully recognizing the many difficulties.

APEC can also place priority on behind-the-border measures, rules of origins, capacity-building, and trade related aspects of Ecotech characteristic of high-quality PTAs, thus complementing rather than competing with areas of WTO competence and traditional leadership.

Extending Outreach: As indicated, APEC should systematically develop stakeholders beyond the current involved communities. Emphasis should be placed on parliamentary and media leaders. Moreover, APEC should make an effort to market the APEC "brand name" more effectively. Too many of APEC initiatives have been named for cities, such as the Busan Road Map, which does necessarily connect to APEC itself in the minds of even the more interested publics in APEC societies.

Undertaking Organizational Reforms: The programme outlined here does not require fundamental change in APEC's modalities or its commitment to open regionalism, but it does require more effective and focused collective leadership, a stronger secretariat, and a more secure and generous funding base.

To carry out an effective APEC 2010 Trade Agenda, there should be a small, but solid core professional staff in the APEC Secretariat. This staff needs to be committed to APEC as an institution (rather than loyalty to a government from which seconded), professionally knowledgeable about trade issues, and capable of commissioning and utilizing needed research.

V. CONCLUSION

APEC co-operation and community-building processes, of course, go far beyond trade. The leaders have extended the APEC agenda into new areas, such as diseases, disasters, and terrorism, which are of mutual concern and where APEC co-operation can make a difference. However, trade in both its liberalization and facilitation dimensions remains a key and core area of economic co-operation because it is a major contributor to regional economic growth.

While our studies include advocates of as well as critics of the FTAAP proposal, the overall weight of our study is that the FTAAP is not politically feasible in the near or medium term. This does not mean that it is not potentially something to work for over the longer term through a series of practical multi-year building blocks, beginning with APEC 2010. We also strongly urge continued efforts to promote regional and global freer trade through more focused support for WTO processes, strengthened efforts to align PTAs, and enhanced outreach both to increase involved sectors of society in APEC process and to build stronger public awareness of the individual economies' and the region's stakes in liberalized trade.

Notes

1. The Mid-term Stocktake of Progress Towards the Bogor Goals reports that average applied tariffs in the region have gone down from 16.9 per cent in 1989 to 5.5 per cent in 2004. See http://www.apec.org/apec/publications.html.
2. In 2005 China's exports to the United States were 21 per cent of all exports (*IMF Direction of Trade Statistics*).
3. "A Free Trade Area of the Asia-Pacific (FTAAP) may have the potential of

bringing significant economic benefit to the region as a whole. We believe that this idea requires and is worthy of further careful study. We therefore recommend the establishment of a high-level task force by APEC Leaders to examine the concept in more detail." ABAC Report to Leaders 2004 "Bridging the Pacific: Coping with the Challenges of Globalization".
4.   The Japanese Origins of PAFTAD: The Beginning of an Asian Pacific Economic Community: http://www.crawford.anu.edu.au/pdf/pep/pep-292.pdf. Lawrence T. Woods, *Asia-Pacific Diplomacy: Non-governmental Organizations and International Relations* (Vancouver: UBC Press, 1993), pp. 41–42.
5.   Pacific Economic Cooperation Council 2005, *The Evolution of PECC: The First 25 Years*, especially Chapter 1, "Building Momentum Toward Pacific Economic Cooperation" by Mark Borthwick.
6.   A phrase often attributed to former United States Secretary of State James Baker.
7.   http://www.apec.org/apec/ministerial_statements/annual_ministerial/ 2005_17th_apec_ministerial.html.
8.   See, for example, Allan Gyngell and Malcolm Cook, "How to Save APEC", Policy Brief (Sydney: Lowy Institute for International Policy, October 2005).

2

A Free Trade Area of the Asia-Pacific in the Wake of the Faltering Doha Round: Trade Policy Alternatives for APEC

C. Fred Bergsten

I. INTRODUCTION AND SUMMARY

The APEC Business Advisory Committee (ABAC) has recommended for the past two years that APEC Leaders launch a study of a Free Trade Area of the Asia-Pacific (FTAAP). The Leaders have been unwilling to do so for at least two reasons: a fear that even such a limited move in the direction of an FTAAP could undercut the ongoing Doha Round in the World Trade Organization (WTO), which remained their trade policy priority and was already in parlous condition, and the (presumably related) unwillingness of the major APEC powers (China, Japan and especially the United States) to endorse the idea. ABAC thus decided to launch its own study of the FTAAP, and alternative trade policy ideas for APEC, in an effort to restore APEC's contribution to global trade liberalization and to revitalize APEC as an institution. The immediate objective is to advance the discussion of these issues at the Leaders Meeting in Hanoi in November 2006 and during the Australian chairmanship in 2007.

This paper argues that the case for studying, beginning an APEC process of intergovernmental discussion and consultation on, subsequently launching negotiations towards, and perhaps ultimately completing an FTAAP is much more powerful in 2006–2007 than when the idea was initially raised in 2004 (or indeed when its conceptual predecessor, the Bogor Goals, were adopted by the Leaders in 1993–94). There are four reasons for this important change.

First, the Doha Round is faltering badly. It now seems unlikely to achieve even minimal success without a "political jolt" of the type that an FTAAP launch by the APEC Leaders could provide. The model is the Leaders' adoption of the goal of "free and open trade and investment in the region", at the first APEC summit in Seattle in 1993, that galvanized the successful conclusion of the Uruguay Round in the General Agreement on Tariffs and Trade (GATT) shortly thereafter.

Second, outright failure or indefinite extension of Doha, which largely amount to the same thing, are now quite possible outcomes (especially without a new "jolt" *à la* FTAAP). Hence a fall-back "Plan B" may become essential to keep the global trading system from relapsing into protectionism as the momentum of liberalization stalls. An FTAAP, in addition to improving the prospect for a successful Doha, is a far more promising "Plan B" candidate than the likely alternative of a renewed explosion of bilateral and subregional preferential agreements within the region (and in the rest of the world).

Third, the continued proliferation of bilateral and subregional (for example, China-ASEAN, Japan-ASEAN, Korea-ASEAN) FTAs within East Asia, which could evolve into a wide-ranging East Asian Community or East Asian Free Trade Area whether called that or not, is again threatening to "draw a line down the middle of the Pacific". The expansion of U.S. subregional FTAs in Latin America, from North American Free Trade Agreement (NAFTA) to Central American Free Trade Agreement (CAFTA) and now into most of the Andean Community, projects a similar pattern from the eastern edge of that ocean (whether or not a full Free Trade Area of the Americas is ever concluded). Such disintegration of the Asia-Pacific region, with East Asia and the Western Hemisphere raising increasingly discriminatory trade barriers against each other, would raise severe political and even security, as well as economic, problems for many countries in the region. It is essential to embed any new East Asian and Western Hemisphere integration schemes within the broader trans-Pacific context to avoid such a risk. APEC is the only institutional foundation for such an initiative, and the FTAAP is the only operational instrument that could mobilize its potential to that end.

Fourth, the United States and China are experiencing intense and growing trade tensions within the context of a bilateral imbalance that exceeded US$200 billion in 2005 and will continue to rise rapidly. The United States has already imposed a number of new barriers against Chinese exports and many more, including across-the-board Congressional sanctions, are being seriously considered. Macroeconomic policy changes, especially substantial revaluation of the renminbi, will be essential to head off or at least limit an economic conflict between the two economic superpowers that could otherwise engulf the entire region. A fresh approach to the trade policy dimension of the relationship is needed as well, however, and an FTAAP would embed any bilateral China-United States confrontation within a broader trans-Pacific context. It would thus offer a more promising response than the bilateral route, which to date has proved largely fruitless and indeed confrontational and dangerous.

For all these reasons, the United States could come to endorse the idea of an FTAAP in the near future (as some of the smaller APEC member economies already have). Especially if pushed by some of its Asian neighbours, China could do so as well. An FTAAP is a natural for Japan, the third leading trader in the region, to avoid being drawn into an East Asian zone dominated by China and to counter the U.S. drive to complete bilateral FTAs with many of the other major countries in the region (Korea, Thailand, Malaysia, Singapore, Australia and perhaps soon Indonesia as well). An FTAAP could become quite feasible fairly soon.

This paper argues that the APEC Leaders, depending on the actual status of the Doha talks when they meet in 2006 and 2007, should therefore initiate an official study of an FTAAP and an intergovernmental discussion/consultation/negotiation to pursue the substance of the idea. The preferred sequence would be to launch the study in 2006 and the action programme a year later, but it might be necessary to fuse these two steps if a collapse, or indefinite delay, of the WTO round were already evident by the time of the Hanoi meetings in November. The paper provides an updated analysis of the case for an FTAAP, relates the idea to the three most likely scenarios for the Doha Round, and addresses directly the prospect that the three largest APEC economies, especially the United States, could become supporters of the idea in the changed circumstances discussed.

II. THE CASE FOR A FREE TRADE AREA
OF THE ASIA-PACIFIC

The substantive case for an FTAAP is well known and very powerful. First, implementation of an FTAAP would represent a gigantic liberalization of trade in the world's largest and most dynamic region. All member economies would derive large welfare gains as a result. An earlier study prepared for ABAC shows that every APEC economy gains more from an FTAAP than from non-discriminatory liberalization by APEC, the only alternative modality for pursuing the Bogor Goals on a region-wide basis and for revitalizing APEC's trade agenda, and that almost all East Asian economies (including the three large Northeast Asians) gain more from an FTAAP than from an "ASEAN Plus 3" FTA.[1]

A truly Free Trade Area of the Asia-Pacific would indeed achieve much greater economic benefits, for the world as a whole as its sizeable gains for the large number of participating economies more than offset the losses to some non-members, than any conceivable multilateral/WTO liberalization. The Doha Round, like the Uruguay Round and its other predecessors, would at best achieve marginal liberalization of 25 to 30 per cent of existing barriers. Since APEC economies account for more than half of world output and trade, elimination of *all* barriers between them would provide a much larger *global* payoff than any realistic Doha outcome. Even if APEC were to achieve liberalization of only 80 to 90 per cent in goods, which would be necessary to meet the WTO test of covering "substantially all trade", the gains for the global economy as a whole would be far superior to those attainable via any plausible WTO negotiation. Those gains would of course accrue primarily to the members of the FTAAP itself, and some non-members would lose, due to the resulting discrimination against them, which is why the latter would then be likely to promptly seek significant further multilateral liberalization via the standard logic of "competitive liberalization".

Second, serious pursuit of the FTAAP idea by APEC is much more likely to promote than undermine the prospects for a successful Doha Round. The countries that represent the primary barriers to a successful

Doha all lie outside APEC — the European Union, Brazil, India, and some of the Africans. Hence the prospect that a new APEC liberalization initiative would strengthen the outlook for Doha, by focusing the recalcitrants on the risk of facing substantial new discrimination if they continue to block a successful WTO outcome, is even greater than at the end of the Uruguay Round when "only" the EU needed to be shocked into co-operation by APEC's initial Seattle summit and "free trade in the region" commitment.

A parallel launch of the FTAAP idea at this time would, at a minimum, thus enhance the prospects of achieving the modest but highly desirable trade liberalization that could result from a successful Doha Round — as long as the APEC members made clear that this outcome remained their top priority as they surely would (and as their predecessors did vis-à-vis the Uruguay Round in 1993–94). If APEC would then follow through and actually create an FTAAP, to maintain the forward momentum of liberalization by building on a successful Doha, its far larger "WTO plus" gains would accrue in addition to those produced by Doha. The resulting discrimination against outsiders would in turn be likely to prompt insistence by those outsiders, led by the EU, to launch another multilateral WTO round to reduce the new preferences (just as the United States insisted on the three major post-war GATT rounds in large part to reduce the preferences stemming from EU creation and subsequent expansion). An effective FTAAP process in APEC could thus make a huge double or triple contribution to global trade liberalization and economic welfare.

If Doha were to fail anyway, despite an APEC effort to revive it via the launch of an FTAAP process, the FTAAP initiative would provide the APEC member economies with a ready "Plan B" to restore momentum for trade liberalization. This would be extremely important, especially for the trade-dependent economies of the Asia-Pacific region, in a world in which the global bicycle had stalled out. The FTAAP idea thus simultaneously offers a spur to Doha and a ready alternative if it were to fail.

Third, an FTAAP could, at least over time, sweep under one roof the exploding proliferation of bilateral and subregional preferential trading arrangements (PTAs) throughout the area (and help head off the further proliferation that is highly likely in the absence of an FTAAP alternative if Doha fails). It would eliminate, in whole or in part (since some PTAs would probably continue to exist even with an FTAAP), the increasing discrimination that such pacts are producing within the region. In particular, it could start rolling together the conflicting rules of origin (ROOs) that are becoming so costly to business and trade throughout the region.

This benefit of an FTAAP is vitally important in light of the steady movement of the East Asian members of APEC towards establishing their own region-wide PTA. The creation of an East Asian Community, or even an East Asian Free Trade Area (EAFTA), could contribute substantially to liberalization and thus have a positive impact on the world economy.[2] It would also generate a major new source of discrimination within the broader Asia-Pacific setting, however, and thus, as with the Mahathir proposal for an East Asian Economic Group in the early 1990s, threaten to "draw a line down the middle of the Pacific".[3] Initial studies suggest that the United States would immediately lose at least $25 billion of annual exports solely from the static discriminatory effects of an EAFTA.

This outcome will occur whether or not the East Asian regional integration process formally produces a single economic entity, per Japan's recent "ASEAN Plus Six" FTA proposal, because the overlapping network of existing and potential agreements, especially the "10+1+1+1" arrangements between ASEAN and the three Northeastern Asian powers, will move substantially in the same direction. Such new trade discrimination across the Pacific could also have important security effects, inevitably loosening the current trans-Pacific alliances (for example, U.S.-Japan), not least because of negative Congressional reactions to such Asia-only initiatives (regardless of the parallel Western Hemisphere-only initiatives being conducted by the United States itself). With the rise in economic and political importance of the Asian economies, and the tensions already existing over some elements of U.S. foreign policy, the impact of such Asia-Pacific disintegration would be far more costly today — to both sides of the Pacific — than would have been the case in the early 1990s.

Similar implications would accrue from the de facto completion of a Free Trade Area of the Americas (FTAA) as is occurring on the eastern edge of the Pacific. Formal negotiations for a full-blown FTAA have stalled, along with the Doha Round, because its conclusion has always been inextricably linked to the Round's outcome on agricultural trade. Hence a failure of Doha would probably mean a failure for the formal FTAA too.

However, the de facto integration of the Western Hemisphere is already far advanced. The United States has expanded its FTA ties beyond NAFTA to include Chile, all of Central America and the larger parts of the Andean Pact (Colombia and Peru). A failed Doha Round could prompt U.S.-Brazil negotiations. Asia-Pacific disintegration is being fed from the eastern as well as western edge of the Pacific in equally messy but also equally discriminatory ways.[4]

The United States has no basis for asking to participate in the East Asian summits. Asians are not invited to the Summits of the Americas. Neither Americans nor Asians are invited to the summits of the European Union. Both the United States and the Asians do, however, have a clear right to be consulted about the hemispheric initiatives of their trans-Pacific neighbours, especially in light of their commitments to each other to move to "free and open trade and investment" in the Asia-Pacific region as a whole. They have an obligation to conduct such consultations with full faith and transparency and to consider new ideas, such as an FTAAP, that would obviate the major costs and risks of East Asia-only or Western Hemisphere-only integration. APEC is of course the natural venue for such consultations. A failure to pursue them would be extremely risky for all APEC economies.

One clear lesson from the history of large regional economic initiatives is that it is important to embed them in broader geographic contexts to avoid the risk that they may subsequently resist liberalization towards non-members and become closed blocs. The European Union and its predecessors, by far the most important preferential trade agreement ever implemented, have been sufficiently nested in the GATT/WTO system that they could not resist global steps to temper their discrimination against outsiders. In addition, the integrating Europeans were embedded in an extremely thick network of trans-Atlantic relationships with the United States and Canada, including most importantly the Marshall Plan, NATO and the OEEC/OECD but many more as well, which virtually obviated the risk of "drawing a line down the middle of the Atlantic" despite the historic depth of integration that the EU was in the process of achieving.

By contrast, MERCOSUR's apparent desire to maintain its subregional preferences, and resist reducing them in any broader framework even with full reciprocity, probably derives at least partly from this absence of broader nesting. The faltering of the WTO system likewise reduces its potential for limiting the risks inherent in a preferential de facto EAFTA or FTAA. Especially in light of the salience of trans-Pacific relationships traced above, and drawing on the historical lessons from the trans-Atlantic relationship, it is essential to embed new Pacific Asia and Western

Hemisphere subregional agreements within a broader Asia-Pacific context. (For the same reason, an FTAAP should be embedded in an effective WTO system, and FTAAP members should do everything they can to strengthen or, if necessary after a failure of Doha, to revive that global institution.)

Fourth, launch of an FTAAP initiative would revitalize APEC itself. Whatever its record in other areas, APEC has declined steeply in both regional and global relevance as its inability to effectively pursue its own Bogor Goals has become (painfully) apparent. In choosing to become solely a cheerleader for the WTO and Doha, without any trade agenda of its own, APEC has abdicated the significant role that it played in global as well as regional trade policy from 1993 at least through 1997 (vis-à-vis the Uruguay Round, as already noted, and in both negotiating most of the hugely liberalizing Information Technology Agreement [ITA] and teeing up nine important sectors for complete liberalization [which unfortunately failed later] in the teeth of the Asian financial crisis). It has looked on helplessly as its member economies pursue their own PTAs without reference to, or even notice of, APEC and the commitments they had supposedly accepted under its aegis.

This weakening of APEC should be of major concern to all its member economies. The rapid growth of economic (and broader) tensions between the United States and China, and the increased risks of "drawing a line down the middle of the Pacific" due to the advent of Asia-only (and perhaps Americas-only) economic arrangements, underline the enhanced need for effective trans-Pacific linkages and institutional ties for security as well as economic reasons. ASEAN, in particular, seeks to maintain active U.S. engagement in the region as a "hedging strategy" against the rise, and possible hegemonial intentions, of China.

APEC is the only existing organization that can fill that role, in contrast to the large number of trans-Atlantic institutions that precluded the parallel risk of "drawing a line down the middle of the Atlantic" as the European Union formed and steadily deepened its integration. To pursue an FTAAP, it would have to acknowledge that it is already a "negotiating forum" and be prepared to point towards binding rather than purely voluntary commitments. This would ultimately strengthen the organization, however, and would in fact be nothing new for APEC since it already negotiated *inter alia* the Bogor Declaration, the ITA in 1996 (which subsequently became binding via the WTO) and the original sectoral liberalization agenda in 1997. Any new initiative that would restore purpose and credibility to APEC would generate benefits that range far beyond the gains, substantial as they would be, for that initiative itself.[5]

In sum, the substantive case for an FTAAP initiative in APEC is far stronger than when the idea was initially broached two years ago. There are powerful political and security, as well as economic and institutional, reasons for pursuing it. We must always be careful to distinguish among the three operational phases of the proposal: studying it, launching discussion/consultation/negotiation on it, and actually implementing the concept. It will be necessary to carefully calibrate these three phases, to the global and regional contexts that exist at the time of the crucial APEC decisions, but each sequential phase of the project could have at least some of the beneficial effects described here. The substantive case is very strong and argues for serious consideration of APEC's moving ahead on the idea in the near future.

III. THE FTAAP AND THE DOHA ROUND

I have already suggested that the launch of an FTAAP initiative by APEC (building on the current study by ABAC) could both have a highly positive effect in galvanizing a successful outcome for the Doha Round and offer a fall-back "Plan B" if Doha were to fail. The relationship between the FTAAP and Doha is so central, however, and has been such a major factor in inhibiting APEC consideration of such an initiative, that it deserves more detailed analysis. I will do so by tracing the implications for the FTAAP idea of the alternative scenarios that now seem plausible for the Doha talks as they approach their current deadline, driven by the expiration of U.S. negotiating authority, of late 2006/early 2007.

My colleagues Gary Hufbauer and Jeffrey Schott have developed a careful analysis of the three most likely outcomes for Doha in their paper "The Doha Round After Hong Kong" (Institute for International Economics, Policy Briefs in Institute Economics Number PB06-2, February 2006), and the prognosis seems even gloomier now in June 2006 in light of events that have transpired since they wrote earlier this year. The three possibilities are:

- outright failure or collapse;
- a minimalist "success"; or

- a substantial further delay, at least until the end of 2007 and perhaps beyond the U.S. elections in late 2008.

My colleagues at the Institute, especially Hufbauer and Schott, and I are very strong supporters of the Doha Round. We have indeed participated actively in developing many of its components, and have testified and written incessantly in an effort to promote a substantively successful outcome. We fully realize, from our long experience with earlier GATT rounds, that all such multilateral negotiations have looked exceedingly bleak prior to their more or less successful conclusions. But our best analytical judgements now lead us to see a strong possibility of a demise of Doha, which we do with great reluctance and only because we believe it is imperative for the world to begin planning on the basis of the real prospects for such an outcome.

We doubt that the major governments, especially the United States and the European Union, would want to explicitly admit the failure of the Doha Round and accept a formal collapse of the negotiations. However, the developing countries could trigger such an outcome by again rejecting the offers of the rich nations as grossly inadequate — as they correctly did at the Cancun Ministerial in 2003. Even the United States negotiators, pushed by the Congress and the U.S. business community, might reject a deal that failed to achieve at least a substantial portion of their negotiating objectives. Hence the first option is, unfortunately, a real possibility.

The consequences for the world trading system of an outright failure of Doha would be devastating. Protectionist relapses could be expected everywhere, especially as the global trade imbalances (which always spawn protectionism in the United States) continue to expand and as most economies soften, with unemployment rising, over the coming couple of years.[6] A further proliferation of PTAs could be expected as governments tried to find some politically viable modality for resuming trade liberalization. Under these circumstances, a "Plan B" would be desperately needed. Launch of an FTAAP should be extremely attractive in this context, especially as trans-Pacific trade ties would be the most likely to suffer in the context of a renewed outbreak of (especially U.S.) protectionism.

A minimalist outcome, the second possibility, is clearly possible. WTO Director General Pascal Lamy signalled such a strategy in his report on Hong Kong to a large conference at the Institute for International Economics on 17 February 2006, and Deputy Director General Rufus Yerxa repeated the concept in a speech in Washington on 24 May 2006. Their message has essentially been that, facing profound difficulties in meeting the original goals of the Round or even advancing the negotiations beyond where they have stalemated over the past year, the WTO membership should "declare victory and go home".

There are two problems with this approach. The first is that the offers to date are quite minimal, and it is doubtful that the world as a whole — as opposed to the ministers who would try to sell such an outcome — would view it as much better than an explicit failure. The second, which compounds the first, is that some of the present "offers", such as the U.S. willingness to limit agricultural subsidies in its next farm bill if the EU and others significantly expand market access in that sector, will almost certainly be withdrawn unless substantially better proposals emanate from their trading partners.

Hence any "declared victory" would be quite hollow and extremely difficult to sell. The global trade policy consequences might not be quite as bad as under an outright failure but neither would they be attractive to contemplate. All of the major trade problems would remain unresolved and the developing countries, in particular, would (rightly) feel betrayed for a second time. The resulting bad taste all around would make it virtually impossible to contemplate another WTO round,[7] or even any major sectoral negotiations, in the foreseeable future. The bicycle might not topple completely but it would become very wobbly. A "Plan B" would still be sorely needed.

The third option, which Hufbauer and Schott regard as the most likely, is extension of the talks from the current "deadline" of late 2006/early 2007 until anywhere from the end of 2007 (after the next French elections) to 2009 (after the next U.S. elections) or even beyond. This would be similar to the end game of the Uruguay Round, which was initially scheduled to conclude in 2000 but continued until late 2003 (after completion of NAFTA and the initial Seattle summit of APEC, as described above). It would be tantamount to the failure outcome in the short run but without the definitive finality thereof, and indeed with some prospect of ultimate success or at least renewed effort down the road.

The global trade policy consequences of this quite plausible "outcome" are the most conjectural. They would depend partly on whether credible new deadlines could be set. They would also depend heavily on whether the Congress seemed likely to extend the President's Trade Promotion

Authority (TPA), which would be highly uncertain with Doha in suspense
due to lack of success and hence unlikely to provide much motivation for
the United States to resume the talks. Victories by the Democrats in the
Congressional elections of 2006 or 2008, or in the Presidential election of
2008, could inject huge additional uncertainties into the picture.

The launch of an FTAAP in this context could provide a quadruple
benefit. It would represent a new driver of liberalization to maintain
forward momentum. It would offer a major incentive for Congress — and
the U.S. business community, which is its most important constituent on
these issues — to renew TPA and thus enable the United States to remain
involved, and hopefully provide the needed leadership, in the related sets
of global trade negotiations. It would offer a credible "political jolt" to the
rest of the world, providing substantial motivation for others to make new
offers that would revive Doha.[8]

If an FTAAP proceeded to fruition even in the wake of a reinvigorated
and successful Doha Round, produced in part by the launch of the FTAAP
itself, it could also galvanize a future WTO negotiation to reduce the new
"Doha plus" discrimination that it created. The creation of the EU, and its
subsequent broadening and deepening, were likewise important triggers
for all three of the major GATT rounds (Kennedy, Tokyo, Uruguay) of the
past half century. The formal launch of the Bogor Goals in 1994, coming
just after the completion of the Uruguay Round, clearly stimulated
successful multilateral/WTO negotiations (on telecom and financial
services, in particular) for several more years; Sir Leon Brittan, the chief
EU trade negotiator at the time, said repeatedly and publicly that "the EU
will not be left behind if APEC does what it says it will do" and used the
specter of APEC discrimination to bring his more recalcitrant member
states into all these global liberalization packages.

IV. THE UNITED STATES AND THE FTAAP

The FTAAP idea must be credible if it is to provide the numerous
substantial benefits suggested above. This does not require the United
States and the other major APEC powers, especially China and Japan, to
fully endorse the idea at this time. It does require them to accede to at
least the first stages of the process, an official APEC study and/or
exploratory discussion of the concept, and it requires a plausible prospect
that they will eventually come to embrace it. The most salient criticism

of the FTAAP to date has been that "it will never fly" with the big countries, especially the United States.[9]

The United States is probably the most important single variable in this equation. It remains not only the largest APEC economy and trading nation but the traditional leader, to which most of the other members (including even China and Japan) look, on trade policy issues at both the global and regional levels. It was the chief driver of the Bogor Goals at Seattle and at Bogor itself, and their very positive interaction with the Uruguay Round in the GATT, and would probably have to play that same role again if Bogor were to be revived via an FTAAP.

On the other hand, in view of its huge trade deficits and the unique role of the Congress, the United States is in many senses the largest problem for APEC (and broader) trade policy at this time. Any significant U.S. adoption of new protectionist measures, especially against China or Asia more broadly as is all too possible, would accelerate the Asia-only trade co-operation momentum and thus deepen the conflict across the Pacific.

Top U.S. officials to date have clearly not endorsed an FTAAP. Neither have they rejected the idea, however, seeking to keep it alive as a possible alternative. They have indeed encouraged private Americans, including leaders of the business community, to promote the idea for that purpose. They have reiterated this stance very recently to the author ("we neither embrace nor discount the idea and genuinely want to see the ABAC report").

Prior to the Presidential election in 2004, and thus in the run-up to Santiago, the Administration was deterred by the implication that an FTAAP would produce "free trade with China". This fear has continued since the election, in light of the huge and rapidly growing trade imbalance between the countries, and remains the major U.S. hang-up on the issue. I will return to it below.

The key point regarding the U.S. attitude towards an FTAAP, however, is how it will be affected by the likely paths for the Doha Round analysed above. My colleagues at the Institute for International Economics and I often criticize the Bush Administration, and do not always support its trade policy, but it is clear to us that the Administration and the President personally are deeply committed to freer trade. They have led the way on Doha; indeed, there would be no Doha without the United States, including the major battle conducted by the Administration to win the TPA from the

Congress by the narrowest of margins in 2002. The Round would have no chance for even a minimal success if not for the bold initiatives taken by the Administration, as recently as just before the Hong Kong Ministerial, to liberalize agricultural and non-agricultural goods, and services restrictions around the world including its own. As recently as last summer, it again mobilized all its (admittedly waning) political muscle to win Congressional acceptance of CAFTA in the latest pitched battle between globalization and anti-globalization forces in the United States. The United States has also caused problems for the Round, to be sure, especially with its unwillingness to consider serious reform of its anti-dumping regime or immigration rules, but overall it has been by far the strongest single source of support for Doha.

Moreover, the Administration clearly sees trade policy as an integral part of its overall foreign policy and would be unwilling to let that central dimension of its global strategy disappear. In the specific case of East Asia, it is clearly concerned by the increased risk of "drawing a line down the middle of the Pacific", especially between the United States and China, and has recently launched a major inter-agency review of the "East Asian architecture" movement, how that will affect U.S. interests, and how the United States should respond. It is virtually inconceivable that the Administration would accept any of the three posited outcomes of Doha without mounting a major successor initiative, especially with respect to its chief trading partners/competitors in East Asia. It would surely want to restart the liberalization momentum, maintain its strategy of competitive liberalization and find a basis for extending the TPA when it expires in July 2007.[10]

One possible U.S. response is to launch additional FTAs with individual Asian partners. Korea and Malaysia have recently been added to the list that already included Singapore, Australia and Thailand. Indonesia is a favoured candidate for subsequent inclusion. Subsequent USTRs have offered to pursue an FTA with Japan once it, like Korea has now done, is ready to put agriculture seriously on the table.

Another U.S. alternative would be to offer "docking rights" to its existing FTAs for APEC members that were willing to accept the obligations of the existing agreements. NAFTA, for example, has an explicit "open accession" clause that has never been used. This might be a more practical way to achieve an eventual FTAAP than an "all in" negotiation from the outset. At the commencement of the APEC strategizing that ultimately produced the Bogor Goals, Senior Minister Lee Kuan Yew of Singapore in fact proposed that the United States open NAFTA to accession by all APEC members and argued that, since some would immediately accept, the entire membership would eventually have to do so via the logic of competitive liberalization. The United States is already employing a variant of this strategy in its Enterprise for ASEAN Initiative, through which it is pursuing bilateral FTAs with individual ASEAN members as they become ready with an ultimate goal of consolidating the bilaterals into a single agreement.

It would surely be superior for the United States, however, and even more so for its Asian partners, to pursue an FTAAP instead of adding further to the "spaghetti bowl" (or "noodle bowl") of PTAs in the regions. More U.S. FTAs, including via "docking" to existing U.S. FTAs by current non-members, would increasingly create a "hub-and spoke" network centred on the United States (and thus encourage further proliferation of similar "hub-and-spoke" configurations centred on other major trading powers) rather than an integrated Asia-Pacific economy. Moreover, this approach would leave unresolved the central issue of U.S.-China trade and broader economic relations. Indeed, U.S. pursuit of FTAs throughout East Asia that excluded China would be likely to further exacerbate the Washington-Beijing tensions: it would add an economic dimension to the "surround China" strategy that the United States is already clearly pursuing in the security sphere, with its new overtures to India along with the deepening of the Japan alliance, that could trigger additional Chinese pushback in both the economic (more PTAs) and security arenas.

Both the international and domestic politics of the FTAAP issue in the United States will thus turn importantly on how it will be seen as affecting the U.S.-China relationship. That relationship is clearly on a very risky path. The bilateral trade imbalance, which now exceeds $200 billion annually and can only increase because U.S. imports from China are six times greater than U.S. exports to China (twice as large as the U.S.-Japan imbalance ever became), is irrelevant per se in economic terms but toxic in domestic political terms. Moreover, the bilateral position accurately reflects the global position of the two countries: each is now running a multilateral imbalance that exceeds 7 per cent of its GNP and is rising rapidly (in China's case, the global surplus doubled in 2005 and rose another 55 per cent in the first five months of 2006). The currencies of both countries are severely misaligned, with dollar overvaluation and renminbi undervaluation of at least 20 per cent and probably more on the order of 30–40 per cent.

Such conditions in the United States have always been accurate predictors of major protectionist reactions. At the present time, the United States has already slapped new controls on six sectors of Chinese exports (apparel, colour television sets, furniture, semiconductors, shrimp and textiles). The House of Representatives has passed anti-China legislation (the English bill in July 2005) and the Senate is considering at least two sweeping across-the-board proposals (Grassley-Baucus and Schumer-Graham) — some of which, if implemented, would violate U.S. commitments under the WTO and thus justify Chinese retaliation. This could trigger a trade war between the two chief drivers of the world economy over the past five years and would almost surely provide added impetus for China and the rest of East Asia to pursue their Asia-only trade initiatives.[11]

All this is occurring with a booming U.S. economy that is enjoying full employment. The prospect for U.S. trade policy is frightening if in a year or two we face a combination of slowing growth (or even a recession), rising joblessness, a global current account deficit of $1 trillion and a bilateral imbalance with China of US$300 to US$400 billion. President Hu Jintao's visit to Washington in April 2006 produced no serious discussion of these issues, let alone any resolution of them.

At the same time, China can make a powerful case that its trade policy is not a major problem. China is one of the most open of all developing countries: its trade to GDP ratio is more than 60 per cent, double that of the United States and triple that of Japan. Its realized tariff average, the ratio of its customs collections to GDP, was 2.2 per cent in 2004. Even its nominal tariff average is only about 10 per cent. Virtually all import quotas have been eliminated and licensing schemes are being simplified. China clearly needs to follow through more aggressively on some of its WTO commitments, especially with respect to intellectual property rights, and would be well advised to respond to the external pressures by leading a new effort to bring the Doha Round to a successful conclusion. But its overall trade policy regime is not the main problem.[12]

The central strategic issue for the United States, with respect to overall China policy as well as trade and foreign economic policy, is how best to head off the potential confrontation despite these realities of China's trade policy.[13] The current bilateral strategy is proving to be largely fruitless; the results, as with Japan for three difficult decades, are at best minimal and on a case-by-case basis while the Chinese partner, even more than Japan, resents overt pressure and may even be less responsive as a result. Resort to the WTO dispute settlement mechanism can help resolve individual quarrels but many of the key issues are not covered by WTO rules and, again, the best possible outcome is case-by-case and drawn out over extended periods of time.

Hence there is compelling logic for the United States and China to bring their trade policy problems within the broader regional construct of APEC and an FTAAP. The idea should not be presented as mainly, or even importantly, aimed at resolving the U.S.-China dispute; doing so might even backfire by making the other APEC members, as well as China and the United States themselves, uncomfortable with the prospect. Fortunately, the rationale for the FTAAP is straightforward and clear as developed in the first part of this paper.

But it would greatly behoove both the United States and China to embed their trade policy disputes into a broader context that would promise eventual elimination of most or all barriers between them. For the United States, the standard logic that has always persuaded the Congress to support such agreements would again prevail: that the partner country's barriers are higher and thus the United States can only gain on balance from their mutual elimination, even if further adjustment is required in a few U.S. sectors. For China, a phased-in liberalization of its remaining restrictions would produce the culmination of its brilliant strategy to join the WTO in the first place: full integration with the world economy with the catalysing effect thereof on its domestic reform process and the creation of the globally competitive firms that it so desperately desires.[14] For both countries, the leavening presence of the rest of the APEC membership should help dilute and diffuse bilateral tensions and thus promote productive outcomes.[15]

It would be incorrect to suggest that the U.S. Administration has accepted this argument at the present time. However, it is thinking very actively about the issues. I believe there is a real possibility that it will move in the proposed direction when it is faced by the confluence of three likely developments:

• indefinite delay, if not outright failure or even a minimalist outcome, of the Doha Round;

- continuing escalation of trade and economic tensions with China, clouding the future of the critical overall relationship between the two countries; and
- further increase of protectionist and mercantilist sentiments in the Congress as a result of the Doha and China developments along with a slowing of the economy and further increase in the global and bilateral trade deficits.

The very real possibility that the United States might adopt a favourable attitude towards an FTAAP in such circumstances should be enough for ABAC, and indeed APEC itself, to begin to lay the necessary foundations for the initiative.[16] Indeed, the other member economies of APEC should make every effort to push the United States in the FTAAP direction under those conditions as it is they who would be hurt most by a United States that was backsliding into protectionism and becoming unable to negotiate internationally because of a lapse of the TPA.

V. CONCLUSION

The FTAAP is an idea whose time is coming if it has not already arrived. Events of the next six months, particularly with respect to the Doha Round but concerning U.S.-China relations and global trade policies more broadly, are likely to clarify the situation in the direction of commending an FTAAP initiative by APEC as the best, or perhaps only, way to:

- catalyse a substantively successful Doha Round;
- offer an alternative "Plan B" to restore the momentum of liberalization if Doha does falter badly;
- prevent a further, possibly explosive, proliferation of bilateral and sub-regional PTAs that create substantial new discrimination and discord within the Asia-Pacific region;
- avoid renewed risk of "drawing a line down the middle of the Pacific" as East Asian, and perhaps Western Hemisphere, regional initiatives produce disintegration of the Asia-Pacific rather than the integration that APEC was created to foster;
- channel the China-U.S. economic conflict into a more constructive and less confrontational context that could defuse at least some of its attendant tension and risk; and

- revitalize APEC itself, which is now of enhanced importance because of the risks of Asia-Pacific and especially China-U.S. fissures.

I thus believe that it is the duty of ABAC, as a trusted advisor to the APEC Leaders, to recommend that the Leaders begin to position themselves to move in the FTAAP direction, depending on the course of the main variables over the coming months. The Leaders should place the issue on their agenda for discussion at Hanoi. At a minimum, they should plan to commission their own study of the topic, drawing of course on the ABAC work to date. If Doha and other external developments evolve poorly, they should have a more extended conversation on both the pros and cons of the idea and on the initial modalities for moving it forward. Again depending on events, and on initial reactions to the idea within key member economies, the FTAAP proposal could then become the centrepiece of APEC deliberations under Australian chairmanship in 2007.[17]

Prior to the initial APEC summits, in Seattle in 1993 and Bogor in 1994, very few observers believed it would be possible or even conceivable for the APEC Leaders to endorse the concept of "free and open trade and investment in the region" by the dates certain of 2010 and 2020. Many member economies were particularly sceptical of the willingness and ability of the United States to take part in such an initiative, let alone lead it. The Leaders did adopt the Bogor Goals, however, and the United States played a central role in that process. They did so for many of the same reasons that seem so compellingly in favour of resuscitating the Bogor strategy via an FTAAP today.

ABAC of course cannot make these decisions. It has already played a vital role, however, in raising the topic and bringing it forcefully to the attention of APEC Leaders and the Asia-Pacific community more broadly.[18] It should now take the next logical steps by developing more fully the case for the idea and how it might work in practice, by urging the Leaders even more strongly to pursue it, and by starting to mobilize domestic support in the member economies. I hope this paper will contribute at least modestly to those critical goals.

Notes

1. "Preliminary Assessment of the Proposal for a Free Trade Area of the Asia Pacific (FTAAP)", an Issues Paper for the APEC Business Advisory Council

(ABAC) prepared by Robert Scollay from the PECC Trade Forum, especially pp. 25–30 and Table 3.

2. A similar case can be made for the Asian Monetary Facility that seems to be emerging as a result of the expansion and multilateralization of the Network of Bilateral Swap Arrangements under the Chiang Mai Initiative.

3. Another possible tendency is for the China-Japan rivalry to create a dividing line *within* Asia — between a "coastline perimeter" consisting of Japan, Taiwan, Australia and perhaps a few others vis-à-vis a China-dominated "mainland bloc". This too would be extremely dangerous, perhaps even more so in terms of possible intra-Asian conflict that (as in the past) could draw in the United States, and an FTAAP would also be of great help in countering this risk.

4. The U.S. network of FTAs is generally of broader coverage and deeper liberalization than those in East Asia so its preferential impact is presumably greater.

5. There is an understandable and laudable desire in many quarters to strengthen both the APEC Secretariat and the level of attention paid to APEC within member economies. The only way to achieve these goals, however, is to restore the substantive importance of APEC and thus raise its priority for members. Serious pursuit of an FTAAP would substantially heighten the salience of APEC to all participating economies and thus inevitably expand their dedication of resources to the institution.

6. Protectionist pressure will rise particularly sharply in Europe if the inevitable large decline in the value of the dollar, which is an essential component of any significant correction of the large and growing international imbalances, takes place mainly against the euro because China and the other Asian surplus countries continue to block significant appreciation of their own currencies.

7. There have been exhausted cries of "never another round" at the end of every previous round negotiated in the GATT/WTO. All three previous major rounds, however, have been widely viewed as extremely successful in advancing global liberalization and improving the rules-based trading system. Hence, whatever the attitudes at the time of their completion, they provided a solid foundation for the next succeeding round. A minimal outcome from Doha, however, let alone its explicit or implicit failure, would radically alter that history and raise serious doubts over the future of the multilateral trading system.

8. It could also induce others, especially the European Union, to accelerate their own FTA strategies instead but the magnitude of an FTAAP would be much more likely to bring those countries back to the multilateral WTO table.

9. It should be noted that a number of smaller APEC member economies have already, especially at Santiago in 2004, endorsed the FTAAP at least conditionally "if the large countries were to do so as well". This group includes at least Australia, Chile, New Zealand, Singapore and Chinese Taipei.

10. Some observers, particularly within the United States, raise doubts about the capacity of the U.S. Government, specifically USTR, to support a major new negotiating effort like the FTAAP. In a world in which the Doha Round was either concluded or suspended, however, the resources now being devoted to that enterprise could readily be shifted to an FTAAP, which would be addressing the same set of issues. A similar shift of U.S. personnel occurred in 1991–92 when the Uruguay Round went into suspended animation and the freed-up resources were largely used to negotiate NAFTA.

11. This would be even more likely if the EU joined the U.S. in applying new trade restrictions to China, and perhaps East Asia more broadly, which could easily result if China continues to block meaningful appreciation of its currency (and thus the currencies of other East Asians) so that the next major dollar decline also occurs primarily against the euro and pushes it to substantial overvaluation against Asia.

12. See Center for Strategic and International Studies and Institute for International Economics, *China: The Balance Sheet: What the World Needs to Know Now About the Emerging Superpower* (New York: Public Affairs Press, 2006), especially Chapter 4.

13. As opposed to its currency policy, which does raise major problems because of the country's massive intervention ("manipulation") to block any substantial rise in the value of the renminbi.

14. A technical but very important question is the differing concept of FTAs maintained by the United States and other APEC members such as Australia, Canada, Chile, New Zealand and Singapore, on the one hand, and by China and some other Asians on the other. The former group insists on "high quality" FTAs, though they sometimes falter in practice as when sugar was totally excluded from the U.S.-Australia agreement, whereas the latter define "free trade" more loosely and seem to place overriding emphasis on political considerations. These differences would clearly have to be addressed in seriously considering an FTAAP. So would some of the U.S. deviations from its own high-standard principles, however, such as the "yarn forward" concept that dominates the rules of origin for textile/apparel trade in U.S. FTAs and would represent a formidable hurdle to rolling the existing U.S. agreements into a single FTAAP.

15. Another major advantage for the United States is that an FTAAP initiative would presumably include Chinese Taipei under the standard rules governing its participation in all APEC non-political activities.

16. One way for the United States to signal its interest in an FTAAP would be for the Administration and/or the Congress to ask the International Trade Commission to conduct a study of the idea. All formal U.S. trade negotiations are preceded by such an "official" analysis.

17. A decision to seriously pursue the FTAAP could also have important

implications for the possible expansion of APEC's membership that will be on the agenda in 2007. Any such effort to deepen APEC co-operation would presumably counsel against broadening the make up of the group, at least to include large new economies such as India, while that process was underway. It might also be desirable, however, to add India to both APEC and an FTAAP before the latter was actually implemented in order to avoid new discrimination between that country and the current membership.

18. It is unfortunate that the APEC Leaders did not pursue the original ABAC recommendation for a study of the FTAAP at Santiago in November 2004. The Doha Round might now be much further along as a result.

3

The Political Economy of a Free Trade Area of the Asia-Pacific: A U.S. Perspective

Vinod K. Aggarwal

I. INTRODUCTION

What are the prospects for a Free Trade Area of the Asia-Pacific (FTAAP)? This paper addresses this question from the perspective of the political economy of U.S. trade policy and the current role of the Asia Pacific Economic Cooperation Forum (APEC). To preview my argument, although such an agreement may well be beneficial from a narrowly economic standpoint, the reality of U.S. trade politics, of relations between Northeast Asian economies, and of APEC's relative institutional weakness make it highly unlikely that an FTAAP will come to fruition in the short to medium term, regardless of whether the Doha Round of the World Trade Organization (WTO) is successful or not. Moreover, even the tactical use of an FTAAP to advance the WTO agenda is likely to backfire and simply further undermine prospects for successful completion of the Doha Round. Instead, I suggest that APEC should play an active role in monitoring the proliferation of bilateral trade agreements in the region and work to promote the multilateral trade agenda.

To briefly elaborate, the logic of my argument runs as follows. With respect to the current U.S. political economy of trade, two developments are of particular significance. First, the U.S. strategy of "competitive liberalization" in which it pursues bilateral and minilateral agreements, both sectorally and broadly, with the intent of stimulating the multilateral path of the WTO has fractured the domestic coalition for free trade.[1] Ironically, in their zeal to push forward the agenda of free trade — an agenda which I share — proponents of competitive liberalization have undermined the very movement to free trade that they so ardently advocate through a politically naïve understanding of trade politics. Creating piecemeal liberalization through open sectoral agreements such as the Information Technology Agreement (ITA) and bilateral trade agreements has undercut the coalition for free trade. By giving specific industries what they wanted, this policy has left protectionists in agriculture, steel, textiles, and others in control of the trade agenda. Thus, those who bemoan the proliferation of bilateral and regional initiatives and the lack of progress in the WTO fail to recognize the obvious unfortunate causality connecting these two approaches to trade. In my view, it is their very advocacy of a policy of competitive liberalization that has been a *key contributor* to the Doha Round's troubles.

Second, the continuing and increasing U.S. trade deficit with China has dramatically increased domestic protectionist pressure in the United States. Many industry groups and their political advocates have seized upon the gargantuan trade deficit, which has been blamed by many on the rigidity of the yuan's exchange rate, to increasingly question the benefits of free trade for the U.S., particularly with countries specializing in low-cost exports. The threat of across-the-board tariffs of 27.5 per cent on all Chinese imports highlights the seriousness of this issue. Although such a tariff is unlikely to pass, it has served as a rallying cry for an assortment of protectionist groups in the United States and allied groups who have linked security concerns, labour rights, human rights, religious freedom, and numerous other issues to trade. Together with the fractured domestic coalition for free trade that has been created by competitive liberalization, any free trade area that involves China will effectively be dead on arrival in Congress for the foreseeable future.

For its part, APEC has failed to significantly move forward the trade liberalization agenda in the Asia-Pacific and is unlikely to do so with its current weak institutional structure. It has, however, continued to play an important and useful role in trade facilitation activities and with respect to other issues such as security and the environment, to name just a few. Using APEC as the key instrument to promote an FTAAP in the current context will lack credibility and will instead further fracture APEC's membership and undermine the useful roles it has been playing.

How might the logic of this pessimistic view on the prospects for an FTAAP be affected by possible success or failure of the Doha Round? If the Doha Round is successful, states will be busy implementing a complex agreement and the FTAAP would be low on everyone's agenda. If the Doha Round fails, the evidence suggests that U.S. industries are much more likely to push for bilateral trade agreements rather than an FTAAP. Asia and the EU are likely to reciprocate the United States' response, further fostering the proliferation of bilateral accords. Having set in motion a pernicious course of competitive liberalization, putting the genie back into the multilateral bottle will be a Herculean task. Here, APEC could play a useful role in attempting to monitor and reconcile such accords and possibly lead a movement to impose a moratorium and roll-back of this disastrous trend. In short, regardless of the Doha Round's success or failure, I believe that an FTAAP is not politically viable at the moment from a U.S. perspective.

The remainder of the paper is organized as follows. Section II characterizes the many different types of trade agreements that might be negotiated, both in theory and in practice. Section III then considers the political problems that have been created through competitive liberalization. Specifically, based on the framework developed in section II, it shows how U.S. policy has moved away from the previous strong commitment to multilateral multi-product trade liberalization as the central approach to bilateral and minilateral broad and sector specific accords. To examine the prospects of an FTAAP, section IV considers the likely domestic political dynamics of current U.S. trade policy, the importance of the U.S.-China trade deficit, and APEC's current role. In conclusion, section V examines the impact of these elements by considering FTAAP's prospects in the scenarios of both success and failure in the Doha Round, as well as positive roles that APEC might play.

II. VARIETIES OF TRADE GOVERNANCE

In the post-World War II period, states have utilized a host of measures to regulate trade flows. Yet in their examination of such accords, analysts have conflated different type of arrangements and used them synonymously. For example, the term "regional agreement" has been used to refer to widely disparate accords such as APEC, the Asia Europe Meeting (ASEM), the North American Free Trade Agreement (NAFTA), intraregional and extraregional bilateral free trade agreements, and even sectoral agreements such as the ITA.[2]

This conceptual ambiguity and under-differentiation of the dependent variable makes it more difficult to develop causal arguments to account for specific outcomes. To more clearly specify different types of trade arrangements, I focus on several dimensions: the number of participants involved in an agreement, product coverage, geographical scope, market opening or closing, and institutionalization. I define the number of participants in terms of unilateral, bilateral, minilateral, and multilateral participation in an agreement. I use the term bilateral to refer to two countries and minilateral to more than two.[3] In terms of product coverage, the range is from narrow (a few products) to broad (multiproduct) in scope. Geographical scope differentiates between arrangements that are concentrated geographically and those that bind states across great distances. A fourth dimension addresses whether these measures have been either market opening (liberalizing) or market closing (protectionist). Fifth and finally, one can also look at the degree of institutionalization or strength of agreements.[4] Table 3.1 summarizes a typology of trade agreements with illustrative examples based on these dimensions but omits discussion of the degree of institutionalization for presentation purposes.

Sectoral Unilateralism

Cell 1 in Table 3.1 focuses on unilateral sectoral market opening or closing measures, the classic example is the British Corn Laws of 1815 and their subsequent removal in 1846.[5] Although some sectoral opening took place in the twentieth century, a variant of sectoral opening that is tied to bilateral bargaining took place in the late 1980s and 1990s. The United States used Super 301, a congressionally mandated trade policy instrument, to threaten

TABLE 3.1
Classifying Varieties of Trade Governance

Product Scope	Number of Participants					
	Unilateral	Bilateral		Minilateral		Multilateral
		Geographically Concentrated	Geographically Dispersed	Geographically Concentrated	Geographically Dispersed	
Few Products (Sectoral)	(1) U.K. Corn Laws (1815) U.K. Corn Law removal (1846) Super 301 (1990s)	(2) U.S.-Canada Auto Agreement (1965)	(3) U.S.-Japan VERs and VIEs (1980s–1990s)	(4) ECSC (1951)	(5) EVSL (1997)	(6) LTA (1962) & MFA (1974) ITA (1997) BTA (1998) FSA (1999)
Many Products	(7) U.K. (1860s) Smoot Hawley (1930)	(8) Canada-U.S. FTA (1989) Japan-South Korean FTA (under negotiation)	(9) U.S.-Israel FTA (1985) U.S.-Singapore FTA (2004) Japan-Mexico FTA (2004)	(10) EC/EU (1958/1992) ASEAN (1967) MERCOSUR (1991) NAFTA (1993)	(11) APEC (1989) AFTA (1991) EU-MERCOSUR (under negotiation)	(12) GATT/WTO (1947/1995)

Source: Adapted from Aggarwal (2001a).

closure of its market and force other countries to "unilaterally" open up their markets in specific products. This particular form of sectoralism sparked a heated scholarly debate. Jagdish Bhagwati and Hugh Patrick, for example, dub this unusual U.S. practice "aggressive unilateralism".[6]

Sectoral Bilateral Regionalism

In cell 2, we have sectoral agreements between a pair of countries that are geographically concentrated. From a market-opening perspective, this approach often reflects pressures from politically strong but narrow interests that are pursuing greater economies of scale. The resulting arrangements tend to promote intra-industry trade.[7] The best example of this kind is the U.S.-Canada Automotive Products Trade Agreement of 1965. Prior to the 1988 Canada-U.S. Free Trade Agreement (CUSFTA), the Auto Agreement was the only major success in the long-standing effort to liberalize bilateral trade between the United States and Canada.

Sectoral Bilateral Transregionalism

Cell 3 refers to sectoral agreements between two countries that are geographically dispersed. Examples of this sort of protectionist agreement include voluntary export restraints (VERs) and potentially market-opening measures such as voluntary import expansions (VIEs), both of which have generally but not always crossed regions.[8] The word "voluntary" is obviously misleading as such agreements are often the result of coercive pressures. These sorts of agreements set off a lively debate about "mismanaged trade" and the notion of a "fair and level playing field".[9] More recently, a less coercive example of bilateral sectoral liberalization can be seen in the negotiations between the United States and EU over the streamlining of testing and approval procedures through the creation of Mutual Recognition Agreements in several sectors.[10]

Sectoral Minilateral Regionalism

In cell 4, we have sectoral agreements between three or more countries that are geographically close to each other. The best example is the European Coal and Steel Community (ECSC), created in 1951. Its main task was to integrate the post-war European coal and steel industry, but it also served as the foundation and stepping stone for the political and economic union of Europe. From the start, the ECSC faced criticism for its inconsistency with Article 24 of the General Agreement on Tariffs and Trade (GATT), which calls for liberalization on a multiproduct basis, rather than only for a few products. Although challenged as being inconsistent with the GATT by Czechoslovakia, the ECSC members managed to obtain a GATT waiver of obligation.[11] After the ECSC evolved into the European Economic Community, the issue of sector-specific accords became moot.

Sectoral Minilateral Transregionalism

Cell 5 provides an example of geographically dispersed sectoral trans-regionalism. One example is the case of the Early Voluntary Sectoral Liberalization (EVSL) under the auspices of APEC. In Vancouver in 1997, ministers agreed to consider nine sectors as a package for fast track liberalization. The United States sought such a sector-specific package deal to discourage countries from picking and choosing sectors based on domestic concerns. This strategy initially appeared viable but quickly ran into difficulties as Japan and several other countries particularly objected to the liberalization of agriculture, forestry, and fishery products in the context of the East Asian financial crisis. In the end, the package was sent to the WTO rather than being considered for liberalization at the APEC level.

Sectoral Multilateralism

Cell 6 provides an example of multilateral sectoral accords. This category includes market-opening measures such as the ITA, the Basic Telecom Agreement (BTA), and the Financial Service Agreement (FSA) as well as market-closing measures such as the Long Term Arrangement on Cotton Textiles and the Multi-fiber Arrangement, the latter expanding managed trade beyond cotton products. The emergence of these types of agreements is a particularly important development. Laura Tyson, for example, has argued that among multilateral trade options, this sectoral approach is a sound alternative to the multi-sector WTO approach.[12] As we shall see below, however, such accords may actually retard progress in trade liberalization by undermining the coalition for free trade and may also lead to economic distortions.

Multiproduct Unilateralism

We turn next to broader multiproduct liberalization and protection. Cell 7 focuses on unilateralism, the most significant example being nineteenth-century Britain. Unilateral liberalization was feasible for Britain, thanks to its industrial strength, its limited investment in transaction-specific assets for trade, and its quasi-monopsony power in raw material and export markets — which contrasted with other countries' limited alternatives to importing British manufactured goods.[13] Contemporary examples include unilateral liberalization measures taken by Australia, New Zealand, Chile, Hong Kong, and Singapore. The most important market-closing measures took place in the United States with the Smoot-Hawley Tariff of 1930 that set a cycle of trade protectionism in motion and aggravated the depression.

Multiproduct Bilateral Regionalism

Bilateral arrangements of both a regional and transregional actor scope have rapidly proliferated over the last few years. Cell 8 refers to bilateral trade agreements covering multiple products between a pair of adjacent countries, such as the CUSFTA of 1988 and Japan-South Korea preferential trade agreement (PTA) (under negotiation). More often than not, such agreements draw upon not only geographic, historic, and cultural affinities but also complementarities in economic structure. In order to reduce the costs related to geographic distance and to maximize the benefits from economic size, analysts argue that neighbouring countries will often form preferential trade agreements (PTAs) with one another, creating a natural trading bloc.

Multiproduct Bilateral Transregionalism

In cell 9, we have cases of geographically dispersed bilateral agreements covering multiple products. Examples include PTAs between the United States and Israel (1985), Mexico and Israel (2000), the United States and Jordan (2001), Japan and Singapore (2001), South Korea and Chile (2002), the United States and Singapore (2004), and Japan and Mexico (2004). Some of these bilateral PTAs — for example, the U.S.-Israel agreement and U.S.-Jordan one — have been clearly motivated primarily by political-strategic rather than economic reasons.[14] Some, such as the PTAs between Japan and Singapore and South Korea and Chile, are largely designed for the purpose of "training" or "capacity-building" for broader and deeper trade liberalization. More recently, this training and capacity-building objective has been widely sought in East Asia as many in the region have begun to seek PTAs with little prior experience in their formation.[15]

Multiproduct Minilateral Regionalism

Cell 10 focuses on geographically concentrated minilateral agreements. For the past decades, these types of accords have attracted the most scholarly attention, commensurate with the rise of regional trading arrangements since the 1960s. Conventional explanations for the move towards minilateral regionalism have focused on both economic and political-strategic motivations. Some economic arguments include: enlarging economies of scale without excessive global competition; increasing the attractiveness of an economy to foreign capital; and creating natural trading blocs according to geographic proximity.[16] Political-strategic economic reasons include signalling or strengthening one's bargaining position in relation to more powerful partners; responding to the erosion of U.S. support for multilateralism; locking in a domestic reform agenda; a domino effect; limiting free rider problems; reducing transaction costs between negotiating parties; and lowering the political salience of negotiations.[17] There has also been a significant amount of work examining regional variations in terms of the nature, strength, depth, and scope of minilateral arrangements. These works usually compare European or North American "success" with Asian or Latin American "failure", focusing on historical, cultural, politico-institutional differences within and between different geographical groupings.[18] It is worth noting that all of these explanations, which have seemingly focused on "regionalism", fall in fact into several cells of my typology, namely 2, 4, and 8 — and, to some extent, cell 11 as well, indicating the conceptual ambiguity and under-differentiation inherent in the existing literature on regionalism.

Multiproduct Minilateral Interregionalism

Another important recent development in trade arrangements concerns links that span countries across continents, as noted in Cell 11. Many analysts lump their examination of "minilateral regional" accords such as NAFTA and the EU with those of "minilateral interregional" arrangements such as the EU's efforts to link up with MERCOSUR, although the causal factors behind minilateral interregionalism are often quite different from those driving minilateral regionalism. The term "interregionalism" can itself be broken down into more specific types, based on the prevalence of PTAs and/or customs unions as constitutive units within interregional agreements. In work with Edward Fogarty, I refer to an agreement as "purely interregional" if it formally links free trade areas or customs unions, as in the case of EU-MERCOSUR.[19] If a customs union negotiates with countries in different regions, but not with a customs union or free trade agreement, we refer to this as "hybrid interregionalism" (for example, the Lomé Agreement). Finally, if an accord links countries across two regions where *neither* of the two negotiates as a grouping, then we refer to this as "transregionalism" (for example, APEC). These sub-categories of interregionalism suggest the importance of taking into account the diverse driving forces and effects of interregionalism — as opposed to more "garden-variety" regional arrangements.

Multiproduct Multilateralism

Finally, cell 12 refers to the case of global, multiproduct trading arrangements such as the GATT and its successor organization, the WTO. Neoclassical trade theory argues that unilateral trade liberalization is the best means by which to promote overall economic welfare. Though theoretically solid, this option is often not politically feasible. As a second-best option, therefore, economists have preferred multilateral trade strategies to sub-multilateral, preferential approaches. Though highly successful throughout the post-war period, multilateral trade forums at the global level have increasingly encountered difficulties in hammering out new terms of trade liberalization. This, in turn, has fuelled interest in preferential arrangements at the sub-multilateral level.

III. THE EVOLUTION OF U.S. TRADE POLICY

What trends have we seen in U.S. trade policy strategy in the post-World War II period? As we shall see, the decisive shift in the types of trade arrangements from multiproduct multilateral negotiations to a variety of other forms came in the mid to late 1980s in the midst of the Uruguay Round negotiations. This analysis and categorization of the evolving landscape of U.S. trade policy based on Table 3.1 helps to provide the necessary background to understand the current political economy of U.S. trade policy and its implications for attempting to create an FTAAP, a topic discussed in Section IV.

Multiproduct Multilateralism: U.S. Trade Policy from the Post-World War II Period to the Early 1980s[20]

With a dominant military force, a large market, enormous productive capacity, and a strong currency and financial system, the U.S. was well positioned to assume global responsibility at the end of World War II. It acted as military leader of the Western alliance, served as the world's central banker, and provided the major impetus for international trade liberalization. As a result, the 1950s and 1960s were marked by unprecedented economic growth and development. In particular, the nested context of the international trading system within the overall security system gave the U.S. executive leverage to resist domestically oriented protectionist groups. The president could resist both Congressional and interest group pressures by raising the spectre of the Soviet and Chinese communist threat to U.S. interests, thereby allowing it to advance Cold War concerns over narrow parochial interests and foster free trade.[21] During this period, the U.S. maintained a coherent approach to the trading system — founded on its interest in promoting multilateralism — and ensured that its trading partners grew to buttress the Western alliance against Soviet encroachment.

The proposed post-World War II trade and monetary systems — consisting of the Bretton Woods regime and the International Trade Organization (ITO) — were cast at a global level and depended on U.S. hegemonic resources and leadership. In addition, with Western Europe and Japan ravaged by the war, the Cold War context further reinforced the U.S. desire for rebuilding these economies. But despite this positive security context, a coalition of protectionists and free traders in the United States, each of whom thought that the ITO was an excessive compromise, prevented the ITO from securing Congressional approval and thus led to its death.[22]

Still, the U.S. executive branch did not simply give up. With the ITO moribund, the United States promoted a temporary implementing treaty,

GATT, as the key institution to manage trade on a multilateral basis in 1948. As a trade "institution", GATT got off to a difficult start, representing a stopgap agreement among "contracting parties" — rather than a true international institution. Originally brokered in parallel with ITO negotiations, the twenty-three GATT members negotiated a series of tariff concessions and free trade principles designed to prevent the introduction of trade barriers. Unlike the ITO, GATT negotiations were successfully concluded and signed in Geneva in October 1947. Under the agreement, over 45,000 binding tariff concessions were covered, constituting close to $10 billion in trade among the participating countries.

As the sole interim framework for regulating and liberalizing world trade, GATT turned out to be highly successful at overseeing international trade in goods and progressively reducing trade barriers.[23] The Kennedy Round of 1962–67 proved to be the most dramatic facilitator of trade liberalization. GATT membership increased to sixty-two countries responsible for over 75 per cent of world trade at the time. New tariff concessions reached over 50 per cent on many products as negotiations expanded from a product-by-product approach to an industry/sector-wide method, while overall tariff reductions were 35 per cent.[24] The Tokyo Round of 1973–79 led to a record ninety-nine countries agreeing to further tariff reductions worth over $300 billion of trade and an average reduction in manufacturing tariffs from 7 per cent to 4.7 per cent. In addition, agreements were reached on technical barriers to trade, subsidies and countervailing measures, import licensing procedures, government procurement, customs valuation and a revised anti-dumping code.

This period is often dubbed the "golden age" of trade liberalization, witnessing a dramatic reduction of border barriers. But while this golden age of globalism was marked by significant coherence, it is worth noting that the 1950s were already marred by exceptions to a multilateral multiproduct approach to negotiations. Indeed, sectoralism emerged in textiles and in oil trade as early as the mid-1950s, while temporary VERs in textiles and apparel evolved into the increasingly protectionist multilateral MFA over a period of forty years.[25]

Yet, however repugnant the development of sector-specific arrangements, the U.S. executive maintained a focus on free trade. For President Kennedy, textiles and apparel protection was simply the necessary price to pay for the broader objective of what came to be known as the Kennedy Round of GATT negotiations. Most crucially, despite deviating from the norms of GATT in some respects, the Long Term Arrangement on Cotton Textiles and the MFA were carefully nested in GATT, and indeed the implementation and enforcement structure were housed in Geneva.

In the context of the negotiation of GATT rounds, the U.S. executive continued to face protectionist pressure from specific industries and was repeatedly forced to accommodate them. Soon after the Kennedy Round was concluded, the steel industry managed to secure VERs to limit steel imports from Japan and the EEC in 1969.[26] These VERs were dropped in 1974, but since then various new accords to limit steel imports have repeatedly been imposed and dropped. In footwear, orderly marketing arrangements were negotiated with Taiwan and South Korea in 1977, but these were dropped in 1981 and have not been reimposed. Similarly, OMAs restricting televisions from Japan, Korea and Taiwan came into effect from 1977 to 1979, but were then dropped from 1980 to 1982. In autos, President Reagan negotiated a VER with the Japanese in 1981, but by 1985, these had also been dropped.

The most important issue to keep in mind when thinking about the implications of sector-specific arrangements is their purpose. For example, as in the case of sectoral arrangements in textiles and apparel, President Kennedy removed opposition by an industry that viewed itself as *losing* from freer trade. By appeasing this potent opponent, Kennedy was able to strengthen the coalition for free trade. Similarly, other agreements as in televisions, footwear, and autos have come into being for similar reasons, but in the case of those industries, were relatively temporary and have not been reimposed. By contrast, as I argue below, competitive liberalization has had the opposite effect, instead *weakening* the pro-free trade coalition. Thus, we must be careful in assessing the pros and cons of sectoral initiatives.

A second key deviation from the multilateral process was the development of regional accords. But the most significant of these — the European Coal and Steel Community, which evolved into the European Economic Community (EEC) and now the EU — were backed by the United States with overall security concerns in mind. Indeed, as we have seen, when some criticized this accord as being inconsistent with GATT Article 24, the United States supported a waiver for the ECSC in GATT. For its part, however, the United States refused to engage in the negotiation of regional trading accords and persisted with its multilateral multiproduct approach, albeit with occasional deviations on a sectoral basis as I have noted.

Table 3.2 illustrates the various trade agreements of which the United States was a part during the period of the 1950s to the early 1980s.

As noted, the dominant U.S. approach during this period was clearly a GATT-based multilateral multiproduct approach, with occasional highly focused deviations. Aside from the sectoral protectionist arrangements, the only other accord of any significance was the U.S.-Canada auto agreement. This agreement, tied to the co-production arrangements across the border, received a formal GATT waiver of obligation.

But in the early 1980s, following the Tokyo Round, change in the traditional approach was clearly in the air. The United States began to fear that European interest was now focused on widening and deepening of its regional integration efforts. With respect to GATT, the 1982 effort to start a new round proved to be a failure, as most countries criticized the United States for attempting to include services and other new issues on the agenda. With problems in GATT, in 1984, following the failed 1982 GATT Ministerial meeting, the U.S. Trade and Tariff Act authorized the administration to actively negotiate bilateral free trade agreements. Soon thereafter, the United States negotiated the Caribbean Basis Initiative (1983) and the U.S.-Israel free trade (1985) agreement, made overtures to ASEAN, and undertook sectoral discussions with Canada in 1984 (which ended in failure). But the direction was now clear: the United States now was willing to shift its own strategy away from pure multilateralism.

Trade Policy after the mid-1980s: One Step Forward, Two Steps Backward[27]

After considerable discussion, particularly over the inclusion of services, the GATT Uruguay Round got underway in 1986. Yet the United States kept up the pressure of using alternatives to GATT to put pressure on other states in the ongoing negotiations. The signal was clear. Treasury Secretary James Baker warned in 1988:

If possible we hope that this ... liberalization will occur in the Uruguay Round. If not, we might be willing to explore a market liberalizing club approach through minilateral arrangements or a series of bilateral agreements. While we associate a liberal trading system with multilateralism, bilateral or minilateral regimes may also help move the world toward a more open system.[28]

TABLE 3.2
U.S. Trade Policy: 1940s to early 1980s

Product Scope	Number of Participants					
	Unilateral	Bilateral		Minilateral		Multilateral
		Geographically Concentrated	Geographically Dispersed	Geographically Concentrated	Geographically Dispersed	
Few Products (Sectoral)	(1)	(2) U.S.-Canada Auto Agreement (1965)	(3) U.S.-Japan, S. Korea, Taiwan, EC VERs (1960s–1980s)	(4)	(5)	(6) Long Term Agreement on Cotton Textiles (1962) Multi-Fiber Arrangement (1974)
Many Products	(7)	(8)	(9)	(10)	(11)	(12) GATT (1947)

Source: Adapted from Aggarwal (2001a).

A high level of contentiousness continuously threatened the conclusion of the round. In part, this reflects the changing balance of power among more actors in the system, the dissolution of the liberal consensus and inclusion of diverse interests, and the unwillingness of the United States to continue to be the lender and market of last resort. The era of détente and the subsequent end of the Cold War further weakened the security argument for continuing economic concessions in broad-based trade negotiations.

After considerable delay, the Uruguay Round came to a conclusion in 1993. But the United States was no longer solely committed to the multilateral route, as illustrated by its policy shift beginning in the mid-1980s. On a multiproduct basis, the United States created its first bilateral agreement with Israel in 1985, and a year earlier had created a preferential trading agreement for the Caribbean countries. But these rather minor deviations were superseded by the very significant 1987 free trade area with Canada, the United States' founding membership in APEC in 1989, the initiation of negotiations with Mexico that led to the 1993 NAFTA agreement, and ongoing negotiations for a Free Trade Area of the Americas.

On a sectoral basis, while continuing to be part of the protectionist Multi-fiber Arrangement, the United States moved to a new tack with the conclusion of "open sectoral" multilateral agreements in information technology, telecommunications, and financial services from 1996 to 1998. It is worth examining the implications of these open sectoral agreements at length. Laura Tyson, for example, has argued that among multilateral trade options, this sectoral approach is a sound alternative to the multi-sector WTO approach. In her words,

> the global-round approach to trade talks, involving all WTO participants in a comprehensive agenda requiring bargains across several sectors, may have outlived its usefulness. Focused negotiations on trade issues in specific sectors among a smaller group of WTO members are a promising alternative. Such negotiations have produced significant agreements in information technology, telecommunications, and financial services.[29]

Yet as I have argued elsewhere, open sectoralism can be politically hazardous.[30] From a political perspective, sectoral market opening is likely to *reduce* political support for multilateral, multisector negotiations. Because sectoral agenda setting involves a limited and easily polarized set of domestic interests, the margin for coalition building and political give-and-take is much slimmer. Moreover, industries that have succeeded in securing sectoral liberalization may pose a threat to a global liberalization agenda. These groups will see little reason to risk their existing benefits by supporting their relocation in the WTO-centred multilateral, multiproduct regime. By giving highly motivated liberal-minded interests what they wanted in their specific sector, this approach contrasts sharply with the long-standing successful policy that we have seen of giving often-temporary relief to strong protectionist interests to remove their opposition to broader liberalization. Thus, while such open sectoral liberalization seems attractive from an economic standpoint, it may actually be one step forward and two steps backward when it comes to securing freer trade.

What about the trend in U.S. policy over the last few years? President Clinton failed to obtain fast track authority during his tenure in the 1990s. Business groups continued to worry that the EU was moving forward in the negotiation of trade accords, particularly with eastward expansion. In 2001, the Business Roundtable argued:

> Obviously, the best policy option is to build on the WTO framework... However, it may take regional and bilateral initiatives to jumpstart the WTO. Alternatively, we may have to undertake the regional and bilateral initiatives just to avoid discrimination by our more active trading partners.[31]

Echoing this view, U.S. Trade Representative (USTR) Robert Zoellick argued that:

> America's absence from the proliferation of trade accords hurts our exporters... If other countries go ahead with free trade agreements and the United States does not, we must blame ourselves. We have to get back in the game and take the lead.[32]

Once President Bush obtained fast track authority (now known as trade promotion authority), the United States proceeded to negotiate a large number of bilateral trade agreements (see Table 3.3), often for strategic reasons with little economic rationale or direct trade benefit. Indeed until the recent initiation of negotiations with South Korea, the total export coverage of all the agreements to this point, excluding NAFTA, was little more than 10 per cent.

What are the international implications of the pursuit of bilateral trade agreements? This so-called competitive liberalization strategy has created an important negative dynamic. As John Ravenhill notes, at the end of 2001, of 144 WTO members, only China, Hong Kong, Japan, South Korea, Mongolia, and Taiwan, had not signed a preferential trading agreement.[33]

TABLE 3.3
US. Trade Policy: Mid-1980s to 2006

		Number of Participants				
		Unilateral	Bilateral		Minilateral		Multilateral
			Geographically Concentrated	Geographically Dispersed	Geographically Concentrated	Geographically Dispersed	
Product Scope	Few Products	(1) Super 301 (1990s)	(2)	(3) U.S.-Japan, VIEs (1980s–1990s) Australia FTA (2004)	(4)	(5) EVSL (1997)	(6) ITA (1997) BTA (1998) FSA (1999)
	Many Products	(7) Generalized System of Preferences (1976, 2002) Andean Trade Preference Act (1991, 2002)	(8) Canada-U.S. FTA (1989)	(9) Israel FTA (1985) Jordan FTA (2001) Chile FTA (2003) Singapore FTA (2004) Morocco FTA (2004)	(10) NAFTA (1993)	(11) APEC (1989) Dominican Republic-Central America FTA (2005) Free Trade Area of the Americas (N)	(12) GATT/WTO (1947/1995)

TABLE 3.3 — cont'd

Product Scope	Number of Participants					
	Unilateral	Bilateral		Minilateral		Multilateral
		Geographically Concentrated	Geographically Dispersed	Geographically Concentrated	Geographically Dispersed	
Many Products	African Growth and Opportunity Act (2000) Caribbean Basin Initiative (1983, 2000)		Bahrain FTA (2005) Oman FTA* (2006) Peru TPA* (2006) Colombia FTA* (2006) Panama FTA* (2006) Korea FTA* (2007) Malaysia FTA (N) Thailand FTA (N) UAE FTA (N)		South African Customs Union FTA (N)	

Note: * indicates that the agreement has been signed but not ratified. "N" means currently being negotiated.

This quickly changed with these members imitating the U.S. strategy of negotiating bilateral accords, and in doing so contributing to the heavily criticized "noodle bowl" in Asia.[34] As was recently reported, "What makes [Japan's] government eager to rush to sign FTAs is the rapid progress elsewhere ... centered on the U.S."[35]

With the Asians and the United States now actively moving forward, we have now come full circle, with the EU now beginning to worry that it has been left behind in the bilateral game. In a recent paper, Peter Mandelson, the European Trade Commissioner noted in July 2006 that the EU needed to ink bilateral deals to increase its competitiveness with Asia and the United States. As the *Financial Times* noted:

> European business has argued that the EU's reluctance to be seen as undermining the World Trade Organization by negotiating bilateral deals has seen it overtaken by competitors such as the U.S. and Japan that are not shy.[36]

In short, the competitive liberal approach has not led to success in the pursuit of broad-scale trade liberalization. Instead, bilateralism has simply fostered more widespread bilateralism.

To summarize U.S. policy after the mid-1980s, Table 3.3 provides a snapshot of the variety of agreements that the United States is now pursuing, and provides a sharp contrast with the agreements that the United States pursued until the early 1980s.

IV. THE POLITICAL ECONOMY OF THE FTAAP: CURRENT U.S. DYNAMICS

With the sharp trend in U.S. policy towards competitive liberalization, and rapid proliferation of bilateral trade agreements in the Asia-Pacific more generally, might an FTAAP be an optimal trade arrangement and reinvigorate APEC? Unfortunately, my analysis suggests that the answer to this question is a resounding "No". Three key factors underlie this pessimism. First, any U.S. domestic political coalition that might support such a move has been undermined by bilateral and sectoral agreements, and these groups have begun to prefer a bilateral route. Second, the U.S. trade deficit poses a significant obstacle to any participation of China in a PTA, whether bilaterally or as part of a broader Asia-Pacific accord. And third, APEC is insufficiently institutionalized to play a role that could foster such an accord. Worse, APEC's current benefits, however limited, are likely to be further undermined by any such effort. Moreover, these arguments apply, irrespective of whether a Doha Round agreement is signed in the near future or not.

The Missing Political Coalition for an FTAAP

With the United States pursuing competitive liberalization, particularly along a bilateral route, the coalition for free trade has begun to fray, making it very unlikely that the U.S. executive will be able to generate support for an FTAAP and secure passage of an implementing bill in Congress.

With respect to general domestic implications of bilateral accords, a number of analysts see the political implications of bilateral agreements along the lines of the problems identified with open sectoralism. As Ravenhill notes:

> By providing a means to achieve liberalization without political pain, the new bilateralism encourages protectionist interests and has the potential to weaken domestic pro-liberalization coalitions and especially demand for multilateral liberalization. From the perspective of comprehensive global trade liberalization, such effects are unambiguously bad.[37]

Turning to the United States specifically, and consistent with my argument about the limited benefit of most U.S. PTAs, Richard Feinberg argues that "bilateralism has opened the door to an explicit introduction of political criteria, in contradiction to GATT/WTO apolitical universalism."[38]

This political dynamic has created a situation where the pursuit of bilateral trade agreements has now given interest groups and their supporters an interest in their continuation. As Feinberg finds from his analysis:

> This range of interests appeals not only to USTR and the Commerce Department, but also to the U.S. departments of State and Defense, as well as to the international offices in the Department of Labor and the Environmental Protection Agency. When such a broad-based coalition of bureaucratic interests gets behind a policy thrust, it is likely to endure.[39]

As the United States pursues a piecemeal approach, the passage of specific accords creates narrow vested interests. For example, with respect to the CAFTA debate, one source commented that the "deal drew concentrated fire from three well-organized constituencies — textile producers, sugar companies and unions. But because the CAFTA economies are so small, U.S. business didn't mount as muscular a campaign as it did in the NAFTA vote."[40] For its part, agricultural groups are interested in a broad agreement and would gain relatively little from a purely Asia-Pacific agreement. The official U.S. advisory committee on agriculture has warned:

> The APAC takes this opportunity to reiterate its belief that highest priority must be given to comprehensive agricultural trade reform in the Doha Development Agenda round of negotiations. Only a WTO agreement can deliver full and equitable reforms in market access, domestic support, and export subsidies. Some APAC members are concerned that a proliferation of FTAs, which only address market access, may have a negative impact on negotiating equitable reform across the three pillars identified in the Doha negotiations. Members are also concerned that Congressional support for trade liberalization could erode through fatigue from constant trade debates over individual FTAs.[41]

Other powerful lobbies are also wary of further opening. The textile and apparel industry has received protection for over 50 years. Although the MFA was terminated at the end of 2004, the textile and apparel industries successfully secured restrictions on Chinese textile and apparel imports in 2005 in the wake of the MFA's removal. Currently, the textile and apparel industry is pushing to create separate negotiations on textiles and apparel once again. In a letter to the USTR, as the *Journal of Commerce* notes:

> ...44 U.S. representatives called for separate negotiations for textiles. Their letter included an implicit threat: If U.S. trade negotiators fail to address the concerns of textile manufacturers, it will "substantially impact" congressional support for a Doha agreement on Non-Agricultural Market Access.[42]

With the textile industry's success in securing new restraints on China in 2005, can one really imagine that this key powerful player would support an FTAAP that would only increase imports from low-cost producers in the Asia-Pacific region? Indeed, even the ratification of bilateral agreements faces bipartisan opposition. With respect to Vietnam, for example:

> A vote in favor of permanent MFN for Vietnam could be controversial for Republicans with textile constituents given the opposition of the National Council of Textile Organizations. NCTO has opposed the bilateral market access deal on Vietnam because it fails to impose safeguards on Vietnamese textile exports which it charges are heavily subsidized by the government.[43]

The increasing opposition to trade liberalization, of any sort, is reflected in the mood in Congress. Although many Republicans have increasing doubts about further trade liberalization, particularly those from states with protectionist-minded industries, the real opposition to trade agreements comes from the Democrats. Since the narrow passage of fast-track authority in 2002, the congressional politics of U.S. trade policy have become increasingly polarized, both in partisanship and in interest-group representation. Democratic opposition to the administration's trade agenda has arisen primarily over concerns about foreign labour and environmental standards, adverse effects for American employment, and human rights issues, aptly seizing trade policy as a tool to mobilize the Democratic base.

Although initial passage of Trade Promotion Authority (TPA) was barely achieved after Republican concession to a programme paying health benefits to workers displaced by trade, most trade accords brought to Congress in the first few years of fast-track generally met bipartisan acceptance. Major contention arose in 2005, however, with the vote to implement the Dominican Republic–Central America Free Trade Agreement (DR-CAFTA). Democrats claimed the agreement would export American jobs overseas without ensuring international labour standards were protected, and allowed U.S. corporations to benefit from low labour costs by exploiting poor workers. A *Washington Post* article rightly called DR-CAFTA "the most fiercely contested trade accord in the past decade", and in the end it passed the House by a vote of only 217 to 215, a far closer victory than even the contentious NAFTA vote in 1993.[44] The partisan nature of the divide was clear from the vote — only fifteen Democrats voted for the agreement, while only twenty-seven Republicans voted against it. What DR-CAFTA revealed was the potential power that a coalition of traditional protectionists (politicians obliged to various local industrial interests) and the champions of "linkage" politics in trade policy (seizing upon labour, environmental, and human rights concerns) might possess if the Republicans are unable to consolidate the party line on trade.

Since DR-CAFTA, Democrats in Congress have prioritized defeating bilateral trade agreements negotiated under the auspices of the "competitive liberalization" strategy, recognizing both the current political weakness of the Bush administration and the potential trade policy has to garner key support from groups like the AFL-CIO in the run-up to mid-term elections. Most recent has been the furor over the negotiated

U.S.-Oman PTA, with House Democrats demanding that a clause be inserted into the agreement to insure against the use of forced labour in production. USTR Schwab responded by asserting that the negotiated text, bolstered by current U.S. law preventing the import of goods produced by forced labour as well as promises by the Omani government to reform its labour laws, was sufficient to prevent labour abuses. Some have argued that the Oman FTA is a "political test drive" for a bigger Congressional battle to be waged over a U.S.-Peru agreement over the next year.[45] And indeed, Democrats appear to be fighting agreements as much for party politics as much as principled opposition.

Most of these pacts are likely to be passed by Congress in the end. But the significant opposition put forward on these limited and, all things considered, rather inconsequential trade agreements reveals the current disbanded state of the much ballyhooed "consensus on free trade" as well as how the deep partisan divide in Congress has affected the feasibility of potential U.S. trade agreements in the future. In this context, an FTAAP involving low labour cost countries, those with human rights violations, low labour standards, and a host of other red flags including religious freedom, democratic rights, environmental policies, and the like is hardly likely to win votes in Congress.

It is worth noting that the growing lack of interest in broad-based accords caused by the pursuit of a competitive liberalization strategy is hardly restricted to the United States. In discussing EU domestic dynamics, the *Financial Times* recently noted:

> unlike the last global round of negotiations, when movie studios, drug companies, software makers, banks and manufacturers coalesced into a formidable free-trade lobby, the enthusiasm this time has been narrower... The lack of business lobbying has been blamed in part by Peter Mandelson, the EU trade commissioner, for the turning of the Doha Round into what he called "the Ag-only round". He said that business had failed to provide "countervailing pressure" to protectionist agricultural lobbies.[46]

The Politics of the U.S.-China Trade Deficit

China's "peaceful rise" as the new engine of the global economy has become a highly charged issue in U.S. domestic politics as economists warn of the ever-growing trade deficit[47] with dire predictions for the dollar and producers lamenting the capturing of their markets by an authoritarian, ostensibly non-market economy. Charges of manipulation in foreign exchange markets to keep the renminbi undervalued have been levied by traditional protectionists and economic forecasters alike who fear either the overwhelming competition to key U.S. sectors or a sudden dollar collapse once Asian banks cease their buying frenzy of U.S. securities.

Since China's full accession to the WTO, cheap goods have flooded the U.S. market, undercutting domestic producers and sending the U.S. trade balance with China into a rapid downward spiral. In 1995, the United States ran a trade deficit with China of US$33.8 billion; by 2005, it had ballooned to over US$201 billion (see Figure 3.1). In the last four years alone, the bilateral trade deficit has nearly doubled while the overall current account situation grows ever worse. Producers particularly harmed by China's emergence include manufacturing, textiles and apparel, and steel, just to name a few. Among other issues, the Steel Trade Advisory committee has been pushing to prevent any PTAs with countries that

FIGURE 3.1
U.S.-China Trade Deficit

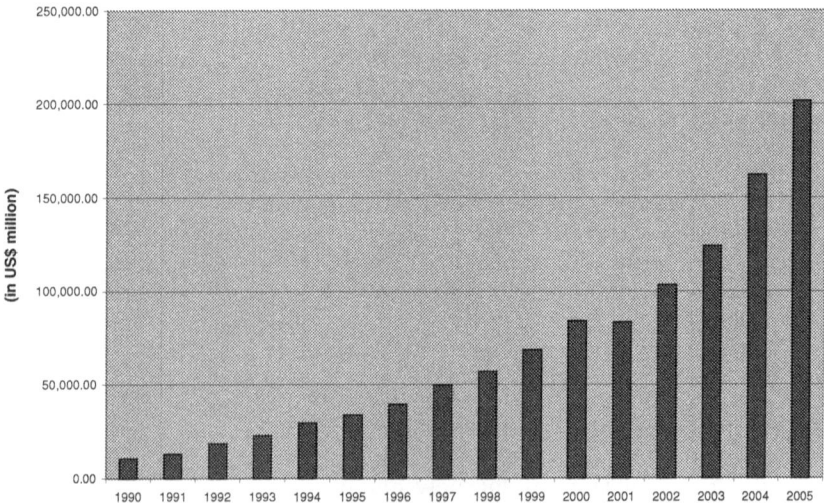

Source: U.S. Census Bureau, Foreign Trade Division, Data Dissemination Branch, Washington, D.C. 20233. http://www.census.gov/foreign-trade/balance/C5700.html.

might be seen to be manipulating their currency (read China) of those engaging in subsidization of the industry. [48] To bolster their coalition, the steel industry has piggybacked on the China deficit and currency issue to garner wider support among producers for protection, attempting to strengthen the ability of domestic producers across the industrial spectrum to tap into anti-dumping (AD) and countervailing duty (CVD) measures.

Many in Congress have seized upon the China issue for political purposes, either in the name of workers or business, introducing a vast array of retaliatory measures that could be taken against the PRC. The most extreme case is certainly the bipartisan Schumer-Graham bill, which would impose an across-the-board tariff of 27.5 per cent (the estimated damage of currency undervaluation) on all Chinese goods. Senator Charles Schumer (D-NY) has said he will bring the bill to a vote in September, or whenever the Treasury declares China's currency policy to constitute "manipulation".

A politically weak Bush administration has not had much luck in fending off pressure against China. In the recent words of a *Washington Post* report: "The Bush administration sought ... to mollify Congress about problems in U.S.-China economic relations ... But the response from Capitol Hill was a mixture of scorn and denunciation, underscoring the pressure from powerful lawmakers for a tougher approach toward Beijing."[49]

APEC's Role

Much has been written about APEC's origin and evolution.[50] Here, suffice it to say that APEC has clearly faced significant problems in fostering free trade in the Asia-Pacific, and the target dates for developed countries of 2010 and 2020 for all countries seems increasingly unrealistic. In particular, the debacle over pursuing a sectoral approach to advance trade negotiations (the Early Voluntary Sectoral Liberalization effort) put APEC's effort to promote trade liberalization in jeopardy, and since 1997, APEC has done little more than serve as a cheerleader for multilateral negotiations.[51] As Charles Morrison and I have argued,[52] much of the weakness of APEC stems from its lack of institutionalization. In recommending changes (in the year 2000), we argued that to realize its role in promoting trade, APEC needs to have a considerably stronger Secretariat, in-house analytical capabilities, greater NGO participation, and a clearer agenda and focus. Many of these recommendations would seem to remain valid.

In terms of APEC's other roles, Elaine Kwei and I have argued that this grouping has played an important role in ensuring that leaders in the Asia-Pacific meet regularly, in setting new agendas, with respect to trade facilitation, and as a means of working towards a greater cognitive consensus on issues of mutual concern. By assigning APEC the clearly divisive task of promoting an FTAAP in view of its current institutional weakness, we risk further marginalization of APEC in an area of the world that remains highly underinstitutionalized. Simply evoking fears of an East Asian economic grouping, as motivation for APEC to play a role in a trans-Pacific free trade agreement does not constitute a compelling argument, and is one that Asian countries may well perceive as simply a cynical American effort to divide them.

V. DOHA OR NO DOHA — PROSPECTS FOR AN FTAPP

What are the prospects of an FTAAP from a U.S. political economy perspective? This paper has argued that a combination of a weak political coalition for an FTAAP, the rising deficit with China, and APEC's institutional weakness make such an accord infeasible for the present. Section I of this paper provided an analytical categorization of trade agreements as an analytical backdrop to examine U.S. trade policy in the post-World War II period. I argued that traditional approaches to looking at trade arrangements have failed to adequately characterize different types of trade agreements, thereby missing the very real political and economic forces driving types of trade accords.

Based on this analytical effort, Section II traced how the United States has moved away from a traditional pursuit of multilateral multiproduct trade agreements to an increasing focus on competitive liberalization including in particular an emphasis on open sectoral and bilateral trade agreements. As I have argued, this approach has systematically undermined the coalition for free trade and diametrically opposed the previously bipartisan effort that bought off protectionist interests with an eye to promoting broad-scale trade liberalization. The result of this failed effort has been to encourage a competitive international dynamic that has delivered an increasing number of pernicious globally negotiated bilateral trade agreements — without any of the claimed beneficial effects on the negotiation of a broad-scale trade agreement that was the original *raison d'etre* of this misguided policy. Ironically, some of the same analysts who promoted the many advantages of the competitive liberal approach now wish to dampen this dismal trend by calling for an FTAAP as yet another halfway house to freer trade.

Yet as Section III has systematically shown, the undermining of the trade coalition through competitive liberalization, the rising trade deficit with China, and APEC's institutional weakness make the likelihood of U.S. support and successful negotiation of an FTAAP unlikely. There is almost no political support for such an idea — or more accurately — active opposition by textile, steel, and other manufacturing elements, as well as agricultural interests. Moreover, the Congress is increasingly moving to a bipartisan consensus *against* freer trade, particularly with respect to China. In this political environment, an FTAAP is simply another pipe dream that may well have as equally pernicious an effect as competitive liberalization for those who wish to promote freer trade and a more open global trading system.

To sum up, we can consider two scenarios, one with possible conclusion of a successful Doha Round and another without, to examine how an FTAAP effort might play out. If a Doha Round is successfully negotiated, the motivation to pursue an FTAAP will rapidly decline as states focus on ratification and implementation of the Round. The likely political struggles to pass an agreement will be high on the agenda of many states, and a new initiative to specifically promote free trade in the Asia-Pacific that goes beyond the WTO ("Doha Plus") would be unlikely to garner support in the United States, particularly in view of the ongoing deficit with China. In this context, APEC could create a study group to identify possible issues that have not been handled in the successful Doha Round, but discussion of an FTAAP would be premature. APEC could also play a role in trying to put the genie of the politically malicious strategy of competitive liberalization back in the bottle through an oversight role.

If the Doha Round fails, might the FTAAP emerge as a second-best solution? This notion also is problematic from a political economy perspective because U.S. goals are widely divergent in the two forums. What the United States is seeking in the Doha negotiations — significant agricultural market access in the EU and industrial market access in large emerging markets such as Brazil and India — are goals that cannot be achieved to any significant extent at an Asia-Pacific bargaining table. Although some might argue that an FTAAP might have better prospects than the currently moribund Doha Round as the number of states involved would be smaller, this view reflects a misunderstanding of the political economy of trade negotiations. In fact, with a larger number of states as in the Doha Round, the horse trading necessary to achieve a successful outcome would yield an agreement that stands a significantly *better* chance of being approved in the United States than a minilateral agreement that narrowly focuses on states with whom the United States runs massive trade deficits.

It is also worth noting that the potential for creating an FTAAP has been hurt by the competitive liberalization efforts that have led to the accelerating negotiation of bilateral trade agreements over the last few years in the Asia-Pacific.[53] This approach has fostered a coalition of pro-liberalization forces in the United States pushing state-specific bilateral accords in the Asia-Pacific, rather than broad-based regional trade initiatives. The agricultural sector, for example, while preferring a multilateral route, has little incentive to push an FTAAP. In fact, Asian and U.S. business groups say it is a "practical reality" that agricultural concessions in the Asia-Pacific region would have to be dealt with on a bilateral basis.[54] More generally, a bilateral path with Korea and Japan avoids the key domestic pitfalls for the United States that marks an FTAAP. The United States still faces significant domestic pressure from the textile and manufacturing industries to prevent a further increase of cheap imports from China, and an FTAAP agreement would open the floodgates not only to Chinese imports, but also to the less developed economies of ASEAN such as Cambodia that present a similar low-cost import threat. The United States has the opportunity to pursue with Korea and Japan the same general goals as it pursued with Singapore — deep trade agreements with high-value economies that avoid many of the domestic political conflicts created by agreements with low labour cost countries.

The increasing promise of U.S.-Korea negotiations has spurred the first serious discussions of a U.S.-Japan integration effort, and pursuing this path would bring many of the economic benefits of an FTAAP with few of the downsides. A deep liberalization agreement with these two countries would mean significant U.S. access to key investment opportunities, an opening of manufacturing and automotive markets, and possibly even much-sought-after access to the agricultural markets of industrialized Asia. With the United States pursuing such a path, an FTAAP would recede to the background. Instead, we would likely see a further unfortunate proliferation of selective bilateral agreements by Asian states in response to U.S. actions, adding more "noodles" to the bowl. From a strategic perspective, the continued prospect of such economic gains with minimal political costs makes other more politically expensive options — like the vaunted FTAAP proposal — far less less attractive than a bilateral path.

In short, with either success or failure in the Doha Round, I believe that an FTAAP is not politically likely at the moment from a U.S. perspective. APEC should not currently be pushing an FTAAP that is infeasible for the time being and that would undermine its positive contributions in other issue areas. Rather, APEC should serve as a forum to institutionalize the administration and negotiation of minilateral and bilateral agreements, so that the "noodle bowl" of liberalizing efforts can be brought into some kind of logical order and into conformity with the WTO. In addition, APEC can usefully pursue a number of functions that have been discussed at length by many scholars and in this volume by Charles Morrison. These include the harmonization of standards, better rules of origin, capacity building, peer assessment of compliance with APEC targets, and serving as a complementary institution to the WTO. Although one might think that promoting schemes such as the FTAAP do no harm, as we have seen, the advocacy of competitive liberalization as a means of securing trade liberalization has been a recipe for disaster. Ideas, both good and bad, do have consequences.

Notes

The author would like to thank David Guarino for his extensive research work and insightful comments and arguments on all aspects of this paper. He also has benefited from Jonathan Chow, Min Gyo Koo, Elaine Kwei, Kun-Chin Lin, and John Ravenhill's suggestions.

1. For a discussion of the pros and cons of competitive liberalization, see Feketekuty (1998), Aggarwal and Lin (2002) and Bergsten (1996, 2002), among others.
2. See, for example, Mansfield and Milner (1999), p. 592, who recognize the problematic nature of the term "regionalism" but then proceed to use this term in their analysis.
3. This usage differs from that of Yarbrough and Yarbrough (1992), which conflates third-party enforcement with these terms so that "bilateral" for them can also mean three countries, a highly counter-intuitive use. Keohane (1990) refers to an agreement among three or more states as multilateralism. Richardson (1987) is consistent with my usage.
4. Of these, the dimension of geographical scope is the most controversial. It is

worth noting that this category is quite subjective, since simple distance is hardly the only relevant factor in defining a "geographic region". Despite the interest that regionalism has attracted, the question of how to define a region remains highly contested. See the discussion by Mansfield and Milner (1999), Katzenstein (1997), and Aggarwal and Fogarty (2004), among others.

5. See Schonhardt-Bailey (1996).
6. Bhagwati and Patrick (1990). This is a somewhat different usage from my own focus on "unilateral" in the sense of removal of restraints by one county without an agreement. As with voluntary export restraints (VERs), the unilateral versus bilateral aspect is often muddied by coercive actions.
7. See Milner and Yoffie (1989).
8. See Aggarwal, Keohane, and Yoffie (1987) on VERs and Bhagwati (1987) on VIEs.
9. See Tyson (1992) and Irwin (1994).
10. See Fogarty (2004).
11. Curzon (1966), pp. 266–68.
12. Tyson (2000).
13. Yarbrough and Yarbrough (1992). McKeown (1983) makes a strong case that Britain did not exhibit hegemonic power in the move to liberalization in the nineteenth century but rather chose to liberalize on its own.
14. Aggarwal and Urata (2006).
15. Koo (2006).
16. On economies of scale, see Milner (1997); on foreign capital, see Lawrence (1996); and on natural trading blocs, Frankel (1997).
17. See respectively Milward (1992); Gilpin (1987) and Krasner (1976); Haggard (1997); Oye (1992) and Baldwin (1997); and Yarbrough and Yarbrough (1992) among others.
18. See Haggard (1997) and Katzenstein (1997).
19. Aggarwal and Fogarty (2004).
20. This subsection draws heavily on Aggarwal and Lin (2002), which focuses on the pitfalls of what we term "opportunistic liberalization" and where we characterize U.S. trade policy as being recently characterized as strategy without vision. See also the excellent concise discussion of historical trends in U.S. trade policy in Bergsten (2002). The classic account remains Destler (2005).
21. See Aggarwal (1985) for a discussion of the nesting of economic issues within a security context.
22. Diebold (1952).
23. While the Annecy Round of 1949 resulted in 5,000 more tariff concessions and the entry of ten new GATT members, the Torquay Round of 1951 led to an overall reduction of close to 25 per cent and the inclusion of four new contracting parties. The 1956 Geneva Round that followed resulted in further agreement of

tariff reductions worth approximately US$2.5 billion. Under the terms of the Dillon Round of 1960–61, for the first time, a single schedule of concessions was agreed for the recently established European Economic Community, based on the Common External Tariff. Also, tariff concessions worth over US$4.9 billion in trade were also negotiated. In total, tariff reductions for the first five rounds amounted to 73 per cent (*Economic Report of the President* 1995, p. 205).

24. *Economic Report of the President* (1995), p. 205.
25. For an analysis of the creation and evolution of the textile regime, see Aggarwal (1985).
26. See Aggarwal, Keohane, and Yoffie (1987), which models the factors that explain why different industries have been able to secure protection of varying length.
27. Adapted from Bergsten's (2002) "One Step Backward, Two Steps Forward" subtitle.
28. *Toronto Star*, 6 January 1988.
29. Tyson (2000).
30. This paragraph draws heavily on Aggarwal (2001*b*) and Aggarwal and Ravenhill (2001).
31. Business Roundtable (2001).
32. Office of the USTR (2001), p. 4.
33. Ravenhill (2003), p. 2.
34. See Aggarwal and Urata (2006) on the proliferation of bilateral trade agreements in the Asia-Pacific.
35. Quoting the *Tokyo Shimbun*, Bernard Gordon, "The FTA Fetish", *Wall Street Journal*, 17 November 2005.
36. *Financial Times*, 10 July 2006, p. 9.
37. Ravenhill (2006), p. 45.
38. Feinberg (2006), p. 113.
39. Ibid., p. 112.
40. "CAFTA Vote Clouds Prospects for Other Trade Deals — Bitter Fight Reveals Fears of Globalization, as Talks in Doha Round Languish", *Wall Street Journal*, 29 July 2005.
41. Agricultural Policy Advisory Committee for Trade, *The U.S.-Peru Trade Agreement: Supplementary Report of the Agricultural Policy Advisory Committee for Trade*, 15 February 2006. http://www.ustr.gov/assets/Trade_Agreements/Bilateral/Peru_TPA/Reports/asset_upload_file570_8967.pdf.
42. "Grasping at straws; Textile industry groups want a special agreement for textiles at the Doha Round", *Journal of Commerce*, 26 June 2006.
43. "McCrery Expresses Doubts About Trade Deals, Including Vietnam", *Inside US Trade*, 9 June 2006.
44. "U.S. Hopes for Momentum from CAFTA; Portman to Push WTO to Negotiate Global Agreement", *Washington Post*, 29 July 2005.

45. "Free Trade and Security", *Wall Street Journal*, 11 July 2006.
46. "US and European officials hope big companies flex their muscles to ensure deadlock is broken", *Financial Times*, 12 December 2005.
47. Bergsten (2005).
48. See Industry Trade Advisory Committee on Steel (ITAC-12) report entitled "The U.S.-Peru Trade Promotion Agreement (U.S.-Peru FTA)", 18 January 2006. http://www.ustr.gov/assets/Trade_Agreements/Bilateral/Peru_TPA/Reports/asset_upload_file765_8986.pdf.
49. "Senators Deride U.S. Position on China; Currency System Is Called Unfair", *Washington Post*, 19 May 2006.
50. See, for example, Funabashi (1995), Aggarwal and Morrison (1998), and Ravenhill (2001).
51. See, for example, Aggarwal and Kwei (2005).
52. Aggarwal and Morrison (2000).
53. See Aggarwal and Urata (2006) on the driving forces leading to the negotiation of bilateral trade agreements in the Asia-Pacific.
54. "U.S., Japan Business Groups Explore Possibility of Bilateral Trade Deal", *Inside US Trade*, 5 May 2006.

References

Aggarwal, V. K. *Liberal Protectionism*. Berkeley: University of California Press, 1985.
———. "Economics: International Trade". In *Managing a Globalizing World: Lessons Learned*, edited by P. J. Simmons and C. Oudraat. Washington, D.C.: The Carnegie Endowment for International Peace, 2001a.
———. "APEC and Trade Liberalization after Seattle: Transregionalism without a Cause?". In *Reforming Economic Systems in Asia: A Comparative Analysis of China, Japan, South Korea, Malaysia and Thailand*, edited by Maria Weber, pp. 149–78. Cheltenham: Elgar, 2001b.
Aggarwal, V. K. and E. Fogarty, eds. *EU Trade Strategies: Between Globalism and Regionalism*, London: Palgrave, 2004.
Aggarwal, Vinod K. and Kun-Chin Lin. "Strategy Without Vision: The U.S. and Asia-Pacific Economic Cooperation". In *APEC: The First Decade*, edited by Jürgen Rüland, Eva Manske, and Werner Draguhn. London: Curzon Press, 2002.
Aggarwal, V. K., Robert Keohane, and David Yoffie. "The Dynamics of Negotiated Protectionism". *American Political Science Review* 81, no. 2 (1987): 345–66.
Aggarwal, Vinod K. and Elaine Kwei. "Asia-Pacific Economic Cooperation (APEC): Transregionalism with a New Cause?". In *Interregionalism and International Relation: A Stepping Stone to Global Governance?* edited by Heiner Hänggi, Ralf Roloff, and Jürgen Rüland. Oxfordshire: RoutledgeCurzon, 2005.

Aggarwal, Vinod K. and Charles E. Morrison. *Asia-Pacific Crossroads: Regime Creation and the Future of APEC.* New York: St. Martin's Press, 1998.

———. "APEC as an International Institution". In *APEC: Its Challenges and Tasks in the 21st Century,* edited by Ippei Yamazawa, pp. 298–324. New York: Routledge, 2000.

Aggarwal, V. K. and J. Ravenhill. "Undermining the WTO: The Case against 'Open Sectoralism' ". *Asia-Pacific Issues* 50 (2001).

Aggarwal, Vinod K. and Shujiro Urata, eds. *Bilateral Trade Arrangements in the Asia-Pacific: Origins, Evolution, and Implications.* New York: Routledge, 2006.

Baldwin, R. E. "The Causes of Regionalism". *World Economy* 20, no. 7 (1997): 865–88.

Bergsten, F. "Competitive Liberalization and Global Free Trade: A Vision for the Early 21st Century". *APEC Working Papers* 96, no. 15. Washington D.C.: Institute for International Economics, 1996.

———. "A Renaissance for U.S. Trade Policy". *Foreign Affairs* 81, no. 6 (2002): 86–98.

———. "The Trans-Pacific Imbalance: A Disaster in the Making?". Speech at the 16th General Meeting of the Pacific Economic Cooperation Council (PECC), Seoul, 7 September 2005.

Bhagwati, J. "Quid Pro Quo DFI and VIEs: Political-Economy-Theoretic Analyses". *International Economic Journal* 1 (1987): 1–14.

Bhagwati, J. and H. Patrick, eds. *Aggressive Unilateralism: America's 301 Trading Policy and the World Trading System.* Ann Arbor: University of Michigan, 1990.

Business Roundtable. "The Case for U.S. Trade Leadership: The United States is Falling Behind". February 2001. http://www.businessroundtable.org/publications/publication.aspx?qs= 2496BF807822B0F19D2.

Curzon, G. *Multilateral Commercial Diplomacy.* New York: Praeger, 1966.

Destler, I. M. *American Trade Politics.* Washington, D.C.: Institute for International Economics, 2005.

Diebold, William, Jr. "The End of the I.T.O.". *Princeton Essays in International Finance,* No. 16, October 1952.

Economic Report of the President. Washington: U.S. Government Printing Office, 1995.

Feinberg, R. "U.S. Trade Arrangements in the Asia-Pacific". In *Bilateral Trade Arrangements in the Asia-Pacific: Origins, Evolution, and Implications,* edited by V. K. Aggarwal and S. Urata. New York: Routledge, 2006.

Feketekuty, Geza. "An American Trade Strategy for the 21st Century". In *Trade Strategies for a New Era: Ensuring U.S. Leadership in a Global Economy,* edited by Geza Feketekuty with Bruce Stokes. New York: Council on Foreign Relations, 1998.

Fogarty, E. "Be Careful What You Wish For: The European Union and North

America". In *EU Trade Strategies: Between Globalism and Regionalism*, edited by Aggarwal, V. K. and E. Fogarty, pp. 180–206. London: Palgrave, 2004.

Frankel, J. A. *Regional Trading Blocs in the World Economic System.* Washington, D.C.: Institute for International Economics, 1997.

Frankel, J. A., E. Stein, and S. Wei. "Regional Trading Arrangements: Natural or Super Natural". *American Economic Review* 86, no. 2 (1996).

Funabashi, Yoichi. *Asia Pacific Fusion: Japan's Role in APEC.* Washington: D.C.: Institute of International Economics, 1995.

Gilpin, R. *The Political Economy of International Relations.* Princeton: Princeton University Press, 1987.

Haggard, S. "Regionalism in Asia and the Americans". In *The Political Economy of Regionalism*, edited by E. Mansfield and H. Milner. New York: Columbia University Press, 1997.

Irwin, D. A. *Managed Trade: The Case Against Import Targets.* Washington, D.C.: American Enterprise Institute, 1994.

Katzenstein, P. J. "Introduction: Asian Regionalism in Contemporary Perspective". In *Network Power: Japan and Asia*, edited by P. J. Katzenstein and T. Shiraishi. Ithaca: Cornell University Press, 1997.

Keohane, R. "Multilateralism: An Agenda for Research". *International Journal* XLV (Autumn 1990).

Koo, M. "From Multilateralism to Bilateralism? A Shift in South Korea's Trade Strategy". In *Bilateral Trade Arrangements in the Asia-Pacific: Origins, Evolution, and Implications*, edited by V. K. Aggarwal and S. Urata. New York: Routledge, 2006.

Krasner, S. "State Power and the Structure of International Trade". *World Politics* 28 (1976): 317–47.

Lawrence, R. Z. *Regionalism, Multilateralism, and Deeper Integration.* Washington, D.C.: Brookings Institution, 1996.

Mansfield, E. and H. Milner. "The New Wave of Regionalism". *International Organization* 53, no. 3 (1999): 589–627.

McKeown, T. "Hegemonic Stability Theory and 19th Century Tariff Levels in Europe". *International Organization* 37, no. 1 (1983): 73–91.

Milner, H. "Industries, Governments, and Regional Trade Blocs". In *The Political Economy of Regionalism*, edited by E. Mansfield and H. Milner. New York: Columbia University Press, 1997.

Milner, H. and D. Yoffie. "Between Free Trade and Protectionism: Strategic Trade Policy and a Theory of Corporate Trade Demands." *International Organization* 43, no. 2 (1989): 239–72.

Milward, A. S. *The European Rescue of the Nation-State.* London: Routledge, 1992.

Nagoka, S. "The economic consequences of VIEs". *Japan and the World Economy* 9 (1997): 557–65.

Office of the United States Trade Representative. *2001 Trade Policy Agenda and 2000 Annual Report*. Washington, D.C.

Oye, K. *Economic Discrimination and Political Exchange: World Political Economy in the 1930s and 1980s*. Princeton: Princeton University Press, 1992.

Ravenhill, J. *APEC and the Construction of Asia-Pacific Regionalism*. Cambridge: Cambridge University Press, 2001.

———. "The Move to Preferential Trade Agreements in the Western Pacific Rim". *Asia-Pacific Issues* 69 (2003).

———. "The Political Economy of the New Asia-Pacific Bilateralism: Benign, Banal or Simply Bad?". In *Bilateral Trade Arrangements in the Asia-Pacific: Origins, Evolution, and Implications*, edited by V. K. Aggarwal and S. Urata. New York: Routledge, 2006.

Richardson, D. "Comment". In *U.S. Trade Policy in a Changing World Economy*, edited by R. Stern. Cambridge: MIT, 1987.

Schonhardt-Bailey, C., ed. *Free Trade: The Repeal of the Corn Laws*. Briston: Thoemmes Press, 1996.

Tyson, L. *Who's Bashing Whom: Trade Conflict in High-Technology Industries*. Washington, D.C.: IIE, 1992.

———. "What Really Sabotaged the Seattle Trade Talks". *Business Week*, 7 February 2000.

Yarbrough, Beth V. and Robert M. Yarbrough. *Cooperation and Governance in International Trade*. Princeton: Princeton University Press, 1992.

4

The Political Economy of a Free Trade Area of the Asia-Pacific: A Chinese Perspective

Sheng Bin

I. INTRODUCTION

APEC has long been relevant for China's economic diplomacy although its significance has been relatively weakened since China's accession to the World Trade Organization (WTO) in 2001. However, China still attaches great importance to the Asia-Pacific Economic Cooperation (APEC) activities because the "APEC approach" that stresses concerted unilateralism, voluntarism and flexibility provides a unique means of regional co-operation on an experimental basis. As such, APEC can serve strategically for China to implement its Asia-Pacific foreign policy in the long run. Meanwhile, with the rapid proliferation of regional trade agreement and free trade agreements (RTAs/FTAs) in the region, China has also started to set up its own RTAs/FTAs network in the manner of a hub-and-spoke system. Among many proposals, the East Asian Free Trade Area (EAFTA) was particularly favoured by Chinese leaders, in contrast to the ambiguous idea of a Free Trade Area of the Asia-Pacific (FTAAP), which was brought forward and widely advocated by the APEC Business Advisory Council (ABAC). On the one hand, there is little doubt that further trade and investment liberalization and facilitation with institutional reforms and a binding treaty would benefit China in terms of enhancing welfare and structural changes. But, on the other hand, it is uncertain whether the proposed FTAAP would challenge China's prevailing strategy for APEC, given the expected institutionalization of the process. Additionally, economic issues, such as the protection of sensitive sectors, and political issues like the U.S.-China relationship and the status of Taiwan, make it more complicated for China to hold a positive attitude towards the FTAAP proposal.

Against such a background, it is important to have an insight of China's policy towards the FTAAP from a political economy perspective. This paper aims to review the current Chinese overall strategy and policies towards APEC and regional agreements, and extrapolate the likely position that China would have for the proposed FTAAP based on a political economy analysis of the benefits and costs of the agreement.

Section II will briefly depict China's trade and economic relations with other APEC member economies in terms of trade, foreign direct investment (FDI), balance of payment and trade barriers. Section III reviews recent Chinese trade policy focusing on its development of an RTAs/FTAs network. Sections IV and V conduct a cost-benefit study of FTAAP by probing the gains, impediments, and concerns China would have in joining the agreement. Finally, section VI concludes with an analysis of some possible scenarios.

II. CHINA'S ECONOMIC RELATIONS WITH OTHER APEC MEMBERS

The Asia-Pacific region is the most important region for China in terms of economic and trading activities. In 2004, 72 per cent of China's exports and 68 per cent of imports were with other APEC economies.[1] The APEC region is also vital in terms of foreign investment with 70 per cent of China's FDI inflows coming from the region.[2] Over the past decade "triangular trade" between China, other East Asian economies and North America (the United States in particular) has emerged that makes up much of China's intra-regional trade in the Asia-Pacific.[3] It means that

China is exporting consumer goods and semi-finished manufactures to the U.S. market, while importing raw materials, intermediary goods and capital goods from the region and then processing them with relatively low value-added. In line with such a large volume of trade flows, there are also huge FDI inflows into China, which makes China the third-largest trader and largest developing country recipient of FDI in the world.

One of the great concerns for China's trade relations with APEC partners is a trade imbalance, particularly with its largest export market — the United States.[4] China has been charged as the main culprit for global imbalances, and immediate actions are called upon in order to make necessary adjustments (Bergsten 2005c). However, China explains that the U.S. trade deficit with China is not only overstated due to some technical reasons, such as rules of origin and transshipment via Hong Kong, but also a "natural" result of "triangular trade" in the region, which moves the U.S.-East Asia trade deficit to a U.S.-China trade deficit, as well as the export control policies imposed by the U.S. government against China.

Meanwhile, trade frictions between China and its trade partners have increased since China's accession to the WTO, many of which are APEC member economies. Regarding WTO disputes, China has been involved in forty-nine cases in total, including one case as a respondent, one case as a complainant, forty-seven cases as a third party to (WTO 2006). China is also currently subject to the greatest number of anti-dumping actions among all WTO members.[5] Furthermore, Chinese enterprises and exporters have expressed great concerns over all kinds of technical barriers and other safeguard measures particularly against China's exports, such as agricultural goods, electronic appliances, toys, footwear, rubber products, and textiles and clothing. Therefore, further trade liberalization initiatives in the Asia-Pacific are expected to ease imbalance, disputes and crises between China and its partners in the region.

III. CHINA'S CURRENT TRADE POLICIES

Unilateral Trade Liberalization and Fulfilling the Commitments of WTO Accession[6]

China has been undertaking significant unilateral trade liberalization since the early 1990s in order to accede to the WTO and meet the APEC Bogor Goals. It has taken major steps to revise and update a large number of laws, and to streamline its trade policy regime to conform to international norms. In accordance with the WTO accession commitments, the average tariff level has been reduced from 15.3 per cent at the time of accession to 9.9 per cent in 2005. In addition, all China's tariffs are bound, and applied rates and bound rates are exactly the same. All non-tariff measures including import quotas, import licences and import tendering had been eliminated by 1 January 2005 with a few exceptions that are also scheduled to be abolished.

On services, China's accession commitments were more extensive than those of other developing countries. Of the 160 services sectors and sub-sectors under the WTO classification, China has opened more than 100, accounting for 62.5 per cent, close to the level of commitments made by developed members. The level of market access and national treatment for foreign services suppliers has also been significantly increased.

Notwithstanding these achievements, China still faces numerous challenges to enhance transparency in policy-making and implementation, dismantle indirect intervention by the authorities, and tackling many "behind-the-border" issues. Many concerns have been raised by other WTO members about anti-dumping and countervailing duties, standards, sanitary and phytosanitary (SPS) measures, export taxes and value-added tax (VAT) rebates. Further measures to liberalize the service sector include relaxed ownership, entry and geographic requirements and a deepening of regulatory and institutional reforms. Several questions have also been raised on the issue of (state directed) investment in certain sectors, particularly in the steel and automotive sectors, as well as the drafting of the Competition Law and enforcement of intellectual property rights.

Participating in the WTO Doha Round

As a member of the "Five Interested Parties Plus" group (eleven countries in total), China is an active player in the current negotiations of WTO Doha Round. China supports the establishment of a fair, more open and dynamic multilateral trading system by enhancing market access, balanced rules, and well-targeted, sustainably financed technical assistance and capacity-building programmes. Up to now, China has submitted more than thirty proposals and position papers in the negotiations, which played a positive and constructive role in advancing the negotiations (Chinese

Government 2006). China affirms that the negotiations should take full account of the level of development and capacity of developing members and should put special and differential treatment into effect to allow them to implement development strategies that suit their own conditions. It also promises to provide assistance to Least Developed Countries (LDCs), including improved market access and debt forgiveness.

As a member of both G-20 and G-33, China supports the elimination of all kinds of export subsidies, the substantial reduction of trade-distorting domestic support, and significant reductions of tariff peaks and tariff escalation of agricultural products. Meanwhile, it stands that there should be an effective solution to the specific concerns of developing members related to special products and the special safeguard mechanism.

In respect of non-agricultural market access (NAMA), the Chinese government supports the reduction of high tariffs by using the Swiss Formula with dual coefficients for developed and developing members respectively to fulfil the principle of "less than full reciprocity". In the negotiations, it also submitted the proposal of a tariff reduction formula, which laid the foundation for the "Chairman's Formula" ("Girard Formula").

In the negotiation of services, China hopes that the export interests of developing members can be recognized, particularly in the field of Mode 4 (movement of natural persons), and that the negotiations are able to strengthen their capacity to participate in world trade in services. China is one of a group that submitted their initial and revised offers at the very early stage of negotiations.

Moreover, China stresses that the negotiations on rules should contribute to further clarify and improve WTO rules, promote trade facilitation and reduce the abuse of trade remedy measures, particularly anti-dumping measures against developing members. It has raised several proposals on the issues of customs procedure, anti-dumping and fishing subsidy.

Finally, China insists that special concerns of newly acceded WTO members should be recognized and respected, taking account of the extensive commitments they have already made and the heavy adjustment pressures in the transition period. It also succeeded in defending its status as a "developing member" as a whole, and therefore is able to enjoy many special and differential treatments regarding "special (non-agricultural) products", *de minimis* exemption of agricultural goods, and favourable disciplines related to state trading enterprises (STEs).

China's RTAs/FTAs Development and Policy Evolution

China has sped up building its own RTAs/FTAs network since 2001 when China signed its first regional trade agreement with other members of the Bangkok Agreement. This is the most important departure from its traditional trade policy which solely relied on the multilateral trading system and adhered to its non-alliance strategy. Currently, China has concluded or has been in the process of negotiating ten RTAs/FTAs involving thirty-two countries and regions in Asia, Africa, Latin America and South Pacific (Table 4.1). For 2005, China's trade volume with these countries and regions was US$344.5 billion, accounting for a quarter of China's total trade for that year.[7] China also started official joint feasibility studies on FTAs with India and Iceland. Other countries, particularly the Republic of Korea and Japan, are also candidates for an RTA/FTA, although the feasibility study still remains at the preliminary academic stage.

China states that it is pursuing and will continue to expand RTAs/ FTAs in an active and steady manner with various forms, focusing on specific partners and issues (Zhao Jie and Han Yi 2005). It also believes that regional trade and economic cooperation is a useful supplement to the multilateral trading system and helps push forward global trade liberalization and investment facilitation, and at the same time, it should not be done at the expense of the multilateral trading system (Chinese Government 2006).

There are a number of distinguishing features that make China's RTAs/ FTAs different from those of other countries. First, following a pragmatic approach to serve particular bilateral or regional commercial and strategic interests, China does not adhere to a common template for each RTA/ FTA. This approach is reflected in the very diverse trade agreements, ranging from the Closer Economic Partnership Arrangements (CEPAs) with Hong Kong and Macau, which contain highly concrete terms and comprehensive issues covered, to the agreements with New Zealand and Australia, which are mainly statements of intent with only broad aspirations for mutual cooperation. Second, instead of the one-off conclusion of a comprehensive treaty, many Chinese RTAs/FTAs are negotiated and implemented in a piecemeal approach from the initial Early Harvest programme that aims to eliminate selected tariffs on goods to further extended topics including services, investment and trade facilitation. It will contribute to the confidence-building process in which all parties are

TABLE 4.1
China's Participation in RTAs/FTAs (up to April 2006)

	Type	Year	Latest development	Areas and issues covered
RTAs/FTAs already signed				
China-Hong Kong	CEPA[a]	The agreement was signed on 29 June 2003, and entered into force on 1 January 2004.	A Supplementary Agreement was signed on 27 October 2004, and has been implemented since 1 January 2005.	• tariff and non-tariff barriers of goods • trade in services • investment • standards conformity • dispute settlement
China-Macau	CEPA	The agreement was signed on 17 October 2003, and entered into force on 1 January 2004.	A Supplementary Agreement was signed on 29 October 2004, and has been implemented since 1 January 2005.	• tariff and non-tariff barriers of goods • trade in services • investment • standards conformity • dispute settlement
Bangkok Agreement[b]	Regional PTA	China acceded to the agreement on 12 April 2001, and started implementing concessions on 1 January 2002.		• reduction of tariff in goods
China-Pakistan	Bilateral PTA	The agreement was signed on November 2003.	The early harvest agreement was signed in 5 April 2005, and entered into force on 1 January 2006.	• reduction of tariff in goods • Pakistan recognized China as a market economy.
China-ASEAN	Regional FTA	The agreement was signed on 4 November 2002, and entered into force on 1 July 2003.	• Early harvest agreement was implemented from 1 January 2004. • The agreement on trade in goods and dispute settlement mechanism entered into force on 1 January 2005. • Tariff reduction process started from 20 July 2005. • Trade in services and investment are still under negotiation.	• tariff and non-tariff barriers of goods • trade in services • investment • customs procedures • mutual recognition • ASEAN member states recognized China as a market economy.

continued on next page

TABLE 4.1 — *cont'd*

	Type	Year	Latest development	Areas and issues covered
China-Chile	Bilateral FTA	The agreement was signed on 18 November 2005.	• The agreement on tariff elimination will start to be implemented in the second half of 2006. • Negotiations on trade in services and investment are to start in 2006.	• national treatment and market access for goods • rules of origin • trade remedies • SPS • TBT • dispute settlement • Chile recognized China as a market economy.
RTAs/FTAs under negotiation				
China-New Zealand	Bilateral FTA	The negotiation was launched on 19 November 2004.	Six rounds of negotiation have been held.	New Zealand has recognized China as a market economy.
China-Australia	Bilateral FTA	The negotiation was commenced on 18 April 2005.	Four rounds of negotiation have been held.	Australia has recognized China as a market economy.
China-GCC[c]	Regional FTA	The negotiation was launched on 6 July 2004.	Three meetings of Trade Negotiation Committee have been held.	
China-SACU[d]	Regional FTA	The negotiation was launched in June 2004.		SACU granted China market economy status.
RTAs/FTAs under joint feasibility study				
China-India	Bilateral FTA	A feasibility study was started in April 2005.		
China-Iceland	Bilateral FTA	On 17 May 2005, China and Iceland agreed to undertake the study.		Iceland has recognized China as a market economy.
Academic Feasibility Study				
China-R. Korea-Japan	Regional FTA	–	–	–
China-R. Korea	Bilateral FTA	–	–	–

Notes:
a. CEPA refers to "Close Economic Partnership Agreement".
b. Other members are India, Republic of Korea, Bangladesh, Sri Lanka and Lao PDR.
c. Gulf Cooperation Council (GCC) includes the following members: Saudi Arabia, United Arab Emirates, Kuwait, Oman, Qatar and Bahrain.
d. Southern African Customs Union (SACU) includes South Africa, Botswana, Lesotho, Swaziland and Namibia.
Source: Antkiewicz and Whalley (2004), Hufbauer and Yee Wong (2005), WTO (2006), Zhao Jie and Han Yi (2005).

able to benefit from trade liberalization from the start. Finally, it is also notable that many agreements exclude sensitive sectors and issues that seem quite difficult to deal with in the short term, such as intellectual property protection, special sectoral liberalization, environment and labour standards, and dispute settlement mechanism. In spite of their relatively low quality, these agreements can well serve both commercial considerations and domestic political interests of both parties with "constructive ambiguity".

Why is China actively pursing RTAs/FTAs? What are the specific political and economic motivations behind China's endeavours to expand its RTAs/FTAs network so fast? The foremost driving force comes from the new wave of RTAs/FTAs proliferation around the world since the early 1990s. Up to December 2004, about 230 countries and regions had notified to the WTO at least one regional trade arrangement. They cover most of WTO members and intra-regional trade accounts for over half of total world trade volume (World Bank 2004). Noticeably, two of the largest developed economies, namely the United States and the EU, have sped up the extension of their own RTAs/FTAs network in recent years. In addition, since the late 1990s many Asian nations shifted from a single-minded dependence on the multilateral trading system to an obvious attempt to consider RTAs/FTAs as part of their trade policy strategy. Under such circumstances, the only response open to China was to launch its own RTAs/FTA initiatives to avoid being excluded from existing regional arrangements and avoid trade diversion.

Secondly, RTAs/FTAs will create a more favourable, stable and foreseeable trade environment for China. China will benefit from better market access in selected economies like ASEAN and India, whose billions of consumers and dynamic economies represent a large potential market for Chinese competitive exports. Moreover, China is increasingly becoming a source of FDI and M&As and the RTAs/FTAs could be an important vehicle for attracting Chinese investment for overseas markets. Chinese bilateral and regional arrangements may, like all other RTAs/FTAs, also manage to lock in protectionism of partners so as to avoid changeable trade barriers in the future.

Thirdly, RTAs/FTAs can be important instruments of commercial diplomacy to realize China's vision of geopolitics and global strategy. Specifically, the CEPAs with Hong Kong and Macau can be regarded as experimental models to institutionalize closed economic partnerships under the "One Country, Two Systems" regime. This approach may give some further indications of an acceptable solution to unify Taiwan economically with the mainland. The ASEAN-China FTA is a typical example of implementing China's good neighbour foreign policy to mitigate those countries' fear of Chinese economic growth and fierce export competition. Other trade agreements, such as those with Pakistan, India, Chile and the South Africa, also demonstrate China's diplomatic endeavours to initiate or consolidate strategic partnerships and promote South-South cooperation with selected countries in different continents.

In addition, China will benefit from more assured supplies of energy and crucial raw commodities under RTAs/FTAs, which partly helps to fulfil national security goals for natural resources. Such a motive is particularly embodied in the bilateral agreements reached between China and Australia, ASEAN and the Gulf countries for crude oil, iron ore and other essential primary materials.[8] The agreements also help to minimize the risk of supply shortages in the event of commodity price increases.

Another significant affect of China's FTAs is to remove those unfavourable results stemming from the legacy of discriminatory clauses in its protocol of accession to the WTO. Among others, the non-market economy provision in determining dumping and transitional product-specific safeguard mechanism had tremendous negative impacts for Chinese labour-intensive and low-skill product exports. Both the Chinese government and export enterprises have long been plagued by the struggle to get full recognition of market economy status. Therefore, FTAs are particularly attractive to China as it has succeeded in pressing partner countries to grant China full market economy status in the negotiations. Such outcomes are well reflected in the agreements with several countries including Australia, New Zealand, Iceland, ASEAN, Chile, Pakistan and SACU (as illustrated in Table 4.1). It can be anticipated that more RTAs/FTAs negotiations will be launched to systematically rectify the "unfairness" which China thinks exists in bilateral trade relations.

It is also argued that China is keen on using RTAs/FTAs to position itself as a free trader when negotiating with industrial countries (Hufbauer and Yee Wong 2005). The treaties with Australia, New Zealand and Iceland can be considered as a first step to initiate such a process, although it is well recognized that these are only small developed nations and the real significance of agreements is still doubted. In other words, those "warm-up" agreements are expected by the Chinese government to bring ample demonstration effects on other industrial countries, particularly on the United States and EU, in the future.

Eventually, RTAs/FTAs are indispensable vehicles to assist the central government to advance trade liberalization, domestic deregulation and industrial restructuring reforms. While the WTO Doha Round seems to have faltered, RTAs/FTAs can provide new momentum to accelerate economic reforms, particularly in sensitive import-competitive sectors like automotive, banking, telecommunication and transportation where strong interest groups and local governments resist further reforms.

IV. POTENTIAL BENEFITS OF JOINING FTAAP

Market Access, Welfare and Dynamic Effect

As described in section II, most Chinese foreign trade and FDI is transacted with economies in the Asia-Pacific region, whereas the main trade barriers and trade frictions are also in the region. Consequently, through the gradual elimination of restrictive trade and investment measures of all countries and regions concerned, the FTAAP may offer China more opportunities to tap overseas markets by taking advantage of its international competitiveness so as to achieve sustained economic growth. Preliminary computable general equilibrium (CGE) simulation analysis indicates that an FTAAP will deliver more favourable economic welfare for China than any other existing arrangement like the ASEAN-China FTA and other scenarios such as ASEAN-China-Republic of Korea-Japan FTA and APEC non-discriminatory liberalization (APEC Most Favoured Nation or MFN) (Scollay 2004). My own estimation based on the gravity model also shows a large amount of welfare gains for China if it participates in the FTAAP (Sheng Bin 2006). These positive economic effects could be even larger if the model captured other elements neglected in the static analysis, such as structural change, externalities, increasing returns, scale effects, and technological progress.

However, any quantitative prediction should be treated with caution because the result depends upon the assumptions, parameters and data selected for the study. More importantly, it should be noted that according to the political economy of trade policy, a considerable part of welfare gains comes from the increase of consumer surplus, which in practice has only limited weight in Chinese government objectives. On the contrary, the losses of producers, particularly of state-owned enterprises (SOEs), which would be incurred by joining the FTAAP, may be given greater weight by the government. Therefore, just like all other cases of trade liberalization, the FTAAP is essentially an "economically right, but politically hard" decision for the central government.

Strengthening APEC Institutionalized Trade Liberalization

The launch of an FTAAP would revitalize APEC itself to pursue trade and investment liberalization, and provide ongoing momentum to achieve the Bogor Goals. Since the failure of the Early Voluntary Sector Liberalization (EVSL) there have been increasing doubts whether APEC will be able to achieve the Bogor Goals. It is also argued that the prevailing APEC process may not be suited to deliver reciprocal trade liberalization commitments. Hence, a more efficient and institutionalized approach, an FTAAP for example, may strengthen the trade liberalization process in APEC. It is also noted that within the APEC process, the emphasis now appears to be placed almost exclusively on the WTO negotiations as the vehicle for achieving APEC's liberalization objectives. Outside the APEC process, APEC economies have turned decisively and increasingly towards preferential agreements as the vehicle for pursuing their liberalization goals (Scollay 2004). Therefore, an FTAAP is urgently needed to boost trade liberalization in the APEC framework and redivert negotiation resources from subregional arrangements to the APEC process. Chinese officials and economists have expressed their dissatisfaction with sluggish APEC trade liberalization on many occasions, and many of them also agree that concrete measures would intensify the APEC process on trade liberalization. However, it is not clear launching an FTAAP would be the best choice for them.

FTAAP and Proliferation of RTAs/FTAs

One of the strong arguments in support of the FTAAP proposal is that a single Pan Asia-Pacific trade pact would effectively end the proliferation and explosion of RTAs/FTAs. (Bergsten 2005b; Scollay 2004). At the same time, the "spaghetti bowl" and the discriminatory effects associated with the current "kaleidoscope" of subregional arrangements can also be eliminated. In this context, there would be no further need for China to continue pursuing its RTAs/FTAs network if an FTAAP were concluded, and hence its regional trade policy could be streamlined and the administrative resources needed for negotiations could be saved.

In spite of such an advantage, there is still a high possibility that Chinese bilateral and regional FTAs will coexist with the FTAAP for some time. One explanation is that the FTAAP negotiation would not be an instantaneous process, and consequently there will inevitably be a period in which the FTAAP and FTA negotiations will proceed in parallel. Moreover, China is not likely to completely abandon new FTA negotiations in case of the failure of the FTAAP. China may still prefer RTAs/FTAs which contain special terms to achieve designated goals or efficiently cope with the issues of both parties, particularly in the scenario where an FTAAP agreement concluded is of a low quality. Finally, China may be reluctant to confine itself into a single template of an FTA which is not able to show preferential and differential treatments for selected partners.

FTAAP and U.S.-China Relations

As two super economies in the region, China and the United States are experiencing a series of intractable problems in bilateral relations, and any problem which is not tackled properly is very likely to trigger a crisis. Specifically, there is an imbalance between the soaring U.S. current account deficit and the huge Chinese trade surplus. China's rigid exchange rate regime has also been heavily criticized, and the U.S. Congress is threatening to take strong measures against China as a "currency manipulator". Furthermore, the Chinese government views the U.S. export restriction on high-tech products and components as political and ideological hostility, the restriction is considered to be partly responsible for the unsustainable U.S. trade deficit with China. The United States has also increasingly imposed new restrictions on Chinese exports of manufactured goods using the anti-dumping and special safeguard mechanism. The Chinese government is also quite annoyed by the U.S. insistence of not giving China a market economy status, even in sectoral cases. The U.S. Congressional rejection of Chinese multinational corporations' bid for American firms and other moves to prevent China'pursuit of FDI or M&A for energy supplies in overseas market are regarded as widespread fears on the part of U.S. politicians against China's rapid growth. The bilateral relationship becomes more worrisome when political and security problems are taken into account. Among others, the issue of Taiwan is the most politically sensitive. Bergsten (2005*b*) also argued that China is likely to perceive a series of U.S. initiatives on economic and security affairs as a "surround China" or even "containment" strategy.

In this context, Bergsten proposed that the only solution to address these fundamental problems between the two locomotives in the Asia-Pacific is to launch FTAAP in order to subsume the China-U.S. bilateral clash into a broader regional framework, when a bilateral FTA agreement can be hardly reached given the U.S. domestic political environment and tremendous trade diversion effect on other Northeast Asian countries. The idea of an FTAAP could be quite attractive to China if a "high-quality" trade pact is concluded, particularly if it includes stipulations on the limited use of trade administrative protection and export controls. It will favourably provide China with a foreseeable open American market by locking in U.S. free trade commitments to China. Moreover, the U.S. trade deficit with China can be possibly curbed or even reduced when the agreement induces more U.S. exports and FDI to China.

Nevertheless, the proposed FTAAP cannot be expected too much to lessen bilateral collisions because none of the problems listed above are easily resolved and dealt with in a pan-regional trade agreement. They are either too particular for both parties concerned or too problematic and sensitive for all other APEC economies at the same time. Thus, the best and most efficient approach of treating the China-U.S. relationship is not in a regional framework, but essentially through a special bilateral senior dialogue mechanism, which aims to build confidence and credibility in mutual cooperation as well as to undertake well-designed structural reforms similar to the U.S.-Japan negotiation in the 1980s.

V. IMPEDIMENTS AND DIFFICULTIES IN JOINING THE FTAAP

WTO, DDA and FTAAP

It is strongly argued that the establishment of an FTAAP would create considerable impetus to the badly faltering WTO Doha Round negotiations and lead to a successful conclusion. Such an implication can be drawn from the catalytic role APEC played in the 1990s in the conclusion of the Uruguay Round and ITA negotiations. Many politicians and economists are therefore earnestly advocating a similar jolt to substantially stimulate the current negotiations (Bergsten 2005b; Scollay 2004). In this regard, the FTAAP plays an imperative role of a "stepping stone" to full global trade liberalization. Meanwhile, the start of an FTAAP negotiation would also be an incentive for non-APEC economies to work constructively in the WTO, given the collective bargaining power of all APEC members. At the least, the FTAAP proposal can serve as an alternative means of trade liberalization across the Asia-Pacific in the event that the Doha Development Agenda (DDA) fails. It is even argued that the FTAAP might not be necessary to be completed if the launch succeeds in bringing an ambitious result for the Doha Round (Bergsten 2005b). In this context, the proposal of FTAAP is just used as a bargaining chip for multilateral negotiations.

Notwithstanding such seemingly convincing arguments of the FTAAP's constructive role, there are still several suspicions of an APEC-wide FTA from the Chinese perspective. As stated above, China considers regional trade integration process as complementary to the multilateral trading system, and hence any RTA/FTA should be WTO-compatible and not undermine the multilateral trading system. In other words, any counter-productive and erosive effect of FTAAP should be avoided. The Chinese government's clinging to WTO principles and rules is derived from the belief that China is able to better settle trade disputes and gain a more favourable position in a multilateral framework, in which developing members can play a more important and active role. Consequently, China would not want the launch of FTAAP negotiations to be perceived as a signal that it has lost confidence and credibility in the WTO. Neither does China want to drain limited executive resources and energy from multilateral negotiations to time-consuming FTAAP negotiations. In short, China has to carefully consider if the support of FTAAP will substantially change its traditional trade policy in which the multilateral trading system remains a central tenet.

The APEC Approach

Many officials and economists have expressed their disappointment with the sluggish APEC trade liberalization process since the failure of the EVSL initiatives. Such an outcome is largely attributed to the current soft APEC approach which is unable to deliver the ambitious Bogor Goals. Some officials have proposed that the APEC process be restructured and institutionally reformed to offer an effective vehicle for trade and investment liberalization. To launch an FTAAP is then such an opportunity. However, others strongly defend the APEC approach saying that it has provided a unique way of maintaining cooperation among members in the past, and should continue to be adhered to. Some of them even suggest that APEC members can leave the negotiation of ambitious binding agreements to other forums like the WTO so that an FTAAP will not destroy the essence of APEC process, while others advise starting the FTAAP negotiation as a separate process, parallel to the development of APEC (Scollay 2004).

What is the Chinese government's stand on the impact of an FTAAP on the APEC approach? If we trace back the history of APEC's development, it is found that China has made great contributions to formulating the APEC approach,[9] which is currently summarized as "concerted unilateralism" and "open regionalism". "Concerted unilateralism" aims to pursue liberalization, facilitation and collaboration of individual economies primarily based on voluntarism and gradualism, and complemented by sharing best practices and expertise, pathfinder initiatives and peer review pressure which is being employed as the main enforcement mechanism. As Scollay (2004) pointed out, the design of APEC process can usefully be viewed as an attempt to reconcile an Asian consensus-based approach with a North American or Anglo-Saxon approach that insists on reciprocity. To achieve "open regionalism", China is determined not to seek to the establishment of APEC as an inward-looking, closed trading bloc, but rather prefers to progressively lower its trade and investment barriers on a non-discriminatory basis.

The APEC approach has long been relevant to China. On the outset of APEC establishment, there were hot debates over the institutional form of APEC. Australia and Japan initially intended to set up an OECD-type organization, a policy forum, while the United States preferred a "New Asia-Pacific Community", a formalized and rule-making free trade arrangement. China has a very clear and confirmed vision of its own, that is, "APEC should keep to its nature as an economic forum and focus on promoting the regional economic cooperation" (Jiang Zemin 1999). This simple self-defined notion has profound policy implications. The function of APEC, from a Chinese point of view, is as a consultative and consensual decision-making entity, and it is neither a venue, like the WTO, for trade negotiation and bargaining, nor an obligatory agreement like the European-approach which relies on the drafting and ratification by all participants of legally binding international agreements or treaties (Table 4.2). In essence, APEC is a loosely structured and minimal institutional organization. China firmly sticks to the APEC approach, indicating that the willingness to cooperate does not imply transferring sovereignty, deepening far-reaching integration and pursuing extensive institutionalization.

TABLE 4.2
Institutional Differences among APEC, WTO and EU

	APEC	WTO	EU
Who are the participants and stakeholders?	inter-government, but also focusing on business and academics participation	inter-government, just beginning to communicate with NGOs	inter-government, also considering interests of social groups
How to become a formal member?	no criteria, no threshold offers	qualification review, downpayment for accession	implicit criteria, approval by all members
What is institutional framework?	no treaty, only some agendas	rules, protocols and schedules	treaties
How to reach an agreement?	consensus and dialogue	negotiations	consensus and voting
How to make commitments?	selected menu (IAPs/CAPs)	package deal	collective actions
How effective for commitments?	voluntary non-binding	compulsory binding	compulsory binding
How are treatments between members and non-members?	open regionalism	MFN among members	custom union and discrimination against non-members
Is there a dispute settlement mechanism?	no	yes	yes
Conclusion	economic forum	multilateral system	regional integration organization

China's approach to APEC is derived from a scrutiny of internal and external political and economic factors. Notwithstanding the projected welfare gains from trade and investment liberalization and facilitation (TILF), Chinese leaders need to "control" the process to accommodate pressure groups and minimize structural adjustment costs in order to have a buffer for future domestic reforms. It can also soften the hard line of some developed members who favour the approach of comprehensiveness and uniformity by compromising "flexibility" with "comparability". China regards the approach as a "unique" collaborative approach of APEC as its own. The practice has clearly shown that this approach is so "viable and effective" that it is "conducive to achieving a balance of rights, interests and needs of various members" and therefore should be maintained" (Jiang Zemin 1999).

However, the FTAAP proposal, which is, on the contrary, based on binding reciprocal commitments, will represent a fundamental and decisive departure from the commonly recognized concept of "concerted unilateralism" and "open regionalism". Hence, this critical change not only needs to be agreed on by all APEC members but also challenges China's long-term strategy for APEC.

High-quality FTAAP?

From the Chinese point of view, if negotiations for an FTAAP are launched, it would be highly desirable to reach a comprehensive and high-quality agreement. Only in this way can the Bogor Goals be achieved and the risk to world trading system be minimized. Several rules, standards or references have been made to regulate the established RTAs/FTAs. GATT Article XXIV and GATS Article V serve as fundamental benchmarks to formulate related rules, albeit with some vague definitions and terms in clauses. Emphasizing conformity to WTO rules, the "Best Practices of RTAs/FTAs in APEC" also provides a good reference and template for APEC members to conduct RTAs/FTAs on a voluntary basis. Moreover, the PECC Trade Forum also proposed an "APEC Common Understanding on RTAs" which can be used as guidelines for RTAs/FTAs that would be consistent with the Bogor Goals.

In Scollay's study paper (Scollay 2004), a high-quality FTAAP agreement is characterized as including few (or preferably no) exclusions in product or sector coverage, simple and transparent rules of origin, clear and minimal safeguard provisions, prohibition on anti-dumping measures and agreement to deal with the relevant issues via competition policy, extensive trade facilitation provisions, full coverage of government procurement, full liberalization of investment flows, and a transparent and effective dispute settlement process. If all these elements could be incorporated in the final treaty, China would undoubtedly benefit from joining the agreement, and therefore it would be likely that China would join. However, achieving a high quality agreement is highly unlikely because of the complexity of the issues as well as the number of sectors involved in the discussions. A low-quality FTAAP with limited coverage and considerable exemptions will just make an APEC-wide FTA like "a new piece of spaghetti in the bowl", and such a situation cannot be considered a useful contribution to both WTO and APEC.

Pressure Groups and Protection of Sensitive Industries

Another explanation of China's reluctance to join the FTAAP comes from concerns over politically sensitive sectors. So far there are several cases of exclusions or exemptions in Chinese bilateral and regional FTAs. For instance, the ASEAN-China FTA has yet to address the issue of the Chinese import restriction on palm oil, in which ASEAN countries have a comparative advantage. Chinese officials are also concerned that agricultural and dairy goods might remain a block to future negotiations with New Zealand and Australia, because China is particularly wary of adverse effects on farmers caused by radical agricultural trade liberalization. The Chinese People's Congress has repeatedly postponed review of the Anti-Monopoly Law which indicates great lobbying pressure from some SOEs, such as service suppliers of banking, telecommunication and transportation, which are stiffly opposed to free competition and further openness to foreign suppliers. All these issues and sectors that have proved difficult to negotiate in the WTO and bilateral FTAs will be just as, if not more, difficult to negotiate in the FTAAP. Therefore, it is inevitable that some exclusions or exemptions would have to be accepted in order to reach agreement on an FTAAP.

Alternative Scenario of EAFTA

While making significant contributions to APEC development, East Asian countries are spontaneously engaging in regional integration among themselves. This process originally derived from then Malaysian Prime

Minister Mahathir's proposal for an East Asian Economic Group in the early 1990s, but it was widely considered as an anti-United States initiative to exclude the U.S. leadership in the Asia-Pacific. Then the proposal turned into a "10+3" cooperative framework including ASEAN, China, Japan and Republic of Korea in 2003. These countries have been holding regular ministerial meetings since 1998 and also successfully held the first East Asia Summit in 2005. Furthermore, many feasibility studies on a pan-East Asian FTA (EAFTA) are being conducted by considering the merger of bilateral agreements between Japan-Korea and the ASEAN-China FTA, although two largest countries, China and Japan, are currently facing political tension and possible military conflict.

The idea of an EAFTA has aroused great concerns for the United States. It is not only worried that an EAFTA would lead to a bi-polar APEC, given the development of EAFTA, but also is feared that EAFTA could have disastrous political and commercial effects on the United States (and also other non-EAFTA APEC member economies) through trade discrimination against outsiders. In this context, Bergsten (2005a) argued that only an FTAAP is able to banish the risk of disintegration of APEC by "embedding both Pacific Asia and the Americas in the Asia Pacific".

China is a firm supporter of the EAFTA proposal. It would benefit from increasing intra-regional trade and FDI flows as well as integrating into a regional production network by further eliminating trade barriers and reducing transaction costs in the region. East Asian countries could also play a more important role in the global economy under an EAFTA, and consequently provide a viable external context for China's regional integration. For China, EAFTA will also give a political expression to the new economic reality with the purpose of fufilling "Asian interests" and "Asian values", while the institutions established since World War II to manage global and regional affairs have long been reflected in the cross-Atlantic order. Even if the FTAAP is launched, China may continue to promote the EAFTA under the framework of "ASEAN+3", particularly in the areas that would not be covered in the FTAAP, such as currency and financial cooperation.

Treatment of Taiwan's Membership

APEC is one of few forums in which both China and Chinese Taipei have memberships. Chinese senior officials and bureaucrats are often puzzled over how to confine the diplomatic activities of Taiwan in the APEC arena. They expect that the influence of Taiwan should be minimized in political terms, and is strictly confined to economic affairs at most. Therefore, China will not anticipate the launch of FTAAP to exacerbate such a problematic issue, because it is impossible for China to negotiate and reach an agreement with a "non-sovereign state". One scenario is that the Chinese government will attempt to insist on the exclusion of Chinese Taipei at the very beginning of negotiations, but it may face the fierce objection of Chinese Taipei and the United States, if an FTAAP is negotiated in the APEC context. Another possibility is to treat Taiwan as an independent tariff territory, just like the practice in the WTO. No matter which solution is chosen, the treatment of Taiwan's membership remains a difficult topic for China and has to be decisively and cautiously addressed in the feasibility study.

Lack of Executive Resources for Possible Negotiations

As a newcomer to FTA negotiations, China still faces many challenges to participate in FTAAP in terms of administrative resources. First, China is now engaging in trade negotiations in a number of dimensions, including the WTO, APEC and various bilateral or regional FTAs. FTAAP negotiations will impose an even greater work load on Chinese trade negotiators and also divert significant resource from current trade talks. Second, China still lacks experience in tackling complex issues in trade in goods, service, investment and other issues, as well as qualified negotiators with sophisticated expertise. Third, capacity-building is urgently needed with sufficient funding for technical and training activities, particularly in the area of trade rules such as rules of origin, technical barriers to trade, and sanitary and phytosanitary regulations.

Transitional Period and Bogor Goals

APEC's Bogor Declaration sets 2010 as the target date for full implementation of trade and investment liberalization by APEC developed economies, and 2020 as the target date for APEC developing economies. Now the first target date is impending, yet a number of challenges are confronted to achieve the ambitious Bogor Goal for developed economies, according to the APEC mid-term stocktaking report (APEC Task Force

2005). With respect to industrial goods, the key issue is how to tackle the residual protection, including tariff peaks in selected sectors such as fish products, leather, rubber, footwear and travel goods, textile and clothing, as well as tariff escalation across manufacturing sectors, in spite of low overall levels of protection in these countries. Furthermore, anti-dumping and safeguard measures against exports which APEC developing economies have interests in are still prevailing on a discriminatory and discretionary basis. Restrictions or prohibitions on FDI and services are also relatively high in some developed economies. Finally, more work needs to be done to deal with "behind-the-border" issues in developed members to implement domestic regulatory and structural reforms. Therefore, if the Bogor Goals are interpreted in a dynamic manner stressing the dismantling of residual border controls and stretching to "behind-the-border" measures, APEC developed members have to pursue ongoing reforms and liberalization to achieve the goal by the deadline. In this regard, Chinese officials are concerned that the launch of an FTAAP would probably dilute the dedication of developed economies on achieving the Bogor Goals or subtly delay the original target date, because the end of transitional period in the FTAAP is widely expected beyond the year of 2010.

VI. CONCLUSION

Following its market-oriented reform strategy, China will continue to pursue trade liberalization by means of multilateral, regional, bilateral and unilateral approaches. Noticeably, in recent years, the Chinese government has increasingly looked to regionalism as a complement to its traditional reliance on the multilateral trading system. RTAs/FTAs seem to be more efficient in tackling special bilateral trade issues and promoting economic cooperation by focusing on selected areas. Moreover, China will benefit from building its own RTAs/FTAs network by positioning itself in the centre of a hub-and-spoke system and achieving non-economic goals in the game of geopolitics. In short, China's evolving strategy RTAs/FTAs strategy will have a significant impact on its attitude to the idea of an FTAAP.

From an economic perspective, there is little doubt that China would benefit from joining FTAAP since both its main trade partners and vital trade barriers in export markets are concentrated in the Asia-Pacific region. Nevertheless, Chinese support for an FTAAP would be curbed by a number of political and diplomatic elements, which are analysed in this paper. Among others, the APEC approach, U.S.-China relations, exclusion of sensitive sectors, the alternative proposal of an East Asian FTA and membership of Taiwan are critical questions that need careful addressing. If the Chinese authorities cannot be persuaded or these problematic issues cannot be handled properly, it is unlikely that China will join the FTAAP negotiation.

Finally, what are scenarios for the Chinese response to the idea of FTAAP? The forecasting is obviously difficult, much depends on Chinese cost-benefit calculus and changeable political and economic configurations in the region. Still, I attempt to make some judgements based on the following three possibilities.

China's Participation in FTAAP

The most optimistic scenario is that China will consent to the idea of FTAAP and positively engage in the negotiations on agreement immediately after the process is launched. A possible motive behind this Chinese decision is to demonstrate that it is not a "spoiler" preventing the agreement from going ahead, particularly when other APEC economies are likely to support the proposal. Moreover, whether China is interested in joining FTAAP crucially depends on how attractive an agreement could be concluded to address the issues central to China's interests, for instance, removing export restrictions, trade remedies and any discrimination against non-market economies. Only if these elements are embodied in the agreement, would the Chinese government be empowered to overcome severe political obstacles and convince domestic constituencies that concessions in the FTAAP are worthwhile.

Another less optimistic scenario could be that China may join at a later date on the voluntary basis, if a "pathfinder" initiative or "APEC-plus" approach is chosen to pursue the negotiation of FTAAP.

China's Reaction if FTAAP Fails

If the FTAAP unfortunately fails, whether due to the opposition of China or not, China would continue to pursue its building of an RTAs/FTAs network, while paying attention to the strengthening of the multilateral trading system and referring to "Best Practice of RTAs/FTAs in APEC". The APEC Best Practices based on consensus among APEC members provide a good reference for all members on how to conduct RTAs/FTAs on a voluntary basis. On one hand, China would launch more RTAs/FTAs negotiations with other countries which it perceives as strategic partners, such as Brazil, Mexico, Singapore, and Russia. Particularly, it is highly likely that China will promote the establishment of EAFTA. On the other hand, China may also make its own contribution by seeking to create an "APEC template" for RTAs/FTAs that would set out a benchmark for individual agreements and negotiations.

The possible failure of FTAAP would also stimulate other APEC economies to continue the proliferation of RTAs/FTAs. In particular, as Bergsten (2005*b*) foresees, the United States is likely to initiate negotiations with the Republic of Korea, Japan or some Southeast Asian countries (most likely Indonesia and/or Malaysia) for a bilateral FTA. If these agreements are reached, China will become losers unless it initiates FTAs with those Asian countries. The United States would be especially annoyed by the proposal of EAFTA so that there must be some political and diplomatic actions to be taken in order to avoid "drawing a line down the middle of the Pacific". All these outcomes will exacerbate the U.S.-China confrontation in APEC.

FTAAP Launched Without China's Participation

A number of proponents have suggested that the FTAAP negotiations could be a separate process independent of existing institutions which would maintain the APEC approach and organization. China would be under substantial pressures in the scenario that the FTAAP is launched outside the APEC framework without Chinese approval, because of the possible significant trade diversion effects and discrimination against non-members. It is obviously not expected by the Chinese government. Therefore, such a "competitive liberalization" pressure, which was first raised by Bergsten, will induce China to seriously consider the possibility of joining the FTAAP at a later time, albeit its reluctance at the very beginning.

Notes

The paper does not represent any standpoint of the Chinese government and the author's home institutes. The author therefore bears sole responsibility of expression in the paper.

1. Calculated based on IMF, *Direction of Trade Statistics*, 2005, and UNCTAD, Comtrade Database (SITC Rev. 3).
2. Calculated based on Chinese National Bureau, *Chinese Yearbook of Statistics*, 2005.
3. For a detailed description of "triangle trade" in the Asia-Pacific, refer to UNCTAD, *Trade and Development Report*, 2005.
4. Bergsten (2005*b*) points that "China's soaring global current account surplus will probably approach $150 billion and 7.5 per cent of its GDP this year, becoming the largest single counterpart to the U.S. global current account deficit of about $800 billion or almost 7 per cent of its GDP."
5. According to WTO statistics, there were 2,743 anti-dumping measures reported during the period from 1995 to first half of 2005, of which 434 were against Chinese products, accounting for 16 per cent (WTO 2006).
6. The data and other information in this section are quoted from WTO trade policy review reports submitted by the Chinese government (2006) and WTO Secretariat (2005).
7. Calculated on the data of MOC, China.
8. Hufbauer and Yee Wong (2005) illustrated several examples of Chinese enterprises' activities in these industries.
9. In 1996, President Jiang Zemin put forward for the first time the "APEC approach" guiding APEC cooperation. In the following summits, he repeatedly emphasized and elaborated on its nature and content from Chinese point of view, and ultimately forged a comprehensive and systematic deliberation of the approach which includes principles as follows: adherence to mutual respect, equality, mutual benefit; recognition of diversity; flexibility and pragmatism; gradual progress and openness; consensus; unilaterism and voluntarism. Detailed description of China's contribution to APEC approach refers to Sheng Bin (2001).

References

Antkiewicz, A. and J. Whalley. *China's New Regional Trade Agreements*. NBER Working Paper 10992 (2004).

APEC Task Force. "Bogor Goals Mid-Term Stocktake". Discussion paper presented at Bogor Goals Mid-term Stocktake Symposium, Jeju, Korea, 28 May 2005.

Bergsten, C. F. "Embedding Pacific Asia in the Asia Pacific: The Global Impact of an East Asian Community". Speech delivered at the Japan National Press Club, Tokyo, 2 September 2005*a*.

――――. "A New Strategy for APEC". Speech delivered at the 16th General Meeting of the Pacific Economic Cooperation Council (PECC), Seoul, South Korea, 6 September 2005*b*.

———. "The Trans-Pacific Imbalance: A Disaster in the Making?". Speech at the 16th General Meeting of the Pacific Economic Cooperation Council (PECC), Seoul, 7 September 2005c.

Chinese Government. *Trade Policy Review Report by the People's Republic of China.* WT/TPR/G/161, 17 March 2006.

Hufbauer, G. C. and Yee Wong. *Prospects for Regional Free Trade in Asia.* Working Paper 05-12. Washington, D.C.: Institute for International Economics, 2005.

Jiang Zemin. Speech by His Excellency President of the People's Republic of China at the APEC Informal Leadership Meeting. Dissemination by the Ministry of Foreign Affairs of PRC, 1999.

Scollay, R. "Preliminary Assessment of the Proposal for a Free Trade Area of the Asia-Pacific (FTAAP)". An Issues Paper for the APEC Business Advisory Council (ABAC), 2004.

Sheng Bin. "Regionalism: Challenge for China's APEC Policy in the 21st Century". *China and World Economy*, No. 11, December 2001.

———. "APEC Trade Liberalization: A Gravity Model Estimation". Memo, 2006.

World Bank. *Global Economic Prospects 2005: Trade, Regionalism, and Development.* 2004.

WTO. "Trade Policy Review Report by the WTO Secretariat". WT/TPR/S/161, 28 February 2006.

Zhao Jie and Han Yi. "China's FTA Strategy and Future Perspective". Economy Report: China. Presentation in the Workshop on Identifying and Addressing Possible Impacts of FTAs Development on APEC Developing Member Economies, Hanoi, Vietnam, 28–30 June 2005.

5

Japan's FTA Strategy and Free Trade Area of Asia-Pacific[1]

Shujiro Urata

I. INTRODUCTION

Japan enacted its first free trade agreement (FTA) in November 2002 with Singapore. The formal name of the agreement is the Agreement between Japan and the Republic of Singapore for a New-Age Economic Partnership, or Japan-Singapore Economic Partnership Agreement (JSEPA). JSEPA is a comprehensive economic partnership agreement (EPA), which includes not only the removal of tariff and non-tariff barriers — the traditional elements of FTAs — but also the liberalization of foreign direct investment (FDI), trade and FDI facilitation, economic and technical cooperation in a wide range of areas including development of human resources, information and communications technology (ICT), small and medium enterprises (SMEs), tourism and others. Both Japan and Singapore realized the importance of a broad-ranging comprehensive agreement, in order to have significant impacts on economic activities in the emerging international economic environment where not only goods but also people, funds, and information cross borders freely. Since then

Japan has enacted two more FTAs (EPAs), one with Mexico in April 2005 and the other with Malaysia in July 2006. Japan is currently negotiating or studying a number of FTAs.

Japan had pursued trade liberalization under the General Agreement on Tariffs and Trade (GATT) and the World Trade Organization (WTO) until the late 1990s, and therefore, the recent pursuit of FTAs by Japan is a reflection of the change in its trade policy from a single track approach based on the GATT/WTO multilateral trade liberalization to a multi-track approach including bilateral and plurilateral liberalization. The White Paper on international trade 2003 published by Japan's Ministry of Trade and Industry argued the need for pursuing a multi-track approach. Several reasons can be identified for Japan's emerging interest in FTAs.

One important reason is new developments in global trade, the scene where multilateral trade negotiations under the WTO are making little progress and regional trade agreements such as FTAs are rapidly increasing. Faced with this situation, the Japanese government recognized FTAs as an option for achieving trade liberalization. To put it differently, the Japanese government expect FTAs to play a role in promoting Japan's economic growth through providing business opportunities for Japanese firms in FTA member countries and promoting domestic policy reforms such as agricultural reform in Japan, which are necessary for achieving sustainable economic growth. Another reason is the expectation that FTAs can play effective roles for the promotion of economic integration in East Asia, in order to contribute to economic growth, and political and social stability, which in turn would have positive impacts on Japan. It should also be noted that the desire to take the initiative in regional affairs in East Asia has motivated Japan to pursue FTAs.

In the light of discussions on the idea of a Free Trade Area of the Asia-Pacific (FTAAP), this paper examines Japan's FTA strategies and attempts to identify possible benefits and costs of the FTAAP. The structure of the remainder of the paper is as follows. Section II gives a review of Japan's FTAs, in order to set the stage for the analysis of Japanese FTA strategy. Section III examines the motives behind Japan's FTA strategy, while section IV discusses the possible impacts of FTAs and the FTAAP by referring to the results of simulation analysis. Section V identifies the obstacles to establishing FTAs and the FTAAP, while section VI provides some several possible policies to overcome the obstacles. Section VII presents Japan's views towards the FTAAP.

II. BRIEF REVIEW OF JAPAN'S FTA DEVELOPMENTS

Japan had been a passive participant in FTA discussions until November 2002 when Japan proposed a possible FTA with the Association of Southeast Asian Nations (ASEAN). Prime Minister Goh Chok Tong of Singapore proposed an FTA to Prime Minister Keizo Obuchi of Japan in December 1999. They decided to set up a study group consisting of government officials, business people, and academics to investigate the contents of a possible FTA and its impacts on their economies. After a series of discussions the study group recommended the prime ministers start FTA negotiations in October 2000. Responding to the recommendation by the study group, the two prime ministers asked their government officials to start FTA negotiations. Negotiations began in January 2001 and reached an agreement in October 2001. After the agreement was signed by Prime Ministers Goh and Junichiro Koizumi of Japan in January 2002, Japan-Singapore FTA (JSEPA) went into effect in November 2002 (Table 5.1). Negotiations appeared to have moved rather smoothly because contentious issues such as liberalization in agricultural trade were limited for both countries.

TABLE 5.1
Japan's FTA Developments

Country	Status	Year
Singapore	In effect	November 2002
Mexico	In effect	April 2005
Malaysia	In effect	July 2006
Philippines	Broad agreement	November 2004
Thailand	Broad agreement	September 2005
Korea	In negotiation	December 2004
ASEAN	In negotiation	April 2005
Indonesia	In negotiation	July 2005
Chile	In negotiation	February 2006
Brunei	Agreed to negotiate	May 2006
GCC Countries	Scheduled to begin negotiation	July 2006
Vietnam	Under study	February 2006
India	Agreed to negotiate	Early 2007
Australia	Under study	November 2005
Switzerland	Under study	October 2005

Source: Ministry of Economy, Trade and Industry.

JSEPA has both strengths and weaknesses. One of the strengths is its comprehensiveness. Another strength is its symbolic nature as JSEPA sent a message to the world about Japan's strong interest in FTAs. One of its weaknesses is the limited coverage of trade liberalization on Japan's side. Singapore removed tariffs on all imports from Japan, while Japan removed tariffs on 94 per cent of imports from Singapore. It should be noted that those imports from Singapore that were not liberalized include not only agricultural products but also selected manufactured products including some petrochemical products and leather goods.

Mexico was the first country that approached Japan for a possible FTA. In November 1998 President Ernesto Zedillo of Mexico proposed an FTA to Japan. Following the proposition by the Mexican president, the committee on Japan-Mexico Closer Economic Relations was set up by Japan External Trade Organization (JETRO) and Mexico's Secretaria de Comercio Y Fomento Industrial (SECOFI). In April 2000, JETRO and SECOFI released a joint report on possible Japan-Mexico FTA. Since the report concluded that a Japan-Mexico FTA would give significant favourable effects on both nations, the Japanese prime minister and the Mexican president agreed to establish a business-government-academics study group to examine a possible approach for strengthening mutual economic ties, including an FTA. The study group was established in September 2001 and examined the contents of a possible FTA. The group presented its recommendation to their national leaders in summer 2002, to start FTA negotiations. The negotiations started in October 2002 with an aim of reaching an agreement in one year. However, the negotiations took much longer than expected and the two countries reached an agreement in September 2004. Japan-Mexico FTA (EPA) was enacted in 1 April 2005.

The most serious obstacle in the negotiations was Japan's strong resistance to liberalization in agricultural products, specifically pork, beef, and chicken products, oranges and orange juice (Table 5.2). After a strong request from the Mexican government, Japan opened up these markets by increasing import quotas, not removing tariffs as it should have been under the FTAs. Mexico agreed to liberalize steel and automobile markets within seven to ten years, responding to Japan's strong request. As a result, Mexico agreed to open its market to all imports from Japan, while Japan agreed to open its market to only 84 per cent of its imports from Mexico. The Japan-Mexico FTA was strongly supported by the Japanese business sector, which felt that their business

TABLE 5.2
Major Contentious Issues for Japan in FTA Negotiations: Selected Cases

Mexico	Trade liberalization in agricultural products including pork, beef, and chicken products, oranges, and orange juice.
Thailand	Trade liberalization in rice.
	Liberalization of the movement of natural persons, specifically cooks, nurses, massage therapist, and care-givers for the elderly.
Philippines	Trade liberalization in bananas.
	Liberalization of the movement of natural persons, specifically nurses, and care-givers for the elderly.
Malaysia	Trade liberalization in plywood.
Korea	Trade liberalization in fish products, refined copper products.

Source: Nihon Keizai Shimbun, 10 October 2004 and hearing from the country officials.

had been suffering from losses of business opportunity due to the lack of an FTA with Mexico. Specifically, the cost in the form of lost business is estimated at 400 billion yen in 1999, amounting close to Japan's exports to Mexico.[2] Mexico on the other hand was interested in exporting its agricultural products to Japan, as the Mexican government was under pressure from Mexican farmers, who were unhappy with the negative impacts of the North American Free Trade Agreement (NAFTA). As can be seen from the results of the negotiations noted above, Japan gained substantially and did not give in much on agricultural liberalization. Although it may be a victory for trade negotiators, it certainly is a defeat for those keenly interested in structural reform.

Regarding the FTA with South Korea, President Kim Dae Jung took the lead in suggesting a closer economic partnership between South Korea and Japan in October 1998. In November 1998 at the Japan-Korea Ministerial Meeting the issue of possible FTA was taken up. Following the meeting, private institutions jointly carried on research activities and released their report in May 2000. The Japanese prime minister and the Korean president agreed to establish the "Japan-Korea FTA Business Forum" in the September 2000 summit meeting. In March 2001, this business forum was established, having both nations' business leaders as core members. In January 2002, after adopting their joint declaration that called for concluding a Japan-Korea FTA as soon as possible, the forum submitted a report to the Japanese prime minister and Korean president. Based on this report's recommendation, Japan and Korea agreed to establish a joint study group comprising government officials, business leaders, and academics. The study group made recommendations to the leaders to start negotiations. FTA negotiations between Japan and Korea started in December 2003, with an aim to conclude the negotiations in two years. Although both Japan and Korea aspired to establish a model FTA for East Asian countries with a high degree of liberalization, the negotiations were deadlocked since the beginning because of their dissatisfaction with the framework of negotiations on market access.

Some specific concerns and problems facing Korea and Japan include the following. Although Korea expects an increase in FDI from Japan from the FTA, Korea is concerned with the possible negative impact on its manufacturing industries except for some electronics products such as semi-conductors, because of their lack of competitiveness vis-à-vis Japanese counterparts. In particular, small and medium-sized enterprises (SMEs) strongly oppose the Japan-Korea FTA, as they fear serious competition from increased Japanese imports. These possible negative impacts have made the Korean government concerned with the worsening bilateral trade balance and increasing dependence on Japan, although these views cannot be justified on an economic basis. Both Japan and Korea generally oppose to liberalization of trade in agricultural products, as has been demonstrated in the WTO negotiations as well as their respective FTA negotiations so far. However, in the Japan-Korea FTA discussions, Korea feels that Japan is not up-to-date in liberalizing agricultural and fishery sectors.

China's Premier Zhu Rongji informally proposed to the leaders of Japan and Korea the establishment of a trilateral FTA among these three countries at the Leaders' meeting in 2002. Japan did not accept China's proposal by indicating that Japan would like to be sure that China, a new WTO member, abides by the WTO commitments and rules before discussing an FTA. At least two reasons could be postulated for Japan's rejection. One is its possible negative impacts on non-competitive sectors such as the agriculture and labour-intensive apparel industries, and the other is its rivalry vis-à-vis China. We will take up these issues in more detail later. It should be noted that government think-tanks from Japan,

China, and Korea have been actively conducting a joint-study project on the possibility of Japan-China-Korea FTA since 2003.

Japan proposed an EPA with ASEAN including an FTA in November 2002, only one day after China and ASEAN signed an agreement on closer economic partnership. Compared with the sensational impact that the China-ASEAN Closer Economic Agreement had, the Japan-ASEAN EPA did not attract much attention, as it did not have any concrete actions. In November 2003 Japan and ASEAN agreed on the framework for comprehensive economic partnership and agreed to start consultations in 2004.[3] Japan and ASEAN started FTA negotiations in April 2005 with a target of concluding negotiations in two years. Japan is eager to establish an FTA with ASEAN because of its importance to Japan not only in economic but also political and strategic aspects. Japan's trade and FDI relationship with ASEAN is still greater than its relationship with China. Japan is interested in improving the business environment in ASEAN by establishing an FTA, through which stable and reliable economic systems such as the protection of intellectual property rights may be developed to benefit Japanese firms operating in ASEAN. It also has to be noted that Japan did not want to be left behind other countries including China, Korea and India, which started negotiations with ASEAN, as the delay in the negotiations would reduce Japan's economic and political presence in East Asia.

While Japan continues to have discussions with ASEAN, some members of ASEAN and Japan started negotiations on bilateral FTAs. Japan's FTA negotiations with Malaysia started in January 2004, while its negotiations with Thailand and the Philippines started in February that year. Indonesia was the last country among the original ASEAN members that started FTA negotiations with Japan in July 2005. Japan-Malaysia FTA was successfully negotiated and enacted in July 2006, while the negotiations with Thailand, the Philippines, and Indonesia are still under way. The contentious issues for its negotiations with these ASEAN countries include liberalization in agricultural imports and liberalization in the movement of natural persons, while Japan is eager to reduce barriers on foreign trade and FDI in these countries. These issues will be discussed in more detail in section VI.

Despite the realization of the need to establish a Japan-ASEAN EPA, Japan has decided to establish FTAs bilaterally with selected members of ASEAN since it cannot establish speedily an ASEAN-wide FTA because of the wide differences in economic and non-economic conditions among ASEAN members. Some argue that bilateral FTAs with selected members of ASEAN would create divisiveness among ASEAN members. Since this is certainly a possibility, Japan needs to conclude its negotiations with ASEAN as early as possible.

Japan is actively participating in discussions on the establishment of an ASEAN+3 (China, Japan and Korea) FTA. The idea of an FTA covering East Asian countries has emerged. At the Leaders' summit meeting of ASEAN+3 in 1998 it was decided that an East Asia Vision Group be set up to study the long-term vision for economic cooperation. The group has presented the leaders with its recommendations, which include the establishment of an East Asian FTA. Currently, the Expert Group, which was set up at the recommendation of ASEAN+3 Economic Ministers, is studying the possibility of an East Asian FTA, comprising ASEAN+3.

Japan's Ministry of Economy, Trade and Industry released a report entitled "Japan's Global Economic Strategy" in April 2006.[4] This report argues for the need to establish an East Asia EPA, whose members include ASEAN+3+3 (the additional three being India, Australia and New Zealand), to achieve economic prosperity in East Asia. The report further calls for Japan's initiative to formulate and implement East Asia EPA.

As for FTAs with other countries, Japan began negotiations with Chile, and expects to begin negotiations with India in early 2007. In addition, Japan is studying the possibility of FTAs with the following countries: Australia, Switzerland, and the Cooperation Council for the Arab States of the Gulf (Gulf Cooperation Council, GCC).

As can be seen from the above discussion, Japan's FTA strategy emphasizes East Asia as a region for establishing FTAs for economic and political reasons.[5] For Japan, economic prosperity, economic growth, and political and social stability in East Asia are critically important because of Japan's geographical proximity and close economic relations. Japan's establishment of FTAs with East Asian countries is expected to promote not only Japan's economic growth but also East Asia's economic growth, contributing to economic prosperity, and social and political stability in East Asia. This in turn contributes to economic growth. The next section discusses the motives of Japan's FTA strategy in more detail.

As noted above, the Japanese government set up a study group consisting of private sector representatives, government officials, and academics to examine possible FTAs before entering negotiations. The idea of a study group was quite useful in formulating the appropriate contents of FTAs because in study group discussions pro-liberalization voices of business and academics rather than pro-protection views of government officials were adopted. Officials of the Ministry of Agriculture, Fishery and Forestry and representatives from agriculture associations oppose any import liberalization of agricultural products by arguing the need for food security and multi-functionality of agriculture. In other words, they argue that the maintenance of agriculture would contribute to the conservation of environment and preservation of rural life. By contrast, business representatives, academics, and in some cases officials of the Ministry of Economy, Trade, and Industry and Ministry of Foreign Affairs present arguments for liberalization.

III. MOTIVES BEHIND JAPAN'S FTA STRATEGY

Japan recognizes FTA as one of its trade policy options in addition to multilateral framework under the WTO. Several factors contributed to this shift in Japan's trade policy. This section investigates these factors.

First, greater access to foreign markets was one of the important motives that aroused Japan's interest in FTAs. Japan was one of few countries that did not have any regional trade arrangements with other countries until the early twenty-first century, where an increasingly greater number of FTAs had become established. Facing a world market with many discriminatory regional trading arrangements, in particular those in Europe and North America, Japan felt the need to secure a market for Japanese firms by setting up FTAs. As FTAs would eliminate trade barriers with FTA partners, Japanese firms are surely able to enjoy more business opportunities. This kind of thinking led to a positive perspective on FTAs, especially when multilateral trade negotiations under the WTO were making little progress.

For internationally competitive Japanese firms, it is very important to have more business opportunities when competing with foreign companies. For example, FTAs with East Asian countries with high growth potential would increase Japan's exports to these countries, which are presently protected with high tariff and non-tariff barriers (Table 5.3). In addition, Japanese firms could expand their business in FTA member countries

TABLE 5.3
Average Tariff Rates in ASEAN+3, 2001
(In percentages)

	Japan	China	Korea	ASEAN	Indonesia	Malaysia	Philippines	Singapore	Thailand	Vietnam
Agriculture and food	30.2	37.6	81.7	13.9	5.0	17.1	9.5	0.4	29.4	30.7
Natural resources	0.1	0.3	3.8	0.8	0.3	1.4	3.1	0.0	0.4	3.2
Textile and apparel	9.0	20.5	10.0	11.1	8.6	12.3	6.5	0.0	18.5	21.4
Wood and paper products	1.1	9.0	4.0	5.4	3.4	6.6	4.7	0.0	11.0	12.0
Chemical products	1.1	13.0	6.7	5.2	4.4	5.9	4.5	0.0	11.7	7.3
Metal products	0.5	7.5	3.8	5.6	5.9	8.5	3.9	0.0	9.3	4.7
Machinery	0.1	13.1	6.1	3.3	3.0	3.9	2.3	0.0	8.2	7.5
Electronic machinery	0.0	10.1	1.1	0.8	2.1	0.4	0.1	0.0	4.7	8.8
Transport equipment	0.0	20.5	3.9	14.6	9.6	31.7	11.5	0.0	24.0	42.1
Other manufacturing	5.3	13.9	8.5	6.1	6.5	6.8	6.1	0.0	7.1	18.4
Trade	0.0	0.0	0.0	0.0	0.0	0.0	0.0	0.0	0.0	0.0
Construction	0.0	0.0	0.0	0.0	0.0	0.0	0.0	0.0	0.0	0.0
Transport and communication	0.0	0.0	0.0	0.0	0.0	0.0	0.0	0.0	0.0	0.0
Public services	0.0	0.0	0.0	0.0	0.0	0.0	0.0	0.0	0.0	0.0
Other services	0.0	0.0	0.0	0.0	0.0	0.0	0.0	0.0	0.0	0.0
Manufacturing	1.7	12.7	4.7	4.2	5.0	4.8	2.4	0.0	9.6	13.0
Total	4.1	11.6	8.5	4.0	3.6	4.7	2.8	0.0	8.8	10.0

Data source: GTAP ver.6 database.

through FDI because an FTA, or EPA, include not only trade but FDI liberalization and economic cooperation, such as human resource development and infrastructure development.

The market access motive clearly played an important role for Japan in pursuing the FTA with Mexico. Thanks to NAFTA and the EU-Mexico FTA, EU and U.S. firms can export their products to Mexico without tariffs. Japanese firms have to pay high tariffs to export their products to Mexico, whose market is protected by high tariffs. Indeed, the simple mean tariff rate for Mexico was very high at 16.2 per cent in 2001.[6] Among Japanese manufacturing sectors, automobile and steel industries were very eager to have an FTA with Mexico. Japan's automobile industry is interested in expanding exports of finished cars to Mexico, while its steel industry is interested in exporting steel products, which are used for the production of electronics, household electrical appliances, general machineries, and automobiles by Japanese assembly firms operating in Mexico. Besides, the Mexican government only allows FTA members to participate in the government procurement market. Mexico can impose such restrictions on government procurement because it is not a signatory to WTO's government procurement code. Faced with these market access problems in Mexico because of its non-FTA member status, Japanese business has rigorously pushed the Japanese government to have an FTA with Mexico.

The stimulation of structural reforms is another motive for Japan to pursue FTAs. Structural reforms are essential to revitalize economic activities and to regain competitiveness for Japan. Since the collapse of a bubble economy in the early 1990s, the Japanese economy was in a long recession. Indeed, the 1990s was characterized as the "lost decade" for Japan. Although Japan's post-war systems contributed to high economic growth in the past, they have recently become ineffective. This is one of the reasons why Japan failed to recover from such long recession. Although the Japanese economy has shown signs of recovery in recent years, it is too early to tell whether the recovery is long-lasting enough to achieve sustainable economic growth. One serious challenge is rapid demographic change reflected in declining population and ageing, which is likely to result in a loss of economic and social dynamism.

To deal with these challenges, many observers agree that further structural reform is necessary for achieving potential growth as it leads to more efficient use of limited resources including human and financial resources. The following sectors can be identified as needing structural reforms: agriculture and fishery and medical, educational, and other services.

In the post-World War II period, Japan had made use of international frameworks (for example, GATT and OECD) and external pressures (especially pressures from the United States) to reform its domestic structures through trade liberalization. Indeed, structural reform contributed significantly to the improvement of the competitiveness of Japan's manufacturing sector. However, in the latter half of the 1990s, liberalization was becoming more difficult under the WTO framework. There are several reasons for the slow progress under the WTO. First, as a result of substantial trade liberalization under the GATT, there remain only difficult areas for further liberalization, which slow down further liberalization. Second, the number of WTO members increased significantly over time to reach 149 (as of December 2005), making it difficult for the WTO to make decision on trade liberalization, because decision-making at the WTO is based on consensus. One seriously contentious issue is the liberalization of agricultural and industrial products, because of different views on these issues among major WTO members including the United States, the EU, Japan, and some developing countries.

The U.S. pressure on Japan concerning trade-related issues weakened after the establishment of the WTO. This is because the U.S., Japan and other WTO member countries began to use the strengthened dispute settlement mechanism under the WTO to settle trade disputes. It should also be noted that Japan undertook a number of policy reforms such as those in financial system, and corporate governance system, which were main causes of U.S. concerns over macroeconomic performance of Japanese economy.

Faced with a lack of external pressures, especially from the WTO's multilateral trade negotiations, Japan became interested in FTAs as one of the policy options to promote structural reform. Japan came to look at FTAs in a positive light after it found that the EU and NAFTA promoted structural reforms in member countries.

Third, Japan is interested in assisting developing countries, especially those in East Asia to promote economic growth by FTAs, because economic growth in East Asia would benefit Japan by providing business opportunities for Japanese firms and by achieving political and social stability in the region. East Asian countries could promote their economic growth by establishing FTAs with Japan, as they can enjoy greater access to Japanese market and also receive various factors such as FDI and economic assistance under EPA. To maximize the benefits from FTAs with East Asian countries, Japan is keen on establishing an East Asian FTA by including all East Asian economies.

Fourth, obtaining an access to natural resources such as oil and foods, which have vital positions in the Japanese economy, is another motive for establishing FTAs. FTA discussions with GCC countries are certainly motivated by the desire to secure oil and natural gas supplies, while one of the motivations for a possible Japan-Australia FTA is to secure food and mineral supplies. Securing natural resources is of critical importance for Japan because it is poorly endowed with natural resources. The importance of this issue is rapidly increasing as highly populated countries — China and India — have been absorbing tremendous amounts of natural resources.

Finally, Japan is keen on using FTAs to strengthen its position in international affairs such as in the WTO negotiations and regional affairs. This is partly in response to the many countries that have been using FTAs for those purposes. Japan would like to contribute to the strengthening of the WTO system by successfully forming EPAs (like Japan-Singapore EPA) that include issues not covered in the existing WTO framework. While GATT/WTO does not have specific rules on competition policies or investments, Japan-Singapore EPA (JSEPA) does cover these fields. Japan has been trying to include these new features in all EPAs including those under negotiations. The WTO and other international organizations may establish specific rules applicable to competition policies and investment in the future by using JSEPA as a model. In this way, Japan may be able to contribute to forming international frameworks through forming FTA and EPA with other countries.

IV. IMPACTS OF FTAS ON THE JAPANESE ECONOMY

The motives behind Japan's FTA strategy are discussed in the previous section. An assessment of the impacts of FTAs on Japanese economy is in order not only to evaluate the fulfilment of such motives but also to help formulate an appropriate FTA strategy. This section briefly discusses the economic effects of FTAs and also examines how much different FTAs will have impacts on Japan and its trading partners based on simulation analysis.

One can classify the economic impacts of FTA into two groups: static effects and dynamic effects.[7] Static effects include "trade creation effect", "trade diversion effect" and "terms of trade effect", while the dynamic effects are "market expansion effect" and "competition promotion effect". The trade creation effect means that FTAs eliminate trade barriers on trade among FTA members and, therefore, creates trade among them. The trade diversion effect means that FTA would replace imports of most efficient non-member countries with imports from less efficient FTA members. The terms of trade effect means that FTA would expand trade volume among its parties, strengthen the parties' influence on non-members and, then improve their terms of trade. The market expansion effect indicates that the elimination of trade barriers among members would expand market size to achieve efficient production/distribution by realizing economies of scale. The competition promotion effect means that market integration would make oligopolistic industries more competitive to achieve higher productivity by introducing competitive pressures.

From the viewpoint of FTA members, the trade creation effect, terms of trade effect, market expansion effect, and competition promotion effect will give positive impacts. However, the trade diversion effect would have adverse effects on them under certain circumstances. On the other hand, from the viewpoint of non-member states, the trade diversion effect and terms of trade effect will give negative impacts, while other effects tend to have positive impacts on them. If FTA expands market size, promotes competition, and encourages economic growth in member countries, its positive effects will spread out to non-member states as well. The FTA option has recently gained popularity, because governments expect FTAs to realize positive dynamic effects. However, if a country gives preferential treatment only to certain trade partners, other countries might form exclusive economic blocs in order to countervail "trade diversion effects" created by such preferential treatment. In this case, the world economy will suffer from significant adverse effects like what happened during the Inter-War era.

Recognizing the negative impacts of trade diversion and excluding non-members, one argues that FTAs should cover a lot of countries and include some highly competitive countries because such FTAs will be able to minimize possible negative impacts from the trade diversion effect.[8] This observation indicates the importance of successful multilateral trade negotiations under the WTO. Indeed, it is the optimal outcome. However, under the circumstances that the WTO falters, an FTA such as the FTAAP with a large number of members can be a viable option. It is better option than FTAs with smaller number of members.

In addition to the impacts on trade, FTAs also affects FDI. As the FTA eliminates regional trade barriers and expands the market size, FDI will flow into the regional market, hoping to sell more products. In addition, if the FTA enables firms to conduct efficient production in the region, foreign firms will undertake investments in the region to take advantage of the more favourable production environment, in order to export their products. This is called FTA's investment creation effect. Investment may be undertaken in member countries at the expense of investment in non-member countries because of increased attractiveness of member countries for investment. This is FTA's investment diversion effect. It should be added that FDI creation and diversion effects can occur in a more direct fashion, if the FTA includes FDI liberalization.

Many empirical studies have been conducted on the economic impacts of FTAs. In these studies the EU and NAFTA have attracted most attention.[9] Although these analyses draw different conclusions to a certain extent, they generally show that FTAs basically expanded regional trade/ investment, encouraged competition within the region and brought some other positive effects to the members. On the other hand, some analyses show that FTAs have diverted trade and investment, and might have given some negative effects on non-member countries. According to the estimation by Japan's Ministry of Economy, Trade and Industry, NAFTA trade diversion resulted in a loss of Japanese exports amounting to 395 billion yen in 1999.[10] Investment diversion was also reported as the NAFTA attracted FDI inflows in electronics and apparel industries to Mexico, which would have otherwise flowed to East Asia.

We are able to measure FTAs' overall economic impacts for the world as a whole by comparing FTA members' benefits and non-members' costs. As a lot of research projects prove that the former exceeded the latter, FTAs would generally bring positive impacts on net basis. Because existing empirical analyses tend to ignore FTA's dynamic effects, they are likely to underestimate FTA's positive impacts. If an FTA has large dynamic effects, it will surely bring more positive impacts on the member countries as well as on non-member countries.

Let us examine the impacts of FTAs on Japan. The results are obtained from a simulation analysis based on computable general equilibrium (CGE) model, specifically GTAP model version 5, which was carried out by Scollay and Gilbert (2001). They conducted a large number of simulation analyses by considering a variety of groupings of the countries involved in FTAs. Figure 5.1 shows the impacts of various FTAs on Japan's welfare. The results show an unambiguous pattern in that an increase in the number of countries involved in FTAs leads to a larger benefit to Japan. The largest gain in welfare (0.98 per cent of GDP) is expected from global trade liberalization, while the smallest gain (0.01 per cent of GDP) is expected from Japan-Korea FTA. Two different types of FTAs are simulated for APEC. One is trade liberalization of APEC members vis-à-vis the rest of the world (APEC MFN), and the other is discriminatory trade liberalization of APEC members vis-à-vis their members only (APEC FTA). The results show that the larger gain can be expected from APEC FTA than APEC MFN. This is due to the terms of trade effect, whose improvement is larger in the case of APEC FTA than APEC MFN. One should note, however, that APEC FTA would result in negative impacts on non-members

FIGURE 5.1
Impacts of FTAs on Japan's Welfare
(% of GDP)

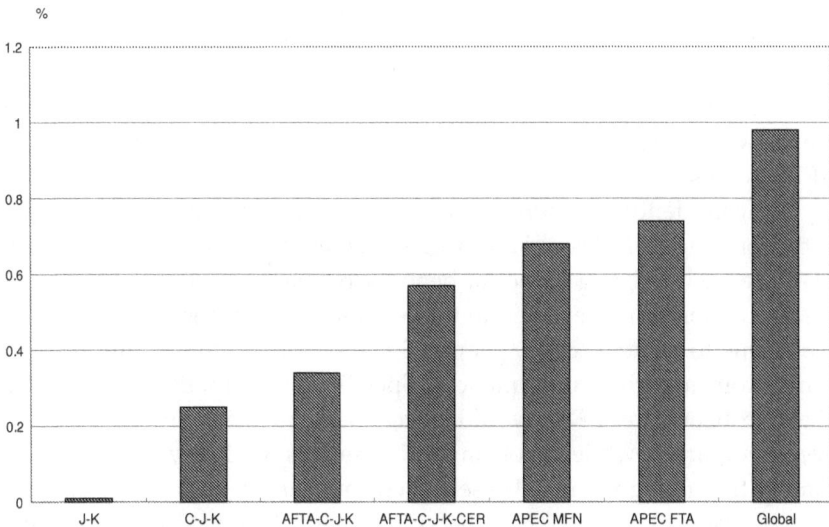

Source: Scollay and Gilbert (2001).

as the welfare impacts of APEC FTA on total world is 0.27 per cent of GDP, significantly smaller than the corresponding value of 0.34 per cent in the case of APEC MFN.

It is worth noting that FTAs with East Asian countries including agricultural products would yield lower benefits than FTAs excluding them because of the trade diversion effect in that imports from efficient agricultural producers such as the United States and Australia are replaced by those from less efficient Asian producers.[11]

It is to be noted that the results are likely to underestimate the true impacts, because the simulation analysis only incorporates static effects but not dynamic effects nor the impacts on FDI due to difficulty in introducing these features in the model. Indeed, many observers emphasize the importance of dynamic effects from the formation of FTAs. Underestimation of the impacts of FTAs using CGE models is likely to be substantial if FTAs include not only trade liberalization but also other features such as FDI liberalization, trade and FDI facilitation and economic cooperation, as in the case of EPA.[12]

V. OBSTACLES TO THE FORMATION OF FTAS AND FTAAP FOR JAPAN

We saw in the previous sections that Japan can expect economic and non-economic benefits from FTAs. Recognizing the benefits from FTAs, Japan has become active in establishing FTAs. However, Japan faces various obstacles in its pursuit of FTAs. This section examines such obstacles for Japan, with a particular focus on obstacles for establishing FTAs with APEC economies.

One can identify economic and non-economic obstacles. Let us begin with economic obstacles and then turn to non-economic obstacles. Although FTAs are likely to bring economic benefits to Japan as a whole as shown by the simulation result reported in the previous section, the benefits would not accrue to all the sectors/people. Some sectors or groups are likely to suffer from negative consequences. Specifically, competitive sectors are likely to benefit as FTAs would bring them business opportunities in overseas market, while non-competitive sectors are likely to lose out to competitive foreign firms. These mixed impacts are expected from any type of trade liberalization, either multilateral liberalization under the WTO or FTAs.

For Japan, the agriculture sector is the most sensitive sector in trade liberalization, regardless of its form, that is, bilateral or regional framework under FTAs, multilateral framework under the WTO, or unilateral framework. Japan has relatively low tariff protection on agricultural products in general, compared with other agricultural product importing countries. Specifically, according to the OECD (1999), average tariff rate for agricultural products for Japan is 12 per cent, significantly lower than the rates for other countries — Norway (124 per cent), Korea (62 per cent), Switzerland (51 per cent), and the EU (20 per cent). What is notable for agricultural protection in Japan is the very high protection given to several products through a complicated protection system, which combines import quotas and high tariffs. For example, the ad valorem tariff equivalent for some selected items are very high as follows: rice (490 per cent), wheat (210 per cent), sugar (270 per cent), butter (330 per cent), and konnyaku potato (990 per cent). In addition, as a part of the Uruguay Round agreement Japan introduced a special safeguard system to deal with the damage caused by import surges, contributing to stronger protection policy on agricultural products.

Among these highly protected items, rice is by far the most difficult item to be liberalized because of several reasons. One is its large share of agricultural production, amounting to approximately 25 per cent of agricultural production.[13] Another is the geographical location of production spreading over more or less throughout Japan. These two factors result in a strong political factor.

Import liberalization of agricultural products has been an obstacle in FTA negotiations for Japan. Japan excluded agricultural products from trade liberalization in the Japan-Singapore FTA, although agricultural production in Singapore is very small. Pork products became a contentious issue in Japan-Mexico FTA negotiations. Despite strong demands from Mexico to reduce the level of protection on pork imports, Japan did not give in. Japan instead increased import quotas on beef, chicken, oranges and orange juice, which was not included in the initial request. Japan's FTA negotiations with other countries have also encountered the problem of import liberalization of agricultural products. Agricultural products, which faced Japan's strong opposition, include the following: Japan-Philippines FTA (bananas, rice, wheat, starch, dairy products, beef, pork, sugar, canned pineapples), Japan-Malaysia FTA (plywood), Japan-Thailand

FTA (rice, sugar, boneless chicken, processed chicken), Japan-Chile FTA (fish products, pork). Besides the sensitive agricultural products listed above for Japan's past and present FTA negotiations, various sensitive agricultural products can be identified in the possible FTAAP negotiations, rice (Australia, U.S., China), beef and pork (Australia, U.S.), sugar (Australia), and dairy products (Australia, U.S.).

Indeed, the possible difficulty in the liberalization of the agriculture sector under an FTAAP can be identified as the shares of agricultural products and food products in Japan's total imports from Australia, Canada, and the United States are high at 16.6, 25.1, and 20.0 per cent, respectively, in 2005. It should be noted that the corresponding shares for imports from China is significantly lower at 7.2 per cent.

The main reason for the difficulty in liberalizing agriculture is its negative impact on employment. It is important to recognize that protection of agriculture sector does not ensure employment of farmers alone, but also the workers engaged in agriculture sector such as construction workers building irrigation systems and workers at farmers' cooperatives.

If the FTAAP covers mobility of natural persons, Japan's Ministry of Welfare and Labour opposes various types of foreign workers. Japan opposed mobility of labour as a part of FTAs with Thailand and the Philippines, even though these countries are keenly interested in "exporting" medical care givers such as nurses and massage therapists. As the ageing of Japanese population is projected to accelerate in the future, Japan is likely to be short of medical care givers for the aged. In light of such future projections, "importation" of medical care givers can be justified. However, nurses associations and medical associations strongly opposed the importation of these people because it would threaten job opportunities for Japanese nurses and other medical care givers. Mobility of labour was included in JSEPA but its coverage and form was very limited in that temporary stay is permitted only for short-term visitors for commercial purposes, intra-firm transferees, investors, and engineers with high technological knowledge.[14]

Let us turn to non-economic obstacles.[15] The issue of national security is an obstacle for Japan and other East Asian countries to form FTAs in East Asia. Japan and Korea have strong security alliances with the United States, while China is not an ally with the United States. ASEAN countries regard the U.S. forces as a security balancer in the region. Because of these different stances on national security, true regional integration based on mutual trust is not likely in the near future. Specifically, the Taiwan issue highlights possible conflict between China and U.S. allies. Somewhat related to the national security issue, differences in political systems, namely democratic states like Japan, and many other East Asian countries on the one hand and authoritarian states like China and Vietnam on the other hand prevents East Asian countries from establishing truly trustful relationship, which is a necessary condition to establish a true FTA. Indeed, Japan's mistrust of China in the areas of national security and political system, coupled with increasing presence of China in the areas of economic as well as political and military areas, is a crucial factor preventing the discussions on a possible FTA.

In the pursuit of establishing FTAs with China and Korea, Japan faces historic problem as Japan colonized these countries (albeit only part of China) during the World War II period. Specifically, a large proportion of people in China and to lesser extent in Korea remember sad experiences under the Japanese occupation and thus do not have a good impression of Japan, making cooperative arrangement such as FTAs difficult to be realized. Despite the historic problem, Japan and Korea have been successful in starting the process towards the establishment of an FTA mainly for two reasons. One is mutual reconciliation over historic issues between the political leaders, and the other is increased mutual understanding of the needs for closer economic and social ties among people of the two countries. Mutual reconciliation between the political leaders was realized thanks to strong political leadership of Korean President Kim Dae Jung who accepted an apology from Prime Minister Keizo Obuchi for Japan's atrocity towards Korean people in the past. Increasing awareness of the need for closer economic and social relationships by the peoples of two countries appears to result from the change in people's perception of mutual relationship from backward-looking to future-looking stance, which in turn results from successful economic growth. This case shows the importance of political leadership and successful economic growth for establishing FTAs.

Finally, there is a view that the establishment of a large FTA such as an FTAAP, which includes two of the world's largest economies, the United States and Japan, and other large economies such as China and Korea, would undermine the WTO trading system, because the FTAAP (with a preferential trading arrangement) is a discriminatory arrangement. To put it differently, the non-members, especially the small countries that are excluded from major FTAs such as the EU would suffer tremendously from discrimination in trade. This is a valid criticism and indicates the importance of FTAAP to become a building block and not a stumbling block to the global trade liberalization.

VI. POLICIES TO OVERCOME THE OBSTACLES

We have identified several obstacles on the establishment of FTAs, which include both economic and non-economic obstacles. This section discusses the policies to overcome these obstacles.

The most difficult problem has to do with displaced workers resulting from FTAs. At least two schemes can be applied to deal with this issue. One is income compensation for the duration of unemployment with the ceiling on the length of payment and the other is provision of technical assistance to improve their skills for getting more productive jobs. With assistance, affected workers should be able to make necessary adjustments. Recognizing that many farmers are very old and would find it difficult to find new jobs, income compensation should be a major policy.

For Japan, the agricultural sector is likely to suffer as imported agricultural products would cause a decline in output and employment. A more forward-looking, proactive agriculture policy, specifically rice policy, can be considered such as providing subsidy to full-time farmers with large cultivated land.[16] With this policy, cultivated land will be integrated so that farmers can improve productivity. Besides, the market will be liberalized and, as a result, not only will consumers gain from the liberalization, but also one big obstacle for FTAs will be removed. It should be noted that Japan's Ministry of Agriculture, Forestry and Fisheries has been carrying out structural reforms to strengthen competitiveness of Japanese agricultural sector. Although this policy may be considered forward-looking and therefore desirable, the absence of import liberalization is a serious problem. Strengthening agricultural sector is difficult without import liberalization.

To deal with trade adjustment in the agricultural sector, which was necessitated by partial liberalization of rice imports as a result of the Uruguay Round of trade negotiations under the GATT, the Japanese government provided as much as six trillion yen. Although the intention can be justified, the programme was not successful in facilitating adjustment, because a large part of the funds were spent not for upgrading skills of affected workers but for different purposes such as drilling hot springs or paving the country roads. Such mistakes must not be repeated.

Some argue the importance of protecting agriculture in order to achieve various objectives such as food security, and preserving nature, environment and culture. These objectives may be justified but protection of agriculture is a wrong and inefficient policy. Appropriate policies can be designed to achieve these goals. For example, food security may be achieved by establishing FTAs, especially the FTAAP that includes a number of agricultural exporters to assure stable and sufficient supplies of agricultural products. To achieve preservation of nature and environment, direct subsidies are known to be most efficient. In essence, import protection is only a second-best or third-best policy and not the optimum policy to achieve these goals. Coupled with substantial costs of protection discussed above, the discussions in this section strongly indicate that protection of agriculture should be removed, not only to promote FTAs but also to promote Japan's economic growth.

These arguments suggest that liberalizing, rather than protecting, Japan's agricultural sector will help Japan to achieve sustainable economic growth. A major obstacle for FTAs will be removed if this point is understood and shared with the Japanese. Of course, when liberating the agriculture sector, it is necessary to minimize the resultant unemployment and adjustment costs. For example, a possible approach will be to liberalize competitive sectors first and, then, deregulate less competitive sectors after some interval.[17] Many FTAs have such schemes of sequential liberalization for different sectors, depending on their competitiveness. However, it is necessary to specifically decide on the timetable and liberalize the market strictly based on the timetable.

Liberalization of the labour market to foreign workers faces strong opposition basically because of its negative impacts on employment. As such, the policies and measures discussed above to deal with agricultural sector problem can be applied to this problem as well. Despite the similar nature of the problem between liberalization of the agricultural sector and labour market, one has to recognize their differences. One of the serious issues regarding liberalization of the labour market is possible negative impact of foreign workers in the Japanese society. Although it is very often exaggerated, the number of crimes committed by foreigners is rising, giving an impression that foreign workers would cause security problems.

Regardless of the validity of this assertion between foreign workers and security issues, the governments, especially local governments and local community have to provide an environment, under which foreign workers and their family can adapt themselves to the Japanese life by providing various necessary services such as language education.

As to the specific issue of accepting medical care givers, Japan should accept foreign workers who satisfy certain conditions. In the case of Japan-Philippines FTA, the Japanese government imposed the following two qualifications — professional capability and Japanese language proficiency. Both of these qualifications can be satisfied by passing national examinations. As far as those qualifications are concerned, Japanese government policy appears justified. However, policy to set the maximum number of Filipino medical care givers cannot be justified. A more desirable policy is to let the market decide on the number.

To promote FTAs, Japanese people, policy-makers and government officials, in particular, have to have a sense of urgency concerning Japanese economy and Japan's future. Without a sense of urgency, meaningful efforts for the promotion of FTAs cannot be expected.[18] They have to realize the importance of establishing Japan's strong relationship with FTA members, which in turn would bring economic prosperity and political and social stability.

Various means can be used to increase such awareness on the part of Japanese people as well as people in FTA partners for the need of deepening mutual relationship to promote FTAs. One effective way is to increase the interaction of people at all levels. Among those, non-business people need to increase their interaction with their counterparts in FTA partners.

One of the most important factors for the promotion of FTAs is a strong political leadership. To establish FTAs, political leaders have to lead the discussions and policy-making processes of FTA strategies based on deep understanding of the costs and benefits of FTAs. With such strong and capable political leadership, inter-ministerial differences in opinion on FTAs will be overcome, and FTA negotiations will move forward. In Japan inter-ministerial differences in opinions on FTAs between the Ministry of Economy, Trade and Industry and Ministry of Foreign Affairs on one hand and Ministry of Agriculture, Forestry and Fisheries and Ministry of Welfare and Labour on the other hand are well known. The former group is basically in favour of FTAs while the latter is against FTAs. Because of the inability on the part of political leaders, these differences remain unresolved and protract FTA negotiations. It should be noted that various forums involving politicians have been set up to promote FTAs and even some politicians known as "Norin-zoku", or the group supported by farmers, have expressed the positive views towards FTAs. In light of the changing attitude of politicians on agricultural issues in FTAs, it may be the bureaucrats who are taking a firm stand against liberalization of agricultural sectors in FTA issues.

VII. ON FTAAP: A VIEW FROM JAPAN

Currently, the Japanese government is engaged in various bilateral FTA negotiations as well as Japan-ASEAN FTA negotiations. An important FTA that is going to be discussed in the near future is the East Asian FTA (EAFTA), which is likely to begin with ASEAN+3 countries with a possibility of including other countries such as India, Australia and New Zealand, the members of East Asia Summit. The discussions on an FTAAP have to be conducted in the light of these developments.

For Japan, the economic benefits from the FTAAP are likely to be greater than the benefits resulting from any FTAs currently in force, under negotiation or under study. This observation can be supported by various evidences. First, for Japan's foreign trade, APEC has a significantly larger position than East Asia, the next largest grouping considered for FTAs involving Japan after APEC. Specifically, in 2004 the shares of East Asia in Japan's exports and imports are 46.4 and 44.9 per cent, respectively, significantly lower compared to 75.2 and 67.8 per cent for APEC. The greater importance of APEC for Japanese economy is reflected in the results of simulation studies on the impacts of FTAs (Figure 5.1). It should be emphasized that the FTAAP can avoid trade diversion effects, which may arise from smaller FTAs such as EAFTA. Specifically, Japan may lose from EAFTA in that it diverts Japan's agricultural imports from very efficient producers such as Australia, Canada and the United States to less efficient Asian countries. This negative impact can be avoided by the FTAAP.

Another big benefit comes from unified definition of the rules of origin under the FTAAP. Without the FTAAP, many different definitions of the rules of origin are used for trade involving APEC economies, giving rise to the "spaghetti bowl" effect. An FTAAP with a simple and unified definition of the rules of origin results in a large integrated market, resulting in various economic benefits such as those arising from scale economies and increased competition.

In addition to those benefits accrued from trade liberalization under an FTAAP, Japan can expect to gain by the establishment of business friendly environment in APEC via FTAAP if it includes other components such as trade facilitation, FDI liberalization and facilitation, and economic cooperation, as those in an EPA. As the FTAAP includes developed economy members along with Japan, we can expect comprehensive and high-quality FTA including competition policy, protection of intellectual property right and others, which contribute to the establishment of a business friendly environment. Furthermore, FTAAP could contribute to establishing economic and social environment, under which transparency, accountability, and important principles can be appreciated.

One major obstacle for the establishment of an FTAAP for Japan is the liberalization of the agricultural sector because of its possible negative impacts on employment and other aspects of agricultural production such as preservation of the natural environment. On this point Japan's decision on the FTA negotiation with Australia, which is expected to take place soon, can be the litmus test to see the attitude of the Japanese government towards FTAs and in particular towards the FTAAP. Liberalization of the labour market may arise if the FTAAP includes such components. The discussions on this issue in sections V and VI indicate several ways to overcome these obstacles by adopting gradual liberalization and appropriate adjustment policies to deal with negatively impacted workers. On liberalization of agricultural imports under FTAAP one important positive impact for Japan is to ensure stable supply of food and some natural resources. In this regard it is important to have an agreement in the FTAAP to assure the strict implementation of business contracts on import and export transactions, and not to restrict export of these products.

One of the most important factors for the promotion of FTAs is strong political leadership as argued in the previous section. To establish an FTAAP, APEC Leaders have to lead the discussions and policy-making processes. In order for the leaders to exercise their leadership, they need support from the general public. Various means can be used to increase the awareness of the general public for the need of an FTAAP. One effective way is through mutual understanding, specifically, increasing the exchange of people of all levels is important to achieve this objective. Since business people have developed close networks, it is non-business people that need to increase their exchange with their counterparts in FTAAP member economies.

The need to revitalize APEC has to be emphasized to promote the FTAAP. One can expect that discussions on FTAAP would reinvigorate APEC, but policy-makers' interest in APEC as an economic forum have to be revived, since their interest in APEC as an economic forum have been quite low after its failure to deal with financial crisis and with an increase in interests in political issues such as terrorists' attacks. One important contribution that the business sector can make towards increasing awareness of the need for an FTAAP is to appeal to political leaders that the emergence of bilateral and minilateral FTAs in the Asia-Pacific region is making their business difficult due to the different rules associated with different FTAs and thus the establishment of an FTAAP, which adopts unified rules, is needed.

Finally, considering that moves towards establishing East Asian FTA (EAFTA) are gaining momentum and a lack of active interest in establishing an FTAAP in Japan, it seems natural to assume that an FTAAP is considered as an agenda after EAFTA. However, it is in the interest of Japan to promote an FTAAP as it generates substantial benefits for Japan.

Notes

1. This paper expands Urata (2005) extensively.
2. Keidanren (2003)
3. Ministry of Foreign Affairs, http://www.mofa.go.jp/region/asia-paci/asean/pmv0310/framework.html.
4. The Ministry of Economy, Trade and Industry (2006).
5. The Ministry of Foreign Affairs of the Japanese government released a document entitled "Japan's FTA Strategy" in November 2002. http://www.mofa.go.jp/mofaj/gaiko/fta/senryaku_05.html.
6. World Bank, World Development Indicators 2003, publication.
7. For the impacts of RTAs, see, for example, Winters (1991).
8. See Schiff and Winters (2003) for useful discussions on the dos and don'ts of regional trade agreements.
9. METI (2001) also provides detailed analysis on economic impacts of EU and NAFTA.

10. METI, an internal document.
11. Scollay and Gilbert (2001).
12. See, for example, Kawasaki (2003) and Ando and Urata (2006) for the impacts including some dynamic impacts.
13. Ministry of Agriculture, Forestry and Fisheries website, http://www.maff. go.jp/hitokuti/top.htm#mokuji1.
14. Ministry of Foreign Affairs, Japan-Singapore Economic Partnership Agreement, http://www.mofa.go.jp/mofaj/area/singapore/kyotei/pdfs/f-6.pdf.
15. It may not be appropriate to take up non-economic obstacles in the discussions of FTA, because all APEC economies are WTO members and thus can be FTA partners. However, some politicians and observers regard non-economic factors to be important in discussing FTAs because to them FTAs, being policies built on mutual trust are more than trade policies.
16. See Yamashita (2004) for the discussion.
17. The GATT/WTO rules allow ten years to complete trade liberalization under FTAs.
18. In Japan, various forums have been established for the promotion of Japan's FTAs mainly involving business and academics. Although such activities are gaining momentum and therefore are likely to increase the awareness of the importance of FTAs among Japanese people, there is still a need for further and greater efforts to make the FTA issue as high-priority agenda.

References

Ando, Mitsuyo and Shuijro Urata. "The Impacts of East Asia FTA: A CGE Model Simulation Study". Keio COE Discussion Paper, 2006.
Kawasaki, Kenichi. "The Impacts of Free Trade Agreements in Asia". RIETI Discussion Paper Series 03-E-018, Research Institute of Economy, Trade and Industry, Tokyo, Japan, 2003.
Keidanren (Japan Business Federation). "Request for Bilateral Negotiations on a Japan-Mexico Economic Partnership Agreement". 16 June 2003.
Ministry of Economy, Trade and Industry (METI). "White Paper on International Trade". 2001.
———. "Global Keizai Senryaku: Higashi Ajia Keizai Togo to Nihon no Sentaku" [Japan's Global Economic Strategy: Economic Integration in East Asia and Japan's Policy Choices]. 2006.
Schiff, Maurice and L. Alan Winters. *Regional Integration and Economic Development*. Oxford: Oxford University Press for the World Bank, 2003.
Scollay, Robert and John P. Gilbert. *New Regional Trading Arrangements in the Asia Pacific?* Washington, D.C.: Institute for International Economics, 2001.

Urata, Shujiro. "Free Trade Agreements: A Catalyst for Japan's Economic Revitalization". In *Reviving Japan's Economy*, edited by T. Ito, H. Patrick, and D. E. Weinstein. Massachusetts: MIT Press, 2005.

Winters, L. Alan. *International Economics*. 4th ed. London: Harper Collins Academic, 1991.

Yamashita, Kazuhito. "Chokusetsu Shiharai de Nogyo Kaikaku" [Restructuring of Agricultural Sector with Direct Payment]. *Nihon Keizai Shinbun*, 26 August 2004.

6

Lessons From the Free Trade Area of the Americas For APEC Economies

Sherry M. Stephenson

I. INTRODUCTION: THE FREE TRADE AREA OF THE AMERICAS

The proposed Free Trade Area of the Americas (FTAA) has larger economic dimensions than any of the numerous subregional agreements in the Western Hemisphere or the individual bilateral free trade agreements (FTAs), grouping thirty-four of the thirty-five countries in the region that together comprise about 870 million people and constitute over one-fourth of the world's GDP (around US$14 trillion) and one-fifth of the world's trade. However, it also has important political dimensions. The FTAA has been viewed as the means to unite the Hemisphere economically, and to solidify political ties between the English-speaking and the Spanish- and Portuguese-speaking nations of the region. For this reason, the FTAA process was launched in 1994 within a broad social and political agenda (the Summit of the Americas) that is absent in the case of other subregional trade arrangements. However, even this political endorsement from the outset at the highest level has not proved enough to allow the FTAA negotiations to be brought to a successful conclusion as they were envisaged.

This paper will review the launching of the FTAA, its challenges and innovative features and the mechanics of the negotiating process, along with the reasons why the FTAA negotiations faltered and the lessons that might be learned from the FTAA experience by the members of APEC.

Placing the FTAA in a historical context, it should be recalled that the idea of a region-wide FTA was not new in the Americas in the early 1990s, having been first proposed by Simon Bolivar — the liberator of the countries of the Andean region — more than 200 years earlier. The idea was sidetracked in the nineteenth century by the independence movement of the former Spanish and Portuguese colonies and by territorial disputes. Towards the end of the twentieth century, U.S. President George H.W. Bush relaunched the concept of hemispheric free trade, under the label "Enterprise for the Americas Initiative". In turn, this initiative was sidetracked during the debate over ratification of the North American Free Trade Agreement (NAFTA), which came into force in January 1994. However it was again revived by President Bill Clinton in December 1994 in the form of the "Free Trade Area of the Americas" initiative, when thirty-four democratically-elected governments in the Western Hemisphere met in Miami to launch the "Summit of the Americas" process.

Thus the FTAA negotiating process in the Western Hemisphere began as an integral component of the Summit of the Americas political process, endorsed by heads of state and government in the Americas. The free trade or FTAA component of the "Partnership for the Development and Prosperity: Democracy, Free Trade and Sustainable Development in the Americas" of the Summit of the Americas is nestled in a commitment to four major objectives and twenty-three very wide-ranging economic, political and social initiatives, of which free trade is only one.

The four major objectives of the broad Summit of the Americas process are to:

- preserve and strengthen democracy;
- promote prosperity through economic integration;
- eradicate poverty and discrimination; and
- guarantee sustainable development.

Although these Summit initiatives range from the promotion of democracy and human rights to sustainable development, improved infrastructure and labour conditions, educational opportunities, control of narco-trafficking, among others, the FTAA was at the time viewed as the centrepiece of the Summit process, through its potential contribution to increased economic prosperity in the region, essential for the realization of the other Summit objectives.[1] Under the title of "Promoting Prosperity through Economic Integration and Free Trade", the Miami Declaration and Plan of Action contains six initiatives to complement the FTAA in the economic area:

- capital markets development and liberalization;
- infrastructure;
- energy cooperation;
- telecommunications and information infrastructure;
- cooperation in science and technology; and
- tourism.

The key difference between trade and the other initiatives, however, is that the FTAA was to be the one component of the Summit process that was to result in a legally binding contract, while the other initiatives consisted of cooperation efforts and voluntary pledges for financial resources.

The FTAA negotiating process was designed to be a lengthy one, as it was felt that many of the participants needed time to prepare adequately for negotiations. The end date for the FTAA negotiations was therefore fixed at the outset as January 2005, making the FTAA a decade-long project. For nine of these ten years the negotiating process was very intensive, as will be described below, and tremendous progress was made. The result of efforts over nearly six years of formal negotiations (to end 2003) can be viewed in the draft text of the FTAA Agreement, found on the official FTAA website, and which contains twenty-four chapters and is no less than 484 pages in length.[2] However, in the very final stretch, the FTAA process ran out of steam as its participants found themselves in a changed macroeconomic context and with differing political priorities. The negotiations have been in a stalemate since early 2004, with little chance of revival. Indeed, since early 2004 the countries of the Western Hemisphere have become increasingly polarized in the conduct of their trade relations.

The ten-year negotiating period envisaged by the drafters of the FTAA turned out to be a very long time, even compared to the pace of multilateral trade negotiations (by way of comparison, the Uruguay Round took seven years to complete). The reason for this long time-frame was the considerable preparatory work that was included, partly in order to allow for the training of negotiators from countries in Latin America and the Caribbean of widely diverging levels of capacity and negotiating readiness. Ironically, this strategy proved highly successful and negotiators from Latin America and the Caribbean have gone on to negotiate numerous FTAs on their own, as well as to participate more fully in the WTO Doha Round negotiations. Becoming increasingly confident of their abilities, however, it has made it more challenging to finalize a hemispheric-wide text.

At the time of the launching of the FTAA the political climate in the Western Hemisphere was very much one in favour of free trade and market opening. The "Washington consensus" on orthodox trade reforms, fiscal and monetary discipline and trade liberalization as the basis for growth was in full sway, and the success stories from Chile and Mexico were on everyone's speaking agenda. The downturn that came with the lull in economic growth and the financial and exchange rate crisis in the southern cone countries would not be felt yet for some years. Governments in the region saw trade objectives through the same lens. The NAFTA had just been brought into effect, and the ramifications of this major innovation in trade relations in the Western Hemisphere — a trade agreement reaching out to include a developing country, Latin American member for the first time — were still reverberating. The successful negotiation and implementation of NAFTA injected a great deal of energy and enthusiasm into the landscape for trade agreements in the Americas at the time.

Moreover, in the 1990s the FTAA was the only major trade initiative in sight in the Hemisphere. The WTO had just come into existence in January 1995, and no one knew at that point how successful the organization would be in implementing the Uruguay Round commitments and in promoting further trade liberalization. The WTO Singapore Trade Ministerial Meeting in 1996 had been a tepid affair, characterized by controversy over incorporating the "new issues" of investment, competition policy and government procurement into the multilateral trade agenda.[3] The WTO Seattle Trade Ministerial Meeting turned out to be a dismal failure at end 1999, and the Doha Development Agenda (DDA) would not be launched until November 2001, over six and a half years after the FTAA negotiating process had been in full swing. And after its launching, it would take a several months, if not a couple of years, to get the DDA properly organized and on track.

Thus all of the negotiating energies in the Americas — after NAFTA and for a while following the launching of the Doha Round — were directed without distraction towards the FTAA in its early years. This, combined with the consensus attitude among political leaders that negotiating a hemispheric-wide FTA was the right thing to do to promote economic growth and development, allowed for tremendous progress to be made in the FTAA negotiations during this period (1995–2002). As will be seen below, the gradual diversion of negotiating attention from the FTAA towards the Doha Round, combined with major changes in the political governance and economic circumstances of countries in the Hemisphere in 2002, changed the focus of key participants and altered the basis of consensus on which the FTAA negotiations had been conducted. Eventually these changes proved to be so large that the FTAA negotiating process foundered before it could be brought to a successful conclusion. It has been stalled since early 2004 and unable to recover.

Current developments (mid-2006) indicate that the polarization of trade relations in the Western Hemisphere is widening rather than diminishing. Lessons from the FTAA experience for the APEC economies who are thinking of launching a Free Trade Area of the Asia-Pacific (FTAAP) should be useful ones to consider so that the same fate will not meet a similarly ambitious undertaking to develop an FTAAP in the Asia-Pacific region.

II. INNOVATIVE FEATURES OF THE FTAA NEGOTIATING PROCESS

The FTAA negotiating process had several innovative features that deserve comment.

1. *Size of the potential free trade area.* The countries that negotiated the FTAA stretch from the Alaskan Yucatan in North America to Tierra del Fuego in South America. The FTAA would have been larger than any other regional trading agreement in the world except for the European

Union (which is a customs union and not a free trade area), although the FTAAP would be an even larger regional grouping. As stated earlier, the thirty-four countries involved in the FTAA process represent a combined population of around 870 million people, a GDP of US$14 trillion and trade flows of nearly US$4 trillion, or approximately one-fourth of the world's output and one-fifth of the world's trade. The FTAAP would be an even larger, more powerful economic grouping, encompassing three of the world's largest economies — the United States, Japan and the People's Republic of China.

2. *Economic diversity of the participants.* The participants in the FTAA negotiating process range from the largest single economy in the world — the United States — to some of the smallest (namely the Caribbean island states). The range in the level of economic development of the participants is also extremely vast, stretching from the two advanced economies of Canada and the United States, to the middle economies of Mexico, Chile, Argentina, Brazil and several of the small Caribbean islands, to the poorer countries of Central and South America. One of the countries in the Hemisphere is counted among the World Bank definition of "least developed", namely Haiti, while Guyana, Honduras and Nicaragua fall in a very low income category. Such a broad diversity among levels of economic development or participants would also be the case for the FTAAP.

3. *Ambition of the negotiating mandate.* The scope of the FTAA negotiations as agreed upon in 1998 was extremely broad, encompassing subjects that were never put on the negotiating table at the WTO but that have been a part of the FTAA since its beginning. The nine negotiating areas included not only the traditional market access areas of tariffs and non-tariff barriers for goods (including a separate negotiating group for agriculture), but also services, investment, government procurement, intellectual property rights, anti-dumping, subsidies and countervailing duties, competition policy, and dispute settlement. In all of these areas draft rules have been developed for the Western Hemisphere. Some 900 trade officials from around the hemisphere met regularly on a bi-monthly cycle for more than six years to negotiate these issues. One non-negotiating group on institutional issues was also created to consider the appropriate institutional and support structure for an eventual FTAA agreement.

4. *Attention to the needs of the smaller economies.* A non-negotiating Consultative Group on Smaller Economies was established from the outset of the FTAA process to deal with the unique situation of smaller economies, a category to which twenty-five of the thirty-four participating countries felt themselves to belong.[4] This group was important in airing the concerns of smaller and relatively less developed economies. While the FTAA negotiations were unique in having established such a group for the first time, this example was subsequently reproduced at the WTO level in the Doha Development Round talks.[5]

5. *Incorporating capacity-building as an integral part of the FTAA negotiations.* Although capacity-building work was carried out from the inception of the FTAA process by the three institutions of the Tripartite Committee (the Organization of American States or OAS, the Inter-American Development Bank or IDB, and Economic Commission for Latin America and the Caribbean or ECLAC), Trade Ministers in the Western Hemisphere agreed to formally establish a Hemispheric Cooperation Program in November 2002 to attend to the technical assistance needs of smaller countries as an integral part of the negotiations. The efforts of this Committee were to continue after the negotiations had been concluded as well, in the form of capacity-building assistance to FTAA members in their efforts to adjust to free trade.

6. *Transparency of the FTAA negotiating process and outreach to civil society.* Lastly, the FTAA was unique in creating a Committee on Civil Society from the outset of the negotiating process. Public submissions were welcomed on an ongoing basis and open meetings were held periodically on the various negotiating issues. Very significantly, the draft text of the FTAA Agreement was made public on three different occasions. This represented a unique step in the history of trade negotiations and the first time that governments involved in a negotiating process agreed to publish a negotiating text.

7. *Rotating the chairmanship and the site of the negotiations and of the FTAA Secretariat.* The governments launching the FTAA decided to introduce a rotating style for the selection of the countries hosting the meetings of the preparatory and the negotiating process. The chairmanship of the negotiating groups as well as the chairmanship of the FTAA process itself (the country chairing the Trade Negotiations Committee) was

changed on a two-to-three year basis. Equally, the site of the FTAA
Secretariat where the negotiations were held was also rotated. Three
sites hosted the negotiations in turn: Miami, USA; Panama City, Panama;
and Puebla, Mexico. The site for the permanent FTAA Secretariat had
not been decided at the time the negotiations stalled, but no fewer than
ten cities in eight countries (three in the United States) had announced
their candidacy to host the Secretariat.

The seven characteristics above that distinguished the FTAA process
— large size of the undertaking, economic diversity, ambition of the
negotiating mandate, attention to the smaller economies, incorporation of
capacity-building, transparency and outreach to civil society, and the
rotating structure of the mechanics of the negotiations — set the FTAA
apart from other regional negotiating efforts. Some of these characteristics
constituted major challenges to the completion of the agreement, while
others were considered as positive innovations and taken over at the WTO
level. This will be commented on further in the paper.

III. THE PREPARATORY YEARS

Because it was felt that the participants were not equally prepared to
enter into serious trade negotiations, governments launching the FTAA
decided to first engage in a three-year preparatory process. This was to
allow the countries time to train their negotiators and to study the issues
under discussion. The preparatory period lasted for three years, from
1995 to 1998.

During the preparatory years, background documents were prepared
and initial discussions were undertaken in twelve working groups that
met on a regular, three-month basis in various parts of the Hemisphere.
The Tripartite Committee institutions (OAS, IDB and ECLAC) played a
key role in providing technical and logistical support during this time,
particularly in assisting the smaller economies. The Tripartite Committee
carried out a variety of tasks, including preparation of inventories of laws
and regulations in all of the negotiating areas; compilation of statistical
data bases; elaboration of studies and background papers in many areas of
the negotiations; coordination of the translation, timing, and distribution
of documents for meetings with the Administrative Secretariat; support to
the chairs of the different working; and maintenance of the Official FTAA

website. In addition, the Tripartite Committee institutions, in particular, the IDB, have financed a large proportion of the operating costs of the Administrative Secretariat in its various locations. Each of the Tripartite Committee institutions also engaged (and continues to engage) in the organization and support of a significant number of educational, training and technical assistance activities throughout the Hemisphere. The technical expertise and support provided to the FTAA participating governments by the Tripartite Committee has proved very important in allowing the negotiating process to move forward smoothly.

During the preparatory phase, four Trade Ministerial meetings took place: in Denver, USA (1995); in Cartagena, Colombia (1996); in Belo Horizonte, Brazil (1997); and in San Jose, Costa Rica (1998), where Trade Ministers agreed to begin FTAA negotiations. These were then formally launched at a political meeting of the Heads of State and Government in the Second Summit of the Americas in Santiago de Chile in April 1998, underlining once again the political as well as economic character of the FTAA process.

In the San Jose Ministerial Declaration (1998), the structure of the negotiations was set out and general principles and objectives to guide the negotiations were agreed upon.[6] The Declaration affirmed that the FTAA Agreement would be balanced, comprehensive, WTO-consistent, and would constitute a single undertaking. Ministers also agreed as part of the principles that the negotiating process would be transparent and would take into account the differences in the levels of development and size of economies in order to facilitate full participation by all countries. The consensus principle for agreeing on decisions by all participants in the negotiating process was set out as the basic means of moving forward, similar to the WTO.

An interesting principle set out in the San Jose Declaration that was particularly important in light of the increasing number of regional trading arrangements in the Western Hemisphere at the time, was the statement that the final FTAA agreement would not displace any pre-existing sub-regional integration arrangement in the Americas. All previously negotiated subregional agreements would continue to exist, but their provisions would prevail only to the extent that "the rights and obligations under these agreements are not covered by or go beyond the rights and obligations of the FTAA" (paragraph f of Annex I of the San Jose Ministerial Declaration).

IV. THE MECHANICS OF THE NEGOTIATIONS
(APRIL 1998 – FEBRUARY 2004)

The structure and organization of the FTAA carried with them some interesting features that might prove instructive to those economies interested in an FTAAP. This section reviews the mechanics of the FTAA negotiating process.

Participants

The participants in the FTAA negotiating process are the thirty-four democratically elected governments in the Western Hemisphere that participated in the 1994 Miami Summit of the Americas meeting.[7] These include all of the independent states in North America, Central America and South America, as well as the members of CARICOM in the Caribbean.[8] All countries in the FTAA process have an equal status in the negotiations and all decisions are taken by consensus.

Structure

The FTAA negotiations are carried out under a structure that was agreed in the San Jose Ministerial Declaration of 1998 and that ensures broad geographical participation in the leadership of the FTAA process itself and of the various FTAA entities. The Chairmanship of the process, the site of the negotiations, and the Chairs and Vice-Chairs of the various negotiating groups were designed to rotate among participating countries during the four phases of the negotiations, as shown in Table 6.1. Chairs of the FTAA process have included Canada, Argentina and Ecuador. Chairmanship of

TABLE 6.1
Chairmanship of FTAA Negotiations

	Chair	Vice-Chair
1 May 1998 to 31 October 1999	Canada	Argentina
1 November 1999 to 30 April 2001	Argentina	Ecuador
1 May 2001 to 31 October 2002	Ecuador	Chile
	Co-Chairs	
1 November 2002 to conclusion of the negotiations	Brazil and USA	

the fourth and final phase of the FTAA process is being jointly shared by Brazil and the United States under a rather unique arrangement that many have considered less than satisfactory, as it has been viewed as one of the stumbling blocks to progress in the negotiations.

The venue or site of the FTAA negotiations was also established on a rotating basis. Three countries were designated as hosts of the negotiations: the United States (Miami) from May 1998 to February 2001; Panama (Panama City) from March 2001 to February 2003; and Mexico (Puebla) from March 2003 to the conclusion of the negotiations.

Ministers Responsible for Trade in the Western Hemisphere were given the responsibility of overseeing the negotiations and met generally every eighteen months. Eight Trade Ministerial meetings took place during the life of the FTAA process : Denver, USA (1995), Cartagena, Colombia (1996), Belo Horizonte, Brazil (1997), San Jose, Costa Rica (1998), Toronto, Canada (1999), Buenos Aires, Argentina (2001), Quito, Ecuador (2002) and Miami, USA (2003). A Ministerial Declaration resulted from each of these meetings, which can be found on the FTAA official website (www.ftaa-alca.org). A final meeting of Trade Ministers was mandated to take place in Brazil in 2004, but this did not occur.

The Vice-Ministers Responsible for Trade were constituted into the Trade Negotiations Committee (TNC) and were tasked with reviewing progress in the FTAA process and giving instructions to guide the work of the negotiating groups and other entities. Additionally, Vice-Ministers had the responsibility for ensuring transparency in the negotiations as well as the full participation of all of the countries in the FTAA process, overseeing the FTAA Administrative Secretariat and deciding on the overall architecture of the agreement and other institutional issues. The TNC normally met three to four times a year, at rotating sites throughout the Hemisphere. No fewer than twenty meetings of Vice-Ministers of Trade took place between June 1998 and February 2004.

Two websites were set up for the FTAA process: an official website on which only official FTAA documents were posted in all four official languages of the negotiations (English, Spanish, Portuguese and French); and an FTAA "Secure site" to be used only by authorized government negotiators who had received a restricted password for access. On the "Secure site" are posted all of the negotiating proposals submitted to the various FTAA negotiating groups and the TNC during the life of the negotiations.

Technical and Analytical Support to the FTAA Negotiations

Important technical and analytical support to the participants in the FTAA negotiations, to the Chairs of the negotiating groups and to the Chairs of the FTAA process, by the three institutions of the Tripartite Committee: the IDB, the OAS and the ECLAC. The three Tripartite institutions also received a mandate from the outset of the process to provide technical assistance related to FTAA issues, particularly for the smaller economies of the Hemisphere, and to carry out capacity-building activities. They have been actively involved in elaborating and supporting the implementation of the Hemispheric Cooperation Program officially endorsed by Ministers as part of the process in 2002.

Administrative and Financial Support to the FTAA Negotiations

Administrative and logistical support was provided to the FTAA process by the FTAA Administrative Secretariat, which also served as the host site for the meetings of the negotiating groups (but not necessarily the meetings of the TNC or the Trade Ministerial meetings). The Secretariat was tasked with keeping the official archives of the negotiations, and providing conference services as well as translation and interpretation, as all meetings are conducted in the two working languages of English and Spanish.[9]

Key financial support for the FTAA negotiating process was provided by the three institutions of the Tripartite Committee, particularly the IDB. Financial contribution from the IDB has covered the salaries of the staff of the FTAA Administrative Secretariat, while the country hosting the Administrative Secretariat has covered the cost of the infrastructure, maintenance, guards and other operating expenses. The Government of Mexico has been financing these costs since February 2004, even as the negotiating groups have not met.

V. NEGOTIATING GROUPS CREATED FOR NINE ISSUE AREAS

Nine negotiating groups were created for the FTAA talks to address issues in the following areas:

1. market access (tariffs and non-tariff barriers, rules of origin, safeguards);
2. agriculture;
3. services;
4. investment;
5. government procurement;
6. subsidies, anti-dumping and countervailing duties;
7. intellectual property rights;
8. competition policy; and
9. dispute settlement.

The first five negotiating groups were given a mandate to negotiate market access as well as trade rules; the latter four negotiating groups were given a mandate only to negotiate trade disciplines. The nine negotiating groups met regularly between May 1998 and November 2003 (the date of the Miami Trade Ministerial) at an intensive pace, on average five to six times a year.

The FTAA negotiations moved forward in these nine groups through negotiating proposals that were submitted by the participants, very similar to the process at the WTO level. Many of these proposals mirrored the text and disciplines of existing subregional agreements in the hemisphere (NAFTA, MERCOSUR, the Andean Community Agreement, and/or CARICOM), while others incorporated elements of newer sub-agreements such as the ones between Chile and Central America (2002), Panama and Central America (2003), Chile and the United States (2004). As previously stated, the text of the third draft version of the entire FTAA agreement can be found on the official FTAA website, and various negotiating proposals can therefore be publicly verified by any interested person or group.

It was agreed in the San Jose Ministerial Declaration that the benchmark for the FTAA negotiations would be the WTO disciplines; however, all parties recognized that it would be necessary to go further in order to reach a "WTO-plus" agreement.[10] The Declaration stated that the FTAA "should improve upon WTO rules and disciplines wherever possible and appropriate." However, considerable latitude existed at the time (and continues to exist) in interpreting what can qualify as "WTO-plus" for a regional agreement.

Three non-negotiating Committees and Groups also met as part of the FTAA process to address horizontal issues related to the negotiations, namely: the Consultative Group on Smaller Economies; the Committee of Government Representatives on the Participation of Civil Society, and the Technical Committee on Institutional Issues (TCI).

Preparations for an FTAA agreement were well advanced within the Technical Committee on Institutional Issues at the time the negotiations stalled. This Committee was created to consider the overall architecture of an FTAA Agreement and was given a mandate to draft text on the institutions required to implement the FTAA agreement, the funding mechanisms and administrative rules, among others.[11] The text submitted by the TCI forms part of the draft FTAA Agreement of November 2003 and contains chapters on: General Articles of the FTAA Agreement; Transparency; Treatment of the Differences in the Levels of Development and Size of Economies; Costs of Implementing the Agreement; Institutional Framework; Annexes; and Temporary and Final Provisions. These draft chapters all precede the substantive draft chapters of the various negotiating areas.[12]

Participation of the Private Sector and Civil Society

The crafters of the FTAA negotiations realized from the outset that it would be important to incorporate the views and encourage the participation of both the business sector and of civil society at large into the process. Thus the San Jose Ministerial Declaration contains the following invitation by Trade Ministers:

> We recognize and welcome the interests and concerns that different sectors of society have expressed in relation to the FTAA. Business and other sectors of production, labor, environmental and academic groups have been particularly active in this matter. We encourage these and other sectors of civil societies to present their views...

A Business Forum was established in order to allow for the business community to meet prior to each Trade Ministerial meeting and to discuss and provide recommendations on all of the issues under negotiation. The Business Forum recommended and Ministers adopted a series of Business Facilitation Measures (found in Annex II to the Toronto Ministerial Declaration of 2001).[13] Several meetings of experts were held in order to assure the implementation of the Customs-Related Business Facilitation Measures. A Hemispheric Guide on Customs Procedures was prepared for the business community in the Americas.

A Civil Society Committee was also established to serve an important outreach function in allowing public interest groups and NGOs in the Hemisphere to express their views on the issues under negotiation. FTAA participating governments established an open invitation to civil society to present written contributions on the various FTAA topics, which were then forwarded to the relevant FTAA negotiating group or committee. These contributions were summarized and forwarded to the Ministers of Trade through the report of the Committee presented at each FTAA Ministerial meeting. A Civil Society Forum was organized as well prior to each Trade Ministerial Meeting, and representatives of civil society groups were allowed to present conclusions from their deliberations directly to Ministers. In order to make its deliberations more pertinent and to reach out to more participants, the Civil Society Committee organized issue meetings on specific negotiating topics during what would turn out to be the last year of the FTAA process. These were joint sessions of civil society representatives and government negotiators. Three of these issue meetings took place, on the topics of agriculture (June 2003), services (September 2003) and intellectual property (January 2004).[14] This model of interaction with civil society would serve to inspire the outreach efforts of the WTO Secretariat at the multilateral level, in the early stages of the Doha Development Round of negotiations.

VII. CHALLENGES FACED BY THE FTAA UNDERTAKING

Each set of trade negotiations, whether bilateral, regional or multilateral, faces its own particular set of circumstances and challenges. However, the FTAA undertaking, by its very uniqueness and its large number of participants, faced a considerable number of challenges that were much larger than those that a more reduced group of countries would have been able to face and possibly overcome. This section considers what the author feels, in hindsight, to have been the most formidable of those challenges.

Extended Time-frame for the Negotiations

The time-frame set for the FTAA negotiations turned out in the end to have been too long to reach a successful agreement. Allowing for a decade between start and projected conclusion meant that at least two governments and often three governments would be elected and as many new trade ministers and negotiators would be appointed in the participating countries. While some governments (such as those of the United States, Chile and others) were willing and able to maintain the continuity of policy and vision necessary for such an ambitious undertaking during this extended time period, other governments (such as those of Brazil, Argentina, Venezuela) changed their focus following a change in leadership. In the end, the FTAA turned out to have made its most substantive contribution in terms of its preparatory process and the training ground it provided for negotiators to master their subjects and practice their negotiating techniques. The lengthy preparatory period built into the process (three and a half years formally, four years effectively) meant that the negotiations did not really begin in earnest until January 1999. This allowed too much time to lapse, while other factors appeared to divert interest and attention.

Very Ambitious Negotiating Agenda

The ambitious negotiating agenda agreed in the FTAA process also presented a major challenge to the negotiations. While the future FTAA agreement was viewed as one that would be "state of the art", the very extensive coverage of behind-the-border, trade-related issues would prove to be one of the factors that created a division among participants. The ambition of the negotiating agenda was used by some governments to justify moving very slowly in the negotiations, and during the penultimate year, to request a scaling down of initial objectives.

Large Diversity of Participants

The large number of participants in the FTAA negotiating process included countries in the Americas of extreme differences in size and economic diversity. The latter was measured not only by levels of development and GDP per capita, but also by the sophistication of national institutions and the legitimacy of government itself. This meant that the negotiators faced a huge challenge in reaching an agreement that could be accepted and effectively implemented by all. Although the Tripartite institutions were active in carrying out capacity-building, national government officials and negotiators often changed or were rotated, or left public service, so that training proved to be an ongoing challenge.

Lack of Clarity on What Constitutes "WTO-plus"

One of the challenges facing any group of very diverse countries setting out to negotiate an FTA is the very wide-ranging judgement of what can constitute an acceptable level of "WTO-plus" disciplines. Making this determination is complicated by the fact that the WTO itself (or rather its members) has been unable to set out clear benchmarks for evaluating the compliance of regional trading agreements with WTO requirements — Article XXIV of the General Agreement on Trade and Tariffs (GATT) in the case of goods and Article V of the General Agreement on Trade in Services (GATS) in the case of services.[15] Partly, but not only, for this reason existing regional agreements vary widely in their coverage and disciplines, as well as in their degree of market opening for goods and services.

In the FTAA process, this lack of clarity meant that participants, while agreeing on the general "WTO-plus" principle, had considerable latitude to argue which disciplines and market access conditions would qualify for this status.[16] It is fair to say that as no single template exists for a regional trade agreement, this will pose a challenge to APEC members setting out to negotiate an FTAAP, as the level of ambition of what participating governments would like to see as a final outcome is likely to vary widely in terms their conception of an acceptable "WTO-plus" agreement.

V. THE MOST CONTROVERSIAL ISSUES IN THE FTAA PROCESS

Four issues in particular proved to be very controversial during the life of the FTAA negotiations, and the lack of ability among the major participants to reach a compromise on how to even approach the negotiations in these four areas was one of the causes that eventually led to the breakdown of the FTAA process. These issues were: agriculture; services/investment; intellectual property rights; and trade-related aspects of labour and environmental issues. Each issue is discussed in turn.

Agriculture

The FTAA, like the Doha Round, was given an ambitious agenda in the area of agriculture. Latin American governments agreed to launch the FTAA partly so that these regional negotiations could be used as a forum to make progress on agriculture that would translate over to the WTO.[17] However, this did not happen. The San Jose Ministerial Declaration set out several objectives for agriculture, including the elimination of tariffs and non-tariff barriers on agricultural products, the elimination of agricultural export subsidies, and the identification of other trade-distorting practices for agricultural products (i.e. domestic support), in order to bring them under greater discipline.

This ambitious agenda proved to be the Achilles heel of the FTAA. The inability to agree on agriculture effectively slowed progress in other negotiating areas. The attempt to use a regional forum to try and resolve one of the most sensitive and difficult of the multilateral issues raised unrealistic expectations on what the FTAA could achieve. From the start, the United States and Canada insisted that while the FTAA could discuss domestic support for agriculture, disciplines in this area could only be negotiated at the multilateral level, in the WTO Doha Round. Neither country wished to curtail its subsidy programmes unless the EU accepted similar disciplines. Led by MERCOSUR members, Latin Americans argued strongly that U.S. and Canadian domestic subsidy policies severely distorted the market and that export subsidies limited their commercial opportunities. For their part, the Caribbean countries wished to continue to enjoy the historical preferences they had with the EU, as ACP (Africa, Caribbean and Pacific) former colonies and Overseas Countries and Territories (OCTs).

Priorities in the agricultural area thus remained far apart and controversial during the life of the FTAA negotiations. Increasingly following the launch of the Doha Development Round at end 2001, MERCOSUR members began to link progress in the other areas of the FTAA negotiations (especially services and investment) to progress in the Doha Round on agriculture. As a result the process began to lose momentum.

Services/Investment

The services/investment area proved to be politically very sensitive in the FTAA negotiations. Many Latin American nations feared that they would have to give up their right to regulate in a discriminatory fashion by entering into comprehensive services and investment disciplines. They thus preferred to move more slowly and gradually towards liberalization. Because of this reluctance, the services/investment area in the FTAA was beset with a major difference in vision as to how a trade agreement should be constructed. A large sub-set of countries (the "like-minded" NAFTA countries that had either negotiated with the United States or were in the process of doing so) wished to proceed along the lines of a "negative list approach" or a comprehensive coverage of all services sectors within the disciplines of the agreement (subject to the negotiation of an agreed number of exceptions or "non-conforming measures") and binding of all of these non-conforming measures at the level of current regulatory practice.[18]

However, MERCOSUR members wished to follow a more modest, less comprehensive modality for liberalization of services and investment, similar to what has been done under the WTO GATS (namely the "positive list" approach), with sectors included at choice, and weak disciplines on the level of binding commitments.

An additional problem involving the services/investment areas in the FTAA context was the question of where to deal with investment to supply services — to treat it solely within the services chapter as one mode of service supply, or to deal with it as part of a comprehensive investment chapter covering both goods and services. The answer to this question would also determine how the FTAA agreement would be structured. However, it remained unresolved. Also relating to the investment area was the delicate question whether investor-state disputes would be a part of the FTAA and consequently subject to arbitration, akin to the controversial NAFTA Chapter 11 provisions that were carried (with slight modifications) into the U.S.-Chile and U.S.-CAFTA-DR FTAs.

Lastly, the issue of the inclusion of the temporary movement of skilled and semi-skilled labour was a controversial one in the services/investment area that remained unresolved in the FTAA discussions. This area was of the greatest interest to the countries of the Caribbean, as well as to several of those in Latin America, who wanted FTAA visas from Canada and the United States, akin to H-1B visas, not only for skilled workers and corporate employees, as well but also for an additional category of technical workers.[19] The U.S. negotiators were unable, however, to discuss any type of commitment to temporary movement of persons in the FTAA negotiations, given Congressional objections to including this area within trade agreements (a firm decision since 2003), combined with heightened security worries.

Intellectual Property Rights

The area of intellectual property protection was a negotiating issue pushed primarily by the United States who wished the FTAA to pioneer the next advance in intellectual property rights (IPR) disciplines and hoped that countries in the Americas would agree to stronger steps for IPR protection. The ways in which the United States (and at times other countries) wished for the FTAA to innovate were through: (1) extending protection in those areas already included in the WTO TRIPS Agreement (i.e. the areas of patents, trademarks, copyrights) by signing additional intellectual property right treaties; (2) carrying out enhanced enforcement; (3) taking into account the technological advances of the Internet for copyright protection and related rights; and (4) accepting very strict requirements for the use of compulsory licensing of patented pharmaceuticals provided in the Doha Declaration on TRIPS and Public Health (so that compulsory licensing would only be permitted in the narrowest circumstances).

Latin America and Caribbean governments were not convinced of the benefits for developing countries from adhering to even tougher intellectual property disciplines than those currently in force at the WTO level, with serious questions being raised by the latter as to the desirability of extending IP protection any further by Brazil and Argentina.[20] Other Latin American countries would have liked an IPR chapter to include "rebalancing" disciplines, such as stricter rules on transfer of technology, the protection of folklore and indigenous plant species and varieties along with natural medicines, and long phase-in periods for new enforcement commitments. However, all of these questions were outstanding and remained highly controversial at the time the FTAA negotiations stalled.

Labour and the Environment

No formal negotiating group was established within the FTAA negotiating process to discuss the politically sensitive issues of labour and environment. As these areas were not among those of common agreement for a negotiating agenda at the time of the San Jose Trade Ministerial meeting, a compromise was reached whereby the negotiations agreed:

   a. To strive to make our trade liberalization and environmental policies
      mutually supportive, taking into account work undertaken by the WTO
      and other international organizations.

b. To further secure, in accordance with our respective laws and regulations, the observance and promotion of worker rights, renewing our commitment to the observance of internationally recognized core labor standards and acknowledging that the International Labor organization is the competent body to set and deal with those core labor standards.

Despite (or perhaps because of) the objectives set out above, some FTAA participants argued that neither FTAA Ministers nor Heads of State and Government had been given a mandate to negotiate on these subjects. Nonetheless, the United States, with the support of Canada and Chile, continued to bring the two areas of labour and the environment up for discussion at the level of Vice Ministers. A great deal of time and acrimony was spent in debating whether these two areas could form part of the negotiations and of a final agreement. In the end it was decided that any governments had a right to submit proposals for consideration in any of the areas related to the negotiations, and that these proposals would be in brackets, as would all other negotiating proposals until agreed by consensus.

After the creation of the Technical Committee on Institutional Issues in 2001, the U.S. submitted text for draft chapters on labour and the environment to the Committee (Chapters VI and VII, respectively, of the Draft FTAA Agreement). The draft chapters are very similar to what was agreed in the U.S.-Chile and U.S.-Singapore FTAs. They contain provisions on the application and enforcement of national environmental/labour laws, provisions for environmental/labour cooperation, consultation mechanisms, and disciplines for procedural matters. They allow the right to bring cases before FTAA panels, along with the possibility of trade sanctions if a party does not comply with an adverse panel decision on the enforcement of national laws.

While countries in the Western Hemisphere that had negotiated or were in the process of negotiating FTAs with the United States understood the political necessity of including labour and environmental provisions in any agreement that the United States would enter into, including the FTAA, other countries never accepted this. Thus the controversy surrounding these two issues continued to the time of the breakdown of the negotiations.[21]

Ultimately, though there were other areas of controversy as well in the negotiations, it was the above four issues that proved to be the most contentious and which were never resolved during the life of the FTAA

negotiations. Because of the continued polarization between the
MERCOSUR members and the NAFTA members (particularly Canada
and the United States) on these issues, it is difficult to imagine what type
of compromise solution might ultimately have been found in these
controversial areas.

VIII. THE BREAKDOWN OF THE FTAA NEGOTIATIONS
AND THE EMERGENCE OF ALTERNATIVES

The objective of completing the FTAA was complicated not only by the
failure to reach agreement on several key negotiating and other issues,
including in particular the five described above, but also by the financial
crises and political changes that beset many Latin American countries
during the last four years of the negotiations, as well as fall-out from the
new security imperatives of the post-9/11 world. Additionally and very
significantly, the initiation of the Doha Development Round took much
valuable attention away from the FTAA process after end 2002. Given the
difficulties that the FTAA was confronting, the pursuit of bilateral free
trade agreements increasingly came to be viewed as a plausible and easier
alternative to a hemispheric-wide effort.

Financial Crisis in Argentina and the Southern Cone

The severe financial and exchange rate crisis experienced by Argentina in
the summer of 2002 strongly affected not only Argentina itself, but all of
the other three members of MERCOSUR. The default by Argentina on its
external debt, the move away from dollarization, together with the return
to the use of a tremendously devalued peso and the loss of savings, very
high rates of unemployment and the large surge in poverty levels that this
engendered, were all perceived as having been the result of an erroneous
pursuit of policies promoted under the "Washington consensus". Other
countries suffered as well, particularly Paraguay and Uruguay, through
the downturn in Argentinian demand, bankruptcies and social disruption.
Throughout the Southern Cone region, this financial crisis and its
subsequent impact lasted more than two years and created a strong anti-
northern, anti-capitalist backlash. Any initiative associated with orthodox
economic policies, including free trade, was rejected by the populace. The
FTAA was perceived as the banner or the most obvious symbol of these

orthodox policies, pushed by the United States, and the MERCOSUR members expressed doubts about its potential benefits. Questions were raised by previous and newly-elected governments in Latin America as to whether they could fulfil their lofty Summit of the Americas promises — or whether they still wished to do so.

Changed Political Landscape in the Americas and the Struggle for Influence

The political landscape in the Western Hemisphere changed dramatically as of 2002. Increasingly during the last two years of the FTAA it was apparent that a battle of influence was underway between the countries gravitating around the NAFTA pole and those gravitating around the MERCOSUR pole. It became clear that the two largest countries in the Hemisphere — Brazil and the United States — no longer viewed trade and hemispheric integration after 2002 in the same manner they did when the FTAA process began eight years earlier in late 1994.

The differences in points of view of these two competing visions derived from a divergence in political objectives and priorities. Trade policy was drawn into the fray, becoming an integral part of foreign policy and thus making it more susceptible to political influences and decisions. While priorities with respect to trade had coincided among all participants at the time of the Summit of the Americas in Miami in December 1994 during the period of the "Washington consensus", and had remained convergent for seven years as the FTAA negotiations moved forward, they clearly began to diverge after 2002. Two events occurred at that time that in hindsight represent a watershed with respect to the definition of the national interests of Brazil/MERCOSUR and the United States in trade.

In Brazil, President Lula da Silva of the Workers' Party was elected in the fall of 2002, the first President from a working class background, running on a more populist platform than any previously seen. Although President Lula's government has followed an orthodox line with respect to monetary policy, it has preferred to adopt a more strident rhetoric on trade, associating the FTAA process with a perceived dominance by the United States and the imposition of a negotiating agenda that it considers inappropriate and overly ambitious.

Brazil's new government concluded early on that it had little interest in proceeding with the FTAA in the then existing framework of negotiations and attempted to reshape the negotiating framework and objectives. Brazil's redefinition of its national interest coincided with its political ambitions to exercise leadership in South America. Priority of the Lula government in the trade arena was given to the Doha Development Round under the WTO, where Brazil felt that the prospects for liberalization in agricultural trade were more promising and where it could exercise a greater leadership role. In parallel, Brazil pushed for a regional deal with the EU over one in the Western Hemisphere where it felt that the presence of the United States would dominate the trade agenda.

Inspired by President Lula and by President Kirchner in Argentina, a few other countries in Latin America have turned away from the FTAA to embrace rival paths to economic integration. During 2006 alone no fewer than ten Presidential elections were held in Latin America. Most of these new governments were socialist or populist in name and representation. This change in the political landscape has allowed for new directions in trade relations to be proposed by this new brand of leaders. The Boliverian Alternative for the Americas or ALBA, an initiative put forward by President Hugo Chavez of Venezuela in 2004 as an alternative to the FTAA, was adopted in April 2006 by Bolivia and Cuba in the form of a People's Trade Agreement. Under the ALBA vision, trade constitutes only one component of an economic relationship, of which the most important elements are economic cooperation and product complementarity.[22] This alternative vision opposes neo-liberal theories of free trade and comparative advantage and eschews a market-driven approach in favour of a state-driven one. Under the agreements that have been concluded through ALBA, energy is a critical component.

In the United States the summer of 2002 was marked by Congressional passage of Trade Promotion Authority (TPA) — the first time that the President had been able to obtain this required legislative stamp of approval to engage in trade negotiations since it had expired at the conclusion of the Uruguay Round at end 1993, nearly ten years earlier. This gave U.S. negotiators a new lease on life, but a very short leash within which to manoeuvre, as the content of any new trade agreement was already broadly defined by the terms of the TPA Act. With this in hand, the U.S. Trade Representative (USTR) turned to the pursuit of a very ambitious trade agenda in bilateral FTAs — the post-NAFTA template — that required not only market opening but also the adoption of far-reaching rules in behind-the-border areas. Institutional transformation and strengthening in partner

FTA countries became one of the stated goals of U.S. trade policy, which followed an openly stated strategy of "competitive liberalization".[23]

However, U.S. negotiators were given little room to compromise under the TPA requirements in terms of the desired negotiated outcome of trade agreements, and particularly with respect to sensitive issues such as market access liberalization for certain agricultural products, services and investment liberalization, intellectual property right protection, trade remedy procedures and mobility of labour. Furthermore, the TPA requires that all trade agreements negotiated by the United States contain disciplines on labour and the environment (as previously discussed), with certain very specific criteria on application and enforcement of national laws.[24] This ambitious negotiating agenda was accepted by other Latin American countries after the FTAA negotiations foundered (including in the either completed or ongoing bilateral negotiations with Central America, the Dominican Republic, Peru, Colombia, Panama and Ecuador), but was no longer accepted by Brazil and its close trading partners.

IX. LESSONS TO BE DRAWN FROM THE FTAA EXPERIENCE FOR APEC

A few key lessons may be drawn from the FTAA experience that should be of relevance to the APEC economies as they consider the possibility of engaging in negotiations for an FTAAP. These are summarized below.

1. A Unity of Vision is Necessary among the Major Economies (U.S., Japan, China)

For negotiations on an FTAAP to be successful, there must be a unity of vision on the objective and finality of a regional agreement among the three major economies in the Asia-Pacific region, namely the United States, Japan and the People's Republic of China. This unity of vision must be present at the beginning of the process and must be maintained until the end of the process. If these three economic giants (constituting three of the four largest economies in the world) do not see the objective and the finality of an FTAAP with a positive eye, or do not maintain a common purpose, then the negotiations will either not begin at all, or they will not succeed. It was after the unity of vision between the United States and Brazil disappeared, that the FTAA negotiations stalled. And in spite of the fact that thirty of the thirty-four countries in the Hemisphere continue to actively support this objective, it has not proved possible to put the negotiations back on track. Such a unity of vision may be easier to achieve at the current time after the suspension of the Doha Development Round, when the FTAAP would be the most credible alternative to the unchecked proliferation of bilateral RTAs in the Asia-Pacific.

2. The Time-frame of the Process Must Not Be Too Long

One of the major problems of the FTAA turned out to be its time framework. The decade given for the negotiations proved to be too long. While lesser developed APEC members can always sign on later to an FTAAP, agreement among the major countries must be seized in a time-frame that does not admit too many changes of government. While ten years proved to be excessively drawn out for this process, two years would clearly be too short, so a period not longer than four to five years should probably be a reasonable one for such negotiations. A fixed deadline would be necessary, however, in order to focus efforts from the outset.

3. An Achievable Outcome Must Be Targeted

If the FTAAP is viewed as an agreement of the entire APEC community, then its objectives must be realistic ones. The FTAAP negotiating agenda should not be overly ambitious, or this may derail the process. After the FTAA experience, it is highly doubtful whether a resolution of the issue of the reform of domestic agricultural support policies could be resolved at the regional level, so it would be wise to leave this issue off the agenda. In the area of intellectual property demands, given the experience of the FTAA, these ambitions may need to be set at a more modest but achievable level. Likewise in the area of services and investment, given the even larger diversity of economies in the Asia-Pacific region than in the Americas, the more advanced APEC members may need to consider a more nuanced approach in terms of services/investment commitments. Given the size and dynamic nature of the region and the number of important economies it encompasses, it is possible that the U.S. Congress would accept an FTAAP agreement that would be somewhat different than the template of the bilateral FTAs that have been recently concluded by the USTR.

Reaching a region-wide agreement among so many widely divergent economies will certainly prove challenging. If the United States and other more advanced economies were to insist on an ambitious agreement, then the alternative to an APEC-wide FTAAP in the first instance might be a staggered approach, whereby those economies that consider themselves ready to take on the disciplines of a "state of the art agreement" could do so at the time of completion of the FTAAP, while the other APEC members could do so when they would consider themselves ready. An integral component of the FTAAP would then consist of a strong trade capacity-building programme, much like the Hemispheric Cooperation Program of the FTAA. This programme would be designed to assist those less advanced economies in reaching the necessary levels of institutional sophistication that would allow them to assume the FTAAP disciplines. No specific time-frame would be attached to this accession process, which would be limited to the APEC members.

4. There Should Be Minimal Interference from Other RTA Negotiations

For the FTAAP negotiations to succeed, there should be minimal distraction from outside or other negotiating efforts. The FTAA negotiations proceeded at a rapid clip until the Doha Development Round was launched and attention was diverted as between negotiating arenas. This became even more apparent after the U.S. obtained TPA authority in 2002 and begin to seriously engage in bilateral RTAs. This effort sapped the negotiating attention (and the ability to act in an independent manner) of both the Central American countries and the Andean countries and weakened those in favour of pushing the FTAA forward. And although it is not impossible for negotiators to participate in various negotiating fora, it was clear in the Western Hemisphere that the amount of human resources required for multiple negotiations is much greater and the attention is subsequently less than would otherwise be the case.

For this reason, a standstill agreement at the outset to cease negotiating other RTAs during the period of the FTAAP discussions would be strongly desirable; otherwise too much distraction will be generated by parallel efforts. Additionally, the negotiating leverage of large trading partners with smaller ones in bilateral RTAs could take away their ability to be full participants in an FTAAP negotiating process.

Likewise, a clause similar to what was agreed in FTAA should be included at the outset in the negotiating principles of an FTAAP in order to clarify the status of existing or previously negotiated RTAs and their relationship to a future region-wide agreement. This clause could make it clear that the FTAAP, once finalized and put in place, would prevail over all previous agreements, unless the disciplines of these pre-existing RTAs were deeper and went beyond the FTAAP.

5. Chairmanship of the Process Should Not Be Given to Any of the Major Players

The FTAA experience showed clearly that placing any of the major players in a position of leadership does not lead to a satisfactory outcome. Just as in the Doha Round negotiations where WTO members prefer not to assign the chairmanship of key negotiating groups to representatives of either the United States, the EU or Japan, likewise in a regional negotiating process the chairmanship of the Trade Negotiations Committee should be given to a small but committed participant, who is not likely to try and influence the process for its own national objectives.

6. Prior Understanding on How to Treat Labour and the Environment is Necessary

Given the sensitivity of the two issues of labour and the environment and the difficulties that these issues caused during the entire life of the FTAA negotiations, it would be desirable to come to an agreement prior to the launch of the FTAAP on how these two issues would be treated. Would they be a part of the negotiating framework? And if so, in what form? As the U.S. TPA is very clear on its instruction to U.S. negotiators, the issues should be tackled from the outset and agreement reached between the major actors so that the FTAAP negotiations would not be poisoned by allegations over misunderstanding of meaning and objective in this area.

7. There Must Be a Willingness and an Identified Capacity to Finance and Support the Negotiating Process

Financing for the FTAA negotiations was provided both by the governments hosting the FTAA Secretariat (one-third), as well as by the Tripartite

Committee (two-thirds of the cost of the negotiating process). The cost of providing the technical support to the negotiating groups and chairs, as well as carrying out capacity-building activities, was absorbed by the budgets of the Tripartite Committee institutions (OAS, IDB and ECLAC). The equivalent of this grouping of institutions does not exist in the Asia-Pacific, other than the Asian Development Bank (ADB). Therefore, the question of who would finance this technical and analytical support (professional expertise) and who would provide the administrative support (presumably the APEC Secretariat) would have to be considered in advance. The ADB would need a mandate from its members to contribute to the financing of an FTAAP process, just as the IDB had to obtain one annually from its members. Capacity-building efforts to train and support trade negotiators would be particularly important for the FTAAP negotiations to succeed, given the diversity of economies in the Asia-Pacific region.

APPENDIX
Chronology of Developments in the FTAA from 1998 to 2004

- At the Fourth Trade Ministerial Meeting held in San Jose, Costa Rica in 1998, Ministers adopted the Declaration that set out their agreement to enter into formal FTAA negotiations. The Declaration contains general principles and objectives for the negotiations, elaborates on the structure of the negotiations and the establishment of the negotiating groups, and set out mandates for each negotiating issue areas.
- Heads of State and Government in the Western Hemisphere met at the Second Summit of the Americas in Santiago de Chile in April 1998 and endorsed the recommendation contained in the Ministerial Declaration of San Jose, officially launching the FTAA negotiations.
- At the Fifth Trade Ministerial Meeting held in Toronto in 1999, Ministers instructed the negotiating groups to prepare a draft text of their respective chapters, and approved several business facilitation measures, designed to facilitate trade among countries in the Hemisphere.[25]
- At the Sixth Ministerial Meeting, held in Buenos Aires in April 2001, Ministers took a number of key decisions on the FTAA negotiations. The various negotiating groups submitted draft chapters of their areas, which Ministers agreed to make publicly available. Additionally, in order to move the process forward, the Technical Committee on Institutional Issues was created in order to begin deliberating the overall architecture of an FTAA Agreement and other institutional matters. In order to promote the dialogue with civil society, Ministers directed the Committee on the Participation of Civil Society to forward the submissions received on the various FTAA negotiating issues to the respective negotiating groups, as well as those related to the FTAA process in general. The importance of technical assistance for smaller economies was reiterated.[26]
- The Third Summit of the Americas was held in Quebec City on 20–22 April 2001. At this meeting, the decision to make the first draft of the FTAA Agreement available to the public was endorsed by Heads of State and Government. The Summit Declaration also fixed deadlines for the conclusion and implementation of the FTAA Agreement in the following terms:

> We direct our Ministers to ensure that negotiations of the FTAA Agreement are concluded no later than January 2005 and to seek its entry into force as soon as possible thereafter, but in any case, no later than December 2005. This will be a key element for generating the economic growth and prosperity in the Hemisphere that will contribute to the achievement of the broad Summit objectives.

- A new phase of the negotiations began in May 2002, with the initiation of market access negotiations for the five market access issues, namely tariffs and non-tariff barriers, agriculture, services, investment and government procurement. Principles and guidelines for these market access negotiations were agreed by Vice-Ministers in 2002 and are set out in a public document entitled "Methods and Modalities for Negotiations".[27]
- At the Seventh Trade Ministerial Meeting held in Quito, Ecuador in November 2002, Ministers agreed on a schedule for the exchange of initial market access offers (to take place between 15 December 2002 and 15 February 2003, with improvement to such offers by 15 June 2003 and negotiations on improvement of offers from 15 July 2003 onwards to the end of the negotiations). They also agreed to make public the second draft of the FTAA Agreement as well as the document on "Guidelines or Directives for the Treatment of the Differences in the Levels of Development and Size of Economies".[28] Ministers approved the Hemispheric Cooperation Program (HCP) and made it a permanent feature of the FTAA process.
- The fourth and final phase of the FTAA negotiating process began in December 2002 and was to last until the conclusion of the negotiations in January 2005. It was agreed that two Ministerial meetings would take place during this phase, one in November 2003 in Miami, USA, and one in 2004 in Brazil. The Ministerial meeting in Brazil has not taken place to date.
- At their Eighth Ministerial Meeting in Miami on 20 November 2003, Ministers reiterated their commitment to the FTAA by the agreed deadline with the ultimate goal of "achieving an area of free trade and regional integration", and set out a revised vision of the FTAA as follows:

> We are mindful that negotiations must aim at a balanced agreement that addresses the issue of differences in the levels of development and size of economies of the hemisphere, through various provisions and mechanisms.
>
> Taking into account and acknowledging existing mandates, Ministers recognize that countries may assume different levels of commitments. We will seek to develop a common and balanced set of rights and obligations applicable to all countries. In addition, negotiations should allow for countries that so choose, within the FTAA, to agree to additional obligations and benefits. One possible course of action would be for these countries to conduct plurilateral negotiations within the FTAA to define the obligations in the respective individual areas.

What resulted from the Miami meeting is no longer a one-track, unified agreement but a two-track, double FTAA vision with differing levels of ambition for the two tracks. Gone — at least in the short-to-medium term — is the notion of a single agreement with uniform disciplines for all the thirty-four negotiating governments. The decision by Trade Ministers to bifurcate the FTAA process into two negotiating tracks is found in paragraphs 5 through 10 of the Miami Ministerial Declaration entitled "The Vision of the FTAA". The major innovation in these paragraphs is the introduction of the term "flexibility" in order to accompany the renewed commitment to a "comprehensive and balanced FTAA".

The main text of these paragraphs reads as follows:

> We are mindful that negotiations must aim at a balanced agreement that addresses the issue of differences in the levels of development and size of economies of the hemisphere, through various provisions and mechanisms.
>
> Taking into account and acknowledging existing mandates, Ministers recognize that countries may assume different levels of commitments. We will seek to develop a common and balanced set of rights and obligations applicable to all countries. In addition, negotiations should allow for countries that so choose, within the FTAA, to agree to additional obligations and benefits. One possible course of action would be for these countries to conduct plurilateral negotiations within the FTAA to define the obligations in the respective individual areas.
>
> We fully expect that this endeavor will result in an appropriate balance of rights and obligations where countries reap the benefits of their respective commitments.

- The Miami Ministerial Declaration recognizes — for the first time in the nine-year process — that plurilateral negotiations may be conducted among those countries wishing to take on higher levels of commitments, or those willing to "agree to additional obligations and benefits" (para. 7). The Declaration insists that the FTAA will still be comprehensive in that it will "include measures in each negotiating discipline, and horizontal measures, as appropriate" (para. 9). The Vice-Ministers are to develop a "common and balanced set of rights and obligations applicable to all countries", while interested parties may choose "to develop additional liberalization and disciplines on a plurilateral basis" (para. 10). Countries may choose to be a part of the higher-level negotiations at any time they wish by notifying this intention; if they do not wish to take part in the negotiations, they may still attend as observers and become participants at any time thereafter. Importantly, the "results of the negotiations [presumably both of them but this is not specified] must be WTO compliant" (para. 10). According to several interpretations of the Miami Declaration, the agreements resulting from both tracks will be considered as forming the FTAA Agreement and will be concluded simultaneously. However, others have never been clear as to how this would work in practice.

- At the Miami Trade Ministerial meeting, Ministers agreed to make the third draft of the FTAA Agreement available to the public on the official FTAA website. This draft is still the most current text of the FTAA Agreement, as neither Trade Ministers nor negotiating groups have met since that time (November 2003).

- At the Fourth Summit of the Americas in Mar del Plata, Argentina (November 2005), the question of trade and in particular the FTAA proved to be extremely controversial. In the end it was impossible to set out a common vision on trade in the Declaration of Mar del Plata, so two opposing visions were included. The paragraph 19 of the Declaration sets out these two opposing texts on the FTAA. No consultations on trade have taken place in the Hemisphere since the Summit.

Notes

1. See "Plan of Action" accompanying the "Declaration of Principles of the Miami Summit of the Americas" in date of 9–11 December 1994, which can be found on the OAS website at www.oas.org, which sets out the twenty-three hemispheric initiatives, including the FTAAs, all as an integral part of the Summit Process.

2. See draft text of the FTAA Agreement, available on the official FTAA website at www.ftaa-alca.org. This is the third version of the draft agreement, in date of 21 November 2003 (document FTAA.TNC/W/133/Rev.3), which Ministers of Trade agreed to release for public distribution at the time of the Miami Trade Ministerial meeting in November 2003.

3. These questions had been settled at the time of the launching of the FTAA process and were not controversial in the Americas. Investment, competition policy and government procurement all formed a part of the FTAA negotiating agenda, to which no one had objected. The issues of labour rights and the environment, however, did not form a part of the formal negotiating agenda at the time of the launching of the FTAA in 1998, and continuous controversy surrounded these issues throughout the life of the negotiations.

4. This was done on the basis of "self selection", as the FTAA negotiators never managed to agree formally on what group of countries should be defined as "small economies". For this reason, the term adopted in the FTAA was "small and relatively less developed economies". This allowed the group to encompass countries such as those in Central America, Bolivia, Ecuador and Paraguay.

5. Section 3.7 discusses the issues that are being negotiated in the nine FTAA

negotiating groups, while section 3.8 discusses the issues covered within the three non-negotiating groups/committees.

6. The General Principles and Objectives agreed by Ministers of Trade of the Western Hemisphere to guide the FTAA negotiations are listed in Annex I of the San Jose Ministerial Declaration of March 1998, which can be found on the official FTAA website at www.ftaa-alca.org.

7. The thirty-four participants in the FTAA process are: Canada, the United States, Mexico, Costa Rica, El Salvador, Guatemala, Honduras, Nicaragua, Panama, Bolivia, the Dominican Republic, Colombia, Ecuador, Peru, Venezuela, Argentina, Brazil, Chile, Paraguay, Uruguay, and the fifteen CARICOM member states, namely: Antigua and Barbuda, The Bahamas, Barbados, Belize, Dominica, Grenada, Guyana, Haiti, Jamaica, Saint Lucia, St. Kitts and Nevis, St. Vincent and the Grenadines, Suriname, and Trinidad and Tobago.

8. Cuba has not been invited to participate in the FTAA process, even though it is an independent state in the Western Hemisphere, because it does not currently have a democratically elected government and was suspended from participating in the Inter-American System of the OAS since 1962.

9. FTAA meetings at the Ministerial and the Vice-Ministerial level are conducted in the four official languages of the Summit Process, namely English, Spanish, Portuguese and French. However, the meetings of the negotiating groups, as well as the circulation of documents, are carried out in the two working languages of English and Spanish.

10. The WTO disciplines are those contained in the various Uruguay Round Agreements that were concluded as part of these negotiations in December 1993 and that are to be applied by all WTO Members. They include disciplines in the areas of tariffs, non-tariff barriers, agriculture, technical barriers to trade, sanitary and phytosanitary (SPS) measures, anti-dumping and countervailing duties, subsidies, textiles and clothing, services and intellectual property rights, among others.

11. See the Terms of Reference for the Technical Committee on Institutional Issues in document FTAA.tncmin/2001/02 in date of 4 February 2002, found on the official FTAA website, www.ftaa-alca.org.

12. See the Third Draft Agreement of the FTAA contained in document FTAA.TNC/w/133/Rev.3 of 21 November 2003, found on the official FTAA website, www.ftaa-alca.org.

13. The specific business facilitation measures agreed by the FTAA participating governments, based on the recommendations presented by the private sector representatives at the various Business Forum meetings can be found on the official FTAA website at www.ftaa-alca.org under "Business Facilitation".

14. A summary of the position papers presented at these issue meetings, together with a list of participants by country and institution, can be found on the official FTAA website at www.ftaa-alca.org under "Civil Society".

15. A recent agreement was reached at the WTO in the context of the Doha Development Round on a "Transparency Mechanism for Regional Trade Agreements" in an effort to improve the notification of such agreements to the WTO Committee on Regional Trade Arrangements. The mechanism does not, however, cover the critical and much more difficult issue of how to evaluate RTAs for WTO compatibility once they have been notified.

16. See article by Sherry Stephenson discussing GATS Article V, "GATS and Regional Integration", in *GATS2000: New Directions in Services Trade Liberalization*, edited by Pierre Sauve and Robert Stern (2000), Brookings Institution Press, pp. 509–30.

17. The question of disciplining domestic support has not been raised in any of the other bilateral FTAs negotiated within the Western Hemsiphere, nor does it form a part of their disciplines. Only the FTAA was given such a broad and ambitious negotiating mandate. In NAFTA the agricultural area was treated differently from that of other goods, and there is no mention of export subsidies or domestic subsidies. Agricultural market access is governed by bilateral agreements between the three parties rather than by a common agreement. As between Mexico and the United States, the NAFTA promises "free" agricultural trade, defined as the absence of no tariffs or quotas, after long delays and phase-ins for "sensitive" products like sugar, corn, beans, and several minor crops.

18. However, even within North America there are still important sectors that continue to be reserved by each NAFTA party. For example, the United States exempted maritime transport, Canada protected its cultural industries, and Mexico maintained its nationalized energy sector, including electricity and drilling services. All three sectors were placed outside of the disciplines of the agreement. And all three NAFTA parties continue to limit foreign ownership of TV and radio. Indeed, most of the liberalization in the services area that has taken place in North America has occurred independently of the NAFTA, through voluntary liberalization rather than through negotiated market opening (the telecom sector is an excellent example of this). The main exception to this rule is the financial services sector in Mexico.

19. An H-1B visa is the visa category offered by the United States to skilled professionals from abroad and it is capped at an annual quota of 65,000 new entrants. The majority of H-1B visas are granted to engineers, computer programmers and software developers. The United States did not expand the number of H-1B visas it offered to grant at all in its services offer to the WTO Doha Development Round.

20. The MERCOSUR members (Argentina, Brazil, Paraguay and Uruguay) have still not complied with the terms of the WTO TRIPS Agreement to the satisfaction of the United States.

21. It will certainly be problematic, if not impossible, to have a future FTAA

Agreement approved by the U.S. Congress without provisions on labour and the environment. The United States has gone beyond the formula developed in NAFTA in its more recent FTAs with Jordan, Chile, Singapore and Australia. In those FTAs, provisions on labour and the environment form an integral part of the basic treaty and are subject to its dispute settlement proceedings. Each country commits to enforce its own laws, with the possibility of monetary fines or trade sanctions in the event a country engages in a persistent pattern of non-enforcement. These two areas will be greatly scrutinized by the U.S. Congress as a part of any trade agreement that comes up for approval. On the other hand, it is difficult to imagine that such an important political initiative as the FTAA would be denied on the grounds of too lax labour and environment provisions.

22. See explanation of the ALBA on the official website, www.alternative bolivariana.org.
23. The recent study by Simon J. Evenett and Michael Meier on "An Interim Assessment of the U.S. Trade Policy of Competitive Liberalization", draft of 24 July 2006, is quite instructive in tracing the history and philosophy behind the pursuit of this strategy on the part of the U.S. Government.
24. All the FTAs concluded by the United States since 2002 without exception have followed a similar template, given by the requirements of the TPA.
25. These business facilitation measures can be found in the Annexes to the Toronto Ministerial Declaration of November 1999. They are concentrated in the areas of customs procedures and enhanced transparency. The working group on business facilitation ceased to meet after this Ministerial meeting.
26. See the Buenos Aires Ministerial Declaration of 7 April 2001.
27. The document on "Methods and Modalities for the Negotiations" can be found on the official FTAA website at www.ftaa-alca.org as FTAA.TNC/20/ Rev.1 in date of 18 October 2002.
28. The document on "Guidelines or Directives for the Treatment of the Differences in the Levels of Development and Size of Economies" can be found on the official FTAA website at www.ftaa-alca.org as FTAA.TNC/18 in date of 1 November 2002.

References

Bergsten, C. Fred. *Competitive Liberalization and Global Free Trade: A Vision for the Early 21st Century*. APEC Working Paper No. 96-15. Washington, D.C.: Institute for International Economics, 1996.
Feinberg, Richard. "Comparing Regional Integration in Non-Identical Twins: APEC and the FTAA". *Integration & Trade* 4, no. 10 (January–April 2000) (Buenos Aires, INTAL).

Hufbauer, Gary Clyde and Jeffrey J. Schott. 2005. *NAFTA Revisited: Achievements and Challenges.* Washington, D.C.: Institute for International Economics, 2005.

Hufbauer, Gary Clyde and Sherry Stephenson. "The Free Trade Area of the Americas: How Deep an Integration in the Western Hemisphere?". In *Reshaping the Asia Pacific Economic Order,* edited by Christopher Findlay and Hadi Soesastro. London: Routledge, 2006.

Inter-American Development Bank (IDB). *Integration and Trade in the Americas: A Preliminary Estimate of 2004 Trade,* Periodic Note. Washington, D.C.: Inter-American Development Bank, December 2004.

Schott, Jeffrey J. *Prospects for Free Trade in the Americas.* Washington, D.C.: Institute for International Economics, 2001.

Stephenson, Sherry. "New Trade Strategies in the Americas". Paper for a conference volume by Baylor University, 2006.

United States Trade Representative (USTR). "United States leads the world to liberalize trade through the Doha Round". *Trade Facts.* www.ustr.gov. Accessed in 2005.

Zabludovsky, Jaime. "The Long and Winding Road to Hemispheric Integration: Ten Key Elements". In *Understanding the FTAA in Free Trade in the Americas: Getting There from Here.* Washington, D.C.: Inter-American Dialogue, 2004.

7

Prospects for Linking Preferential Trade Agreements in the Asia-Pacific Region

Robert Scollay

I. INTRODUCTION

The rapid proliferation of preferential trading agreements (PTAs) in the Asia-Pacific region in the early years of the twenty-first century is by now a very well-known phenomenon. In the last five years at least eighteen PTAs between APEC members have been concluded, with at least a further twenty under negotiation. A full list of these initiatives is provided in Table 7.1. A number of others are at various stages of study or discussion, and in some of these cases the opening of negotiations is believed to be imminent. Adding in the five agreements that were already in existence in the region before the turn of the century, a realistic assessment of current initiatives suggests therefore that there could be over forty PTAs operating in the APEC region in the near future, possibly more. This is in addition to the PTAs that APEC members have been pursuing and concluding with partners outside the APEC region.

TABLE 7.1
Preferential Trading Agreements between APEC Economies[a]

Agreements Concluded	*Agreements Under Negotiation[b]*

(a) Initiatives Active since 1999

Bilateral

Singapore-New Zealand	Japan-Korea
Singapore-Australia	Japan-Thailand (substantially agreed)
Singapore-Japan	Japan-Philippines (substantially agreed)
Singapore-U.S.	Japan-Indonesia
Singapore-Korea	Korea-Thailand
Chile-U.S.	U.S.-Thailand
Chile-Korea	Australia-China
Chile-China	Australia-Malaysia
Mexico-Japan	New Zealand-China
U.S.-Australia	New Zealand-Malaysia
Peru-U.S.	Peru-Thailand
Thailand-Australia	Singapore-Canada
Thailand-New Zealand	Korea-Mexico
China-Hong Kong SAR	U.S.-Malaysia
Japan-Malaysia	U.S.-Korea
Thailand-China[c]	Chile-Thailand
	Korea-Canada

Plurilateral

ASEAN-China	ASEAN-CER
Chile-New Zealand-Singapore-Brunei (TPSEP)[d]	ASEAN-Japan
	ASEAN-Korea
	(FTAA)

(b) Agreements in Existence Before 1999

NAFTA	(USA, Canada, Mexico)
ANZCERTA	(Australia, New Zealand)
AFTA	(Brunei, Cambodia, Indonesia, Laos, Malaysia, Myanmar, Philippines, Singapore, Thailand, Vietnam)
Chile-Canada	
Chile-Mexico	

Notes:
a. The agreements are listed by participant members rather than the official name of the agreements.
b. Agreements under study or discussion are not listed here, even if negotiations are believed to be imminent. Proposed agreements for which the negotiations appear to have been suspended without any apparent intention for them to be resumed are also not listed. The proposed New Zealand-Hong

continued on next page

TABLE 7.1 — *cont'd*

Kong and Singapore-Mexico agreements are in this category. On the other hand, the Japan-Korea proposal is listed because while negotiations are suspended they may not have broken down permanently. Likewise there is uncertainty as to whether the Free Trade Area of the Americas (FTAA) negotiations may be revived in the future. The FTAA is bracketed because most of the participants are not APEC members. The FTAA would cover the following trade flows between APEC members that are not currently covered by FTAs: Canada-Peru, Mexico-Peru, Chile-Peru (although the latter two are already covered by more limited preferential arrangements).
c. There is some doubt whether the Thailand-China FTA should be included in this list. Details are scarce and it is sometimes presented as an "early harvest" agreement, linked to the main ASEAN-China agreement.
d. The TPSEP (Trans Pacific Strategic Economic Partnership) is sometimes known informally as the "P4" (Pacific 4) Agreement.
Sources: APEC Secretariat, Member Economies/ FTA/RTA Information, http://www.apec.org/webapps/ fta_rta_information.html;Okamoto, J. (2006).

All but two of the concluded agreements are bilateral free trade agreements (FTAs). Parallel to the spread of these bilateral FTAs there have been ongoing efforts to promote the concept of a regional trade bloc in East Asia. A proposal for an East Asian Free Trade Agreement (EAFTA), covering the members of the ASEAN Plus Three group, has been on the table since 2000, but agreement to move forward on this proposal has not so far been reached. In the meantime the three major Northeast Asian economies (China, Japan and Korea) have each pursued their separate preferential trading arrangements with the Southeast Asian economies of the ASEAN (Association of Southeast Asian Nations) group. China and Korea have concluded FTAs with ASEAN as a group, while Japan initially preferred to pursue bilateral FTAs with individual ASEAN economies, and has only recently taken steps towards an agreement with the full ASEAN group.

Although new PTAs between APEC economies are routinely announced as steps towards achievement of APEC's Bogor goals, in one respect they represent a fundamental departure from the original APEC vision. The Bogor Declaration envisages a region whose markets would be integrated by the establishment of free trade and investment within the region on a non-discriminatory basis. Preferential trading agreements on the other hand are inherently discriminatory. While they result in liberalized trade between their members, they discriminate against non-members. A multiplicity of preferential trading agreements in the Asia-Pacific region gives rise to complex patterns of preference, discrimination and exclusion, and is a recipe for fragmentation of regional markets and trading relationships, thereby denying APEC economies and their businesses the full efficiencies and other benefits that could be attainable through the greater integration of the markets of the region.

The trend to proliferating PTAs is however likely to be irreversible in the short run, since the magnetic attraction of the larger economies as preferential trading partners has given rise to a "domino effect", whereby smaller economies of the region find themselves impelled to seek their own bilateral agreements with major trading partners, to avoid being disadvantaged relative to their competitors. A tendency towards the emergence of "hub and spoke" configurations of PTAs is a further consequence of this effect, in which the benefits of preferential trade liberalisation accrue disproportionately to the "hubs".

From a business perspective, concern over the fragmentation effect of multiplying PTAs has centred on the potential for increased transaction costs associated with the development across the region of a "spaghetti bowl" of PTAs containing inconsistent provisions on matters such as rules of origin. The proposals for a regional trade bloc in East Asia have also drawn concern over the likely consequence of a "split down the middle of the Pacific" between separate trading blocs on either side of the ocean, again limiting the potential for the region as a whole to benefit from the full integration of its markets.

Given these concerns it is not surprising that increasing attention has been given to exploring ways of countering the fragmentation effects of multiplying PTAs. One possible avenue, which is the subject of this paper, is the promotion of "convergence" between existing and future PTAs in the region.

II. MEANINGS OF CONVERGENCE

Convergence among PTAs can be considered in a number of dimensions. One dimension relates to the mechanisms for linkage between the existing PTAs and the likelihood that members of existing agreements will seek such linkages. At the most ambitious level, linkage could involve the formation of progressively larger preferential groupings, including through the expansion and amalgamation of existing PTAs, so that they eventually converge towards regional free trade and investment. A more limited and possibly more complicated process could involve the evolution of parallel agreements with overlapping membership that may co-exist with each other. It is possible, even likely, that both forms of convergence could occur simultaneously prior to the final stage of full regional integration.

The question arises as to whether the spread of such linkages might eventually achieve the objective of full Asia-Pacific integration. If they do not, trade and investment relations in the Asia-Pacific region could remain fragmented by discrimination. Discrimination between the larger groupings that might have emerged through the linkage processes could arguably be more damaging, although the "spaghetti bowl" would be simplified by coalescence into a small number of larger preferential groupings.

A second, and obviously related dimension of convergence concerns the extent to which linkages between agreements require harmonization of provisions and the extent to which such harmonization is feasible. There are a number of possible variants of harmonization of FTA provisions, depending in part on the nature of the linkage that is being pursued.

If convergence is viewed as the creation of a single agreement through the amalgamation or expansion of existing agreements, the neatest solution is of course the establishment of a single set of provisions to which all members of the new larger agreement subscribe. This requires either full acceptance by all parties of the provisions of one of the pre-existing agreements, or agreement by all parties to a modified set of provisions acceptable to all. A possible variant is the adoption of a "variable geometry", or "tiered" approach", with provisions divided into a common "core" set of provisions adopted by all parties, and a further set of provisions from which some members may be allowed to wholly or partly opt out. The conditions under which opting out is permitted might also be the subject of agreement among the parties.

Where convergence takes the form of co-existing agreements with overlapping membership there will inevitably be differences between the provisions of the agreements concerned. If the difference lies simply in the range of issues covered, the position is similar to that of a single agreement with "variable geometry". Where there is inconsistency between the agreements in provisions on a specific issue, potentially more difficult issues arise as to how the inconsistency will be resolved for the parties that are members of both agreements.

Convergence could also involve the adoption of common provisions across the separate PTAs in the region, without necessarily proceeding towards amalgamation of the agreements, at least initially. Adoption of common provisions could be regarded as an end in itself, or a step towards future amalgamation of agreements. Adoption of common provisions has the potential to simplify the "spaghetti bowl", provided that the common provisions embrace issues that give rise to the most costly "spaghetti bowl" effects, such as rules of origin. The extent of the contribution to achieving full regional integration would depend also on the extent to which the common provisions cover the trade flows of the region. Discrimination and consequent fragmentation of regional trading relationships will remain entrenched to the extent that significant regional trade flows remain outside the scope of the common provisions.

III. EXISTING "LINKAGE INITIATIVES"

There are several examples in the Asia-Pacific region of initiatives that involve linkages between pre-existing agreements. The Trans-Pacific Strategic Economic Partnership (TPSEP) widens a zone of free trade that originally embraced only Singapore and New Zealand, to include also Chile and Brunei Darussalam. Some of the ASEAN Plus One initiatives overlap with bilateral PTA initiatives between the non-ASEAN partner and individual ASEAN economies. The ASEAN-China FTA (ACFTA) subsumed an earlier agreement between China and Thailand. Korea has FTAs both with Singapore and with the ASEAN group as a whole.[1] Japan, which has an FTA with Singapore and has been negotiating bilaterally with Thailand, Malaysia, the Philippines and Indonesia, is now moving to negotiate an FTA with ASEAN as a group. Australia and New Zealand each have FTAs with Singapore and Thailand as well as negotiations under way with Malaysia, and are also negotiating for an FTA with the full ASEAN membership. If the EAFTA were to proceed it would effectively represent convergence of the "ASEAN Plus One" initiatives involving China, Japan and Korea.

The case of ACFTA and the China-Thailand agreement is the only example to date of one agreement being fully amalgamated into the other. In this case the relatively narrow China-Thailand agreement, which covered only agricultural products, was treated simply as an "early harvest" precursor of the ACFTA, which has wider coverage.

The TPSEP on the other hand has not superseded the earlier New Zealand-Singapore Closer Economic Partnership (NZSCEP) agreement, which will continue to operate in parallel to it. The rules of origin in the TPSEP and the NZSCEP are quite different, based in the former case on change in customs classification and in the latter case on regional value content. This presumably means that exporters in Singapore and New Zealand will be able to choose the rule of origin regime under which they export to each other's market. Since the TPSEP has not yet entered into force, it is too early to assess how this might work out in practice. Differences in issue coverage between the two agreements are likely to be less problematic. The absence of an investment chapter in the TPSEP, for example, presumably means that investment relations between New Zealand and Singapore will be governed solely by the NZSCEP.

The ASEAN-Japan negotiations and the negotiations for an ASEAN-Australia-New Zealand FTA (AANZFTA) also raise interesting issues. These are the cases where ASEAN's prospective partners have already concluded or are in the process of negotiating bilateral FTAs with individual ASEAN members. It is not yet clear how these bilateral FTAs will relate to the wider agreements with ASEAN as a group. One possibility is a "variable geometry" approach where the prospective ASEAN-Japan FTA and the AANZFTA contain a "core" of provisions in common with the bilateral FTAs, leaving the bilateral FTAs to go further in areas where agreement cannot be reached in the wider agreement.

On the other hand there may be pressure for the ASEAN-wide agreements to adopt provisions that are inconsistent with provisions in the bilateral FTAs, perhaps due to changes in perceptions as to what provisions are desirable. For example, Australia and New Zealand are known to be pressing ASEAN to adopt rules of origin based on the change in customs classification approach in AANZFTA, contrary to the regional value content approach adopted in their respective agreements with Singapore, as well as to the approach followed in AFTA. Adoption of regional value content rules in AANZFTA on the other hand, as preferred by ASEAN, would clash with the rules based on change in customs classification adopted in Australia's and New Zealand's bilateral FTAs with Thailand. In the case of the ASEAN-Japan FTA, ASEAN is pressing Japan to adopt the 40 per cent regional value content rule that is ASEAN's preferred standard, which is significantly more generous than the regional value content rules that Japan has sought in its bilateral FTA negotiations with ASEAN members.

Similar issues will inevitably arise if an EAFTA is to be negotiated. In that case there will be questions of how EAFTA will cohere both with ACFTA, the ASEAN-Korea FTA and the proposed ASEAN-Japan FTA, and with any bilateral FTAs that remain in force between China, Japan and Korea and individual ASEAN members.

The examples that have arisen so far are all cases of how a pre-existing agreement should relate to a new agreement that includes both the members of the pre-existing agreement as well as a number of additional members. Only in the case of Thailand-China and ACFTA has the pre-existing agreement been fully subsumed into the newer agreement, and this was a relatively simple case, as already noted. In the TPSEP/NZSCEP case it has been decided that the two agreements will operate in parallel, even though they contain inconsistent provisions on some issues. It will be interesting to see how this works out in practice. In the other cases the approach to be followed has yet to be clarified, although in the case of the three "ASEAN Plus One" initiatives and AANZFTA it appears fairly certain that the new agreements will be less ambitious than the bilateral agreements with which they overlap, so that the latter will almost inevitably continue in operation in parallel with the new wider agreements. It remains to be seen how potential clashes in provisions between the bilaterals and the wider agreements will be resolved.

The convergence represented by these developments is clearly far from a self-sustaining process, and cannot yet be regarded as a credible route to full regional integration. The trade flows involved in the TPSEP are very small, and although the members have emphasized that the agreement is open to accession by new members, this opportunity is yet to be taken up. In particular it may not be realistic to expect larger economies of the region to be willing to accede to the TPSEP. While ACFTA and the ASEAN-Korea FTAs have been concluded, the outcome of the Japan-ASEAN and AANZFTA negotiations remains to be seen. Prospects of moving forward on EAFTA remain hostage to the troubled political relationships between the three major East Asian economies of China, Japan and Korea. Of these three only Korea has so far moved to open negotiations for a trans-Pacific FTA with the United States.

IV. GAPS IN THE PREFERENTIAL TRADING
ARCHITECTURE OF THE ASIA-PACIFIC REGION

When considering the potential for preferential trading initiatives in the
Asia-Pacific region to evolve into full regional integration, an important
feature of the existing state of preferential trading developments to keep
in mind is that the economic superpowers of the region are lagging behind
in the pursuit of preferential relationships with each other.

Figure 7.1 shows that PTAs already concluded cover 45 per cent of
intra-APEC export flows, and this figure would rise to 55 per cent if all
PTAs currently under negotiation are successfully concluded. On the
other hand, 45 per cent or almost half of intra-APEC export flows remain
untouched by PTA initiatives. Figure 7.2 in turn makes clear that it is
primarily the trade flows between the major "hub" economies and the
flows involving Taiwan (Chinese Taipei) and Hong Kong that have
remained outside the scope of the regional spread of PTAs. Trade flows
between the United States, China and Japan and all trade of Taiwan and
Hong Kong except Hong Kong's trade with China and New Zealand
have yet to be the subject of a serious PTA negotiation. Korea and Japan
have held FTA negotiations but those negotiations are currently
suspended. Prospects for establishment of free trade among the major
Northeast Asian economies in the foreseeable future do not appear bright.

FIGURE 7.1
Coverage by PTAs of APEC Member Exports to Other APEC Economies
(2002–2004 Trade Data)

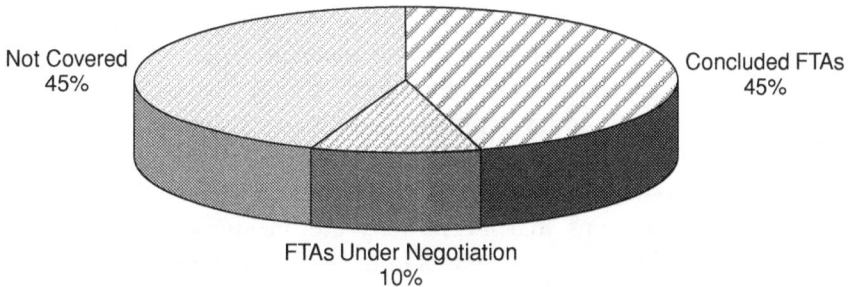

Not Covered 45% — Concluded FTAs 45% — FTAs Under Negotiation 10%

Source: IMF Direction of Trade Statistics.

FIGURE 7.2

Share of Intra-APEC Exports in Main Bilateral Flows Not Covered by Concluded PTAs or PTAs Under Negotiation (2002–2004 Trade Data)

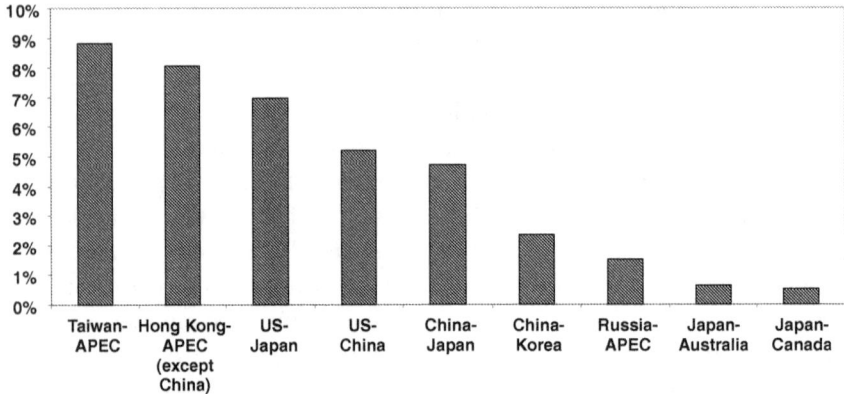

Source: IMF Direction of Trade Statistics.

It remains to be seen whether the recently announced commencement of FTA negotiations between the United States and Korea will catalyse increased interest in PTAs between the major Northeast Asian and North American economies.

V. PROVISIONS OF EXISTING AGREEMENTS: DIVERGENCE AND SCOPE FOR CONVERGENCE

The existing PTAs in the Asia-Pacific region exhibit great diversity in their provisions, reflecting the ways in which the members of each agreement have customized the provisions of their agreements to reflect their political sensitivities and specific aspects of their economic circumstances, especially those related to levels of development. This diversity is found for example in the treatment of sensitive products and sectors in the provisions on trade in goods and trade in services. It is found also in the so-called "trade-plus" provisions that increasingly are an important element in modern PTAs.[2] There are differences in the extent to which "trade-plus" provisions are included and also wide differences in the content and design of the provisions when they are included.

This section of the chapter considers these divergences in greater detail, from the perspective of implications for the prospects for eventual convergence.

Trade in Goods

Provisions on trade in goods in FTAs involving developed economies are constrained to meet the requirements of GATT Article XXIV,[3] which requires the elimination of all duties and other restrictive regulations of commerce on "substantially all trade" between the parties within a "reasonable period of time". Although the interpretation of GATT Article XXIV is notoriously elastic, it does impose a degree of uniformity, in that FTAs involving developed Asia-Pacific economies invariably provide for the complete removal of trade barriers between the parties on most products, even though there is considerable variation in the time period over which the elimination of barriers is to be implemented and in the identity and scope of products excluded from the provisions of the agreement.

Agreements whose membership is confined to developing economies[4] may take advantage of the more lenient provisions of the Enabling Clause of 1979, which allows much greater flexibility, allowing agreements in which tariffs and other barriers are not fully eliminated, and where liberalization provisions may apply to only a very limited range of products, on a "positive list" basis. Although some FTAs between APEC developing economy members have been notified to the WTO under the Enabling Clause, they generally do not take advantage of the full flexibility offered by that provision. Generally these agreements provide for full elimination of trade barriers on products covered by the agreement,[5] and in some cases also have a very limited range of products permanently excluded from liberalization.

Variations in the provisions on trade in goods in Asia-Pacific FTAs reflect different sensitivities attached to particular products. In some cases the sensitive products are simply excluded from the liberalization commitments altogether, as in the case of a range of agricultural products in each of Japan's FTAs or sugar in the case of the U.S. FTA with Australia. In other cases sensitive products are subject to lesser liberalization commitments. In AFTA, for example, the treatment finally agreed for a small range of sensitive products is that the tariff reduction process will end at a positive tariff percentage rather than at zero. Each member is able to choose the products designated as sensitive. This procedure is also followed in the ACFTA, where each member has designated a large number of products as "sensitive products". There is a rather low correlation between the products listed as "sensitive" by each ACFTA member.

An emerging trend, reflected for example in Australia's and New Zealand's FTAs with Thailand, is to avoid permanent exclusion of sensitive products, and to deal with sensitive products in other ways, such as very lengthy transition periods for the phasing out of tariffs, and use of various special transitional measures for sensitive products during the phase-out period. Phase-out periods of up to twenty years, as found for Thailand's sensitive agricultural products in the afore-mentioned two agreements, are becoming increasingly common, along with use of special measures such as special safeguard measures and tariff rate quotas, also used for Thailand's sensitive products in the same two agreements. Bilateral emergency actions are often provided for textile and clothing products. Another technique is to defer decisions on liberalization of sensitive products until some specified future date or until some specified future event has occurred, as for example in the Korea-Chile FTA, where a decision on liberalization of a large number of sensitive agricultural products is deferred until after the conclusion of the Doha Round. The sequencing of the tariff reductions can also vary, from equal annual or bi-annual instalments to heavily back-loaded arrangements where the majority of the liberalization occurs at the end of the phase-out period. The proportion of products on which tariffs are eliminated immediately or early in the phase-out period also varies enormously between agreements, and between partners in the same agreement.

The use of product-specific and usually highly restrictive rules of origin is another technique routinely used for sensitive products in PTAs. Rules of origin however are so important in determining both the trade effects of an FTA and the prospects for convergence, that they deserve separate consideration.

Rules of Origin

There are no WTO rules governing the use of rules of origin (ROOs) in FTAs.[6] The parties in each FTA are thus free to establish whatever ROOs they choose. Rules of origin are now well recognized as a crucial factor in determining the true degree of liberalization of trade in goods provided by any FTA. The costs imposed on exporters by ROOs, for example in record-keeping and documentation, production down time, and switches to more expensive input mixes, count as an offset to the cost advantages provided by tariff preferences. Rules of origin can often be more important than tariff preferences in determining the degree of market access provided by the FTA. One indication of this is the extent to which exporters choose not to use the tariff preferences available under FTAs, and prefer to continue to incur the MFN tariff when exporting to the partner country. This is usually interpreted as an indication that the costs of complying with the ROO exceed the value of the tariff preferences, although there can also be other reasons for non-utilization of tariff preferences.

Rules of origin can vary enormously in the extent to which they restrict or facilitate trade. Some rules are deliberately restrictive, responding to pressures from import-competing producers demanding to be sheltered from the additional competition that would otherwise result from the tariff preferences under the FTA. A sufficiently restrictive ROO can completely nullify the effect of the tariff preferences. In other cases restrictive ROOs may simply reflect poor design. ROOs perceived by one partner in an FTA as unduly restrictive can be an ongoing source of friction between the partners.

Econometric analysis has indicated that restrictive or selective rules of origin have a significant adverse affect on aggregate trade flows, while at the same time there is a marked increase in trade in intermediate goods when restrictive or selective rules of origin are applied to final goods. An indirect indication of the power of rules of origin in influencing trade is the close attention paid to them by commercial interests when FTAs are being negotiated. Insistence on restrictive rules of origin may also be a way for governments to achieve *de facto* exclusion of additional products from liberalization within the FTA, even if those products nominally become duty-free.

Inconsistent rules of origin across the PTAs in a region play a key role in the fragmentation of regional markets that results from proliferation of PTAs. They are also widely seen as the main culprits for the increased transaction costs that are expected to be imposed on businesses in economies that participate in multiple PTAs. Adoption of common rules of region is crucial in any programme to promote convergence across the region's FTAs. However, because of the vital role of ROO in determining the effect of an FTA in liberalizing trade, it is also crucial that any common ROOs that are adopted are designed to facilitate rather than restrict trade.

At one level there is widespread consensus on the desirable features of ROOs that are intended to facilitate trade. These rules "should be as straightforward as possible, and should be transparent, clear and consistent, and should not impose unnecessary compliance costs" (PECC Common Understanding 2006); "easy to understand and to comply with" (APEC "Best Practice" guidelines 2006). At the level of practical application, however, there is intense debate over the type of rule of origin that best meets these criteria, and also wide variations in the way that each type of rule is applied within the region's PTAs.

ROOs are generally of three types. Regional value content (RVC) rules require a specified percentage of the value[7] of the final product to be added in the partner country. Change of customs classification (CTC) rules require a change in customs classification at a specified level between the intermediate inputs imported from outside the area and the final product exported to the partner. A third approach is to specify a part or parts of the manufacturing process that must take place within the area. For example the "triple transformation" rules for garments in NAFTA and some other U.S. FTAs require that each step in the transformation from raw material to yarn to cloth to finished garment must be performed within the area.

The debate over which type of ROO best meets criteria such as those proposed by PECC and APEC focuses on the choice between RVC and CTC rules. One school of thought holds that RVC rules with a low value content requirement and generous cumulation provisions best meet the criteria. This has been the view held by ASEAN, which has used a 40 per cent RVC rule with full cumulation as the basic ROO for AFTA, and has been pressing, with partial success, for the adoption of this rule as the standard rule in all "ASEAN-Plus" FTAs. Another school of thought holds that the apparent simplicity in RVC rules is illusory, and that even an apparently generous RVC rule imposes undue costs on exporters and subjects them to unmanageable risks as to their ability to satisfy the rule on a continuous basis. Supporters of this view point to anecdotal evidence of low preference utilization in PTAs where RVC rules are in use. They hold that CTC rules offer exporters much greater certainty and are consequently more trade-facilitative. Exporters know the tariff classification of their inputs and their final products, and this knowledge is all that is required for complete certainty as to whether their products will satisfy the ROOs.

Unfortunately the Harmonized System (HS) of tariff classification was not designed with ROOs in mind, with the result that a single CTC rule will not be suitable for every product. As a consequence comprehensive application of the CTC approach typically requires that the ROO for each tariff category be specified. This results in extremely lengthy ROO schedules. The complexity of these schedules is however more apparent than real. Exporters are generally interested only in a small number of products and so will be interested in the small sections of the schedules that deal with those products, which provide them with precise guidance as to the requirements for meeting the ROOs on the products they wish to export.

On the other hand it is also the case that the effect of CTC rules for particular products will be understood only by the firms involved in the production and export of those products. The limited extent of understanding of the effect of a particular ROO can assist special interests in taking advantage of this non-transparency to press for ROOs that will severely restrict the ability of competitors in the partner country to export under the preferences. The resulting ROOs may be both restrictive and complex.

CTC rules are used in all U.S. FTAs in the Asia-Pacific region. Australia and New Zealand recently became converted to the advantages of CTC-based rules, and are in the process of converting the CER rules to this basis from their original RVC-based format, and have also pressed for the adoption of CTC-based rules in their more recent FTA negotiations, including in AANZFTA.

This is an important debate. If the arguments of the opponents of RVC rules are correct it would be unfortunate if this type of rule became established as the norm in a large part of the Asia-Pacific region. On the other hand the advocacy of CTC-based rules by the United States, Australia and New Zealand is tarnished by the way that these rules have been deliberately made much more restrictive for products sensitive to themselves, for example, autos and textiles in NAFTA, and clothing in the agreements of Australia and New Zealand with Thailand.

In addition to the fundamental debate over the type of ROO to be used, there are also wide variations in the way that each type of ROO is used in Asia-Pacific FTAs. Variations in RVC rules arise from differences in the percentage of regional value content required, differences in that way that regional value content is calculated, different cumulation provisions, and from the way that for some products RVC rules are combined with a specific process requirement. Variation in CTC rules arise from different levels at which the change in customs classification is defined and differences in the way that CTC rules may be combined with a specific process or RVC rule that must be satisfied simultaneously. Each variation potentially creates additional transaction costs for exporters to the market concerned.

These differences are prevalent both across agreements and for different products within the same agreement. Differences are often explained by the desire to make the ROOs more restrictive for particular sensitive products, for example where a particularly restrictive RVC or CTC provision, or combination of RVC and CTC provisions is used, or where a specific process rule is combined with the basic RVC or CTC rule.

Additional differences that can be costly for exporters are in different documentation and certification requirements. In some agreements, origin must be importer-certified, while in others the requirement is for exporter certification, and in the latter agreements there is a further difference between those where exporter self-certification is allowed and those where certification must be by a designated official agency, with attendant additional costs.

Prospects for Convergence

For the short and medium term the diversity of provisions in Asia-Pacific FTAs relating to liberalization of trade in goods has created a picture of great complexity. Different trade flows covered by these FTAs are subject to different product exclusions, different tariff phase-out profiles for different goods, different application of special safeguards and tariff quotas to different goods, and often different rules of origin.

It would be technically possible to bring some or all of the liberalization provisions within the scope of a single FTA, in which each member has different commitments to different partners. This is in fact already the case, admittedly in a rather minor way, in the TPSEP, where the commitments of each partner are different, and where the commitments for example of New Zealand to Chile and Brunei differ from its commitments to Singapore. Another example outside the APEC region is the DR-CAFTA agreement between the United States, five Central American countries and the Dominican Republic. This however would in no way reduce the complexity of the existing transitional provisions, unless steps were taken to harmonize those provisions themselves.

Further complexity would be introduced if agreements with overlapping membership provided for different tariff rates or different rules of origin to apply to the same product traded between the same partners. In the one existing Asia-Pacific case for which the necessary information is available, the overlap between the NZSCEP and the TPSEP, exporters will apparently be able to choose between the different rules of origin in each agreement, but this will have no implications for tariff treatment, since tariffs on all trade between New Zealand and Singapore were already eliminated under the NZSCEP. Where two agreements provide different tariffs for the same product traded between the same partners, this could be handled by providing that the lower of the two tariff rates should apply, as is done in the case of the overlap between the DR-CAFTA agreement and the Central American Common Market. The issue becomes more problematic however if the rules of origin also differ, so that exporters must choose between two different combinations of tariff rate and rule of origin, as is also the case in the DR-CAFTA agreement. No cases of the latter kind appear to have arisen in the Asia-Pacific region as yet, but they cannot be ruled out for the future.

The picture in the Asia-Pacific will change considerably in the longer term, when the provisions for liberalization of trade in goods in all agreements have been fully implemented. Under these conditions tariffs and other trade barriers will have been removed on most products in trade between the members of the various agreements, although significant exclusions in some agreements may well remain. The discrimination or fragmentation of trading relationships that will remain in the region under these conditions will arise from three sources: differences in the pattern of product exclusions in the different agreements, gaps in the coverage of the region by PTAs, and differences in ROOs. These differences will also stand as obstacles to the establishment of region-wide integration through amalgamation of the different PTAs.

This analysis suggests that three considerations are important for minimizing the longer term obstacles to convergence of the provisions on trade in goods among Asia-Pacific PTAs. First, the extent of permanent product exclusions in each PTA should be minimized. Second, ways need to be found to overcome the existing obstacles to liberalization of regional trade flows that are not yet covered by existing arrangements. Third, steps should be taken to resolve the debate over the preferred type of ROO, and to reach consensus both on the type of ROO to be used in the region and how it should be applied to each industry or sector.

The third of these lines of attack, the move towards a common approach to ROOs, is both extremely important and also an appropriate area for regional consultation and cooperation, for example within APEC. The debate over the relative merits of the two main competing types of ROO ought in principle to be resolvable at a technical level, although the difficulties of doing so in practice should not be underestimated. Reaching consensus on how a given type of ROO should be applied across industries and across agreements will, however, be a very difficult task, since the more restrictive ROO provisions in particular have generally been introduced to accommodate deeply entrenched vested interests, and will not be easily surrendered.

One possible alternative approach may be to consider allowing different ROO to operate in parallel across the region. The availability of the different ROOs in the TPSEP and NZSCEP may provide a limited experiment in using this approach. In this case, however, the situation is greatly assisted by the fact that the tariff remains the same (i.e. zero) regardless of the ROO used. Elsewhere in the region, allowing the operation of different ROOs in parallel would be problematic until the tariffs associated with the use of each ROO are also reduced to zero. Even then, proposals to allow different ROOs to be used in parallel would face opposition from the same vested interests that have supported establishment of the existing divergent ROOs in the first place.

The alternative to reaching agreement on a common regional approach to ROOs is that the fragmentation of regional markets brought about by the proliferation of PTAs in the region will persist indefinitely, to the extent that differences in ROOs remain significant and the liberalization achieved in PTAs is not multilateralized.

Trade in Services

Liberalization of trade in services inevitably involves behind-the-border measures, since most barriers to services trade are regulatory in nature. It will also inevitably be a highly controversial subject, since the barriers to services trade are typically embedded in regulations that have been developed to serve legitimate purposes, and also since there are often deep political and social sensitivities surrounding foreign involvement in some service sectors. Liberalization is also complicated by the different ways that services can be supplied, now generally represented by the four modes of supply recognized in the GATS.

A particular issue that has had to be addressed in the treatment of services trade in PTAs is the relationship between GATS Mode 3 (commercial presence) and investment, since commercial presence necessarily involves investment and many modern PTAs also include an investment chapter.[8] The issue is further complicated by the fact that whereas GATS Mode 3 in principle involves liberalization of both pre-establishment and post-establishment phases of investment in service industries, investment chapters in some PTAs contain only post-establishment provisions, while others contain both pre- and post-establishment provisions. The post-establishment provisions of investment chapters in PTAs may go well beyond GATS-type services measures in the extent of investor-protection provided.

In PTAs in the Asia-Pacific region, as elsewhere, a stylized distinction has come to be recognized between two approaches to the liberalization of services trade and to the relation between services trade and investment provisions, although in reality there are a number of variations on each approach. One approach is known as the GATS approach, in which the services trade provisions essentially follow the structure of the GATS, detailing commitments in each mode of supply for the sectors covered, on a positive list basis. In agreements following this approach the investment chapter may apply only to non-services sectors. If the investment chapter includes post-establishment provisions only, this means that the only pre-establishment commitments on investment in the agreement will be those contained in the services commitments on Mode 3. At the other extreme it would be possible for the services provisions to contain only very limited pre-establishment commitments, while the investment chapter contains much more extensive pre-establishment commitments for other sectors.

The second approach is often referred to as the "NAFTA approach". In this case the services chapter typically covers both GATS Modes 1 and 2 under the heading of "cross-border supply" of services. Investment in all sectors is covered in the investment chapter, which may include both pre-establishment and post-establishment provisions. A negative list approach to sectoral coverage is adopted. GATS Mode 4 (movement of natural persons) may be covered in a separate annex.

There are at least two difficulties involved in linking the services provisions of different PTAs. First, there is the question of excluding commitments in sensitive sectors and modes of supply, and of allowing exceptions to the commitments in the sectors and modes of supply where commitments are made.[9] In the "positive list" modality followed in the GATS approach, the sectors and modes of supply in which commitments are made, and exceptions to those commitments, are specified. Under the "negative list" modality of the "NAFTA approach" sectors and modes of supply in which commitments are not made must be listed, and then a list of "non-conforming" measures details the departures from full liberalization in the sectors and modes of supply that are not excluded. In principle the same exclusions and reservations could be achieved under both approaches, but the "NAFTA approach" is much more demanding since it requires that a decision be made, explicitly or implicitly, for every sector and mode of supply.

In general it is likely that more far-reaching commitments will have been made in agreements following the NAFTA approach. This highlights the second difficulty in linking different agreements, which arises when one of the agreements has followed the GATS approach while the other has followed the NAFTA approach. It may be difficult for members of an agreement that has followed the GATS approach to accept the reduced flexibility likely to be involved in the agreement that has followed the NAFTA approach.

"Trade Plus Provisions"

There is great diversity in both the coverage and content of "trade-plus" provisions in Asia-Pacific PTAs. Developed economies such as the United States, Japan, Australia and New Zealand have typically sought inclusion of a full range of such provisions: investment, standards and conformance, customs procedures, intellectual property, government procurement, competition policy, electronic commerce, and sometimes trade remedies. There are exceptions; for example there is no investment chapter in the TPSEP.

At the other end of the spectrum, ASEAN has sought to limit the issue coverage in the "ASEAN-Plus" agreements to goods, services, investment and dispute settlement, even though individual ASEAN members may have accepted wider issue coverage in bilateral FTAs with the same partners. ASEAN has also favoured a sequential approach to the negotiation of provisions, with trade in goods provisions being negotiated first, followed successively by negotiation of services, investment and dispute settlement. The China-Chile FTA has been concluded initially as a goods-only agreement, leaving other provisions to be possibly negotiated later. Developed economies on the other hand have generally sought comprehensive issue coverage from the outset in their FTAs.

There is however considerable variation in the content of "trade-plus" provisions of the Asia-Pacific FTAs with comprehensive issue coverage. The key difference is between provisions containing "soft" obligations that impose no substantive requirements on the parties and are not usually subject to dispute settlement, and provisions containing "hard" obligations that require the parties to undertake specific actions or refrain from specific actions, and that may be subject to dispute settlement. Provisions with "soft" obligations are generally expressed in terms of "best efforts" and "agreements to cooperate and exchange information", and are likely to represent compromises between the divergent preferences of developed and developing economy partners.

The variation in levels of ambition of the "trade-plus" provisions in Asia-Pacific FTAs may reflect, in unknown proportions, simple differences in degrees of readiness to take on "hard" obligations, and conflicts over what the content of any "hard" obligations should be. One area of clear conflict is over intellectual property provisions. In part, the conflict in this area is over enforcement, but there is also a conflict over the optimum extent of intellectual property protection that should be provided, reflecting divergence between the interests of the producers and consumers of intellectual property, overlaid by considerations such as the importance of adequate intellectual property protection in attracting FDI. Other areas of overt conflict have been environmental standards, labour standards, and capital controls. In the area of environmental and labour standards however, the United States, as the principal *demandeur* in this area, appears to be moving away from an insistence on "hard" obligations, in favour of agreements to cooperate on environmental and labour matters.

"Variable Geometry", Templates, and Prospects for Convergence

The variety of coverage and content in the "trade-plus" provisions of Asia-Pacific FTAs suggests that a "variable geometry" approach might offer the best prospects for convergence. This could involve a single agreement in which the members assume different ranges and levels of obligations, possibly on the basis of agreed criteria that might include levels of development. It could also involve overlapping agreements, where one agreement containing "core" provisions, to which all parties subscribe, coexists with separate agreements in which more advanced obligations are assumed by subsets of the members of the "core" agreement that are in a position to do so. This would appear to be one possible way in which the relations between "ASEAN Plus" FTAs and bilateral FTAs of individual ASEAN members will eventually be defined.

There is however a countervailing tendency for some developed APEC economies, especially the United States, to adhere to an "FTA template", in which the coverage and content of "trade-plus" provisions is fully specified. This "template" is reportedly presented to prospective FTA partners as a "single undertaking" that must be accepted in its entirety, with little variation. Convergence then depends on the willingness of the prospective partner to accept the "template". A prospective partner for whom parts of the "template" are unwelcome is faced with the choice between swallowing its objections and accepting the unwelcome provisions, or opting out of the proposed FTA.

A particular problem for convergence arises if more than one major economy establishes its own FTA "template", and if there are inconsistencies between the different "templates". The outlook then is for the establishment of multiple "hub and spoke" configurations centred on each major economy as a "hub", where the FTAs in each configuration converge on the "template" of the "hub", but where the prospect of convergence between the configurations with their inconsistent "templates" is remote. Other economies may then either seek to follow one of the "hub" templates in their own FTAs, as Mexico has tended to do (essentially following the NAFTA template), or, if they seek to participate in more than one "hub and spoke" configuration, be willing to adapt the design of their FTAs to the "template" of each configuration, as Chile and Singapore have tended to do.

VI. ROLE FOR APEC'S "MODEL PROVISIONS"

APEC is currently embarked on a programme of developing "model provisions" for RTAs/FTAs, with a target of producing a full range of agreed "model provisions" by 2008. Draft model provisions have already been put forward in the following areas: trade in goods, services, investment, trade facilitation, technical barriers to trade, government procurement, safeguards, e-commerce and dispute settlement. Reaction to these drafts suggests that the drafters have done well, but also that consensus on "model provisions" will be difficult to achieve.

These "model provisions" obviously have a potentially valuable role to play in promoting convergence among Asia-Pacific PTAs. The contribution of the "model provisions" will be especially valuable if agreement can be reached on the full range of provisions, and if APEC economies demonstrate a willingness to put the "model provisions" into practice. Given the conflicts that exist over the design of some of the more controversial provisions, such as intellectual property, a substantial degree of compromise is likely to be needed in order for agreement to be reached on a full set of "model provisions", and it remains to be seen whether this will be attainable. The most valuable and most vital "model provision" would be a model provision on rules of origin that specifies in as much detail as possible the approach to be taken to rules of origin in Asia-Pacific PTAs.

A full set of "model provisions" could be very useful in both the "variable geometry" and "template scenarios". Under a "variable geometry" approach, confidence in the eventual outcome could be strengthened if even those FTA members making limited commitments do so in line with the "model provisions", and if it is understood that the further components of the "model provisions" will be adopted in the fullness of time. Under the "template" approach, acceptance of a full set of "model provisions" could overcome the potential problem of inconsistent "templates", highlighted above.

VII. CONCLUSIONS

There has been modest progress towards linking some PTAs in the Asia-Pacific region. It would not be realistic however to suggest that a self-sustaining process leading to full integration across the Asia-Pacific region though linking the region's PTAs is under way.

There are major gaps in the coverage by PTAs of the region's trade flows. The gaps include trade flows between the region's largest economies. The existence of these gaps indicates the existence of serious obstacles to the liberalization of trade flows between these major economies in the region, and these obstacles are in turn major impediments to achievement of region-wide free trade.

There is great diversity in the provisions of the region's PTAs, reflecting the different ways in which members of different PTAs have addressed their particular sensitivities.

In the short and medium term the diversity in the provisions of the region's PTAs relating to liberalization of trade in goods creates very complex patterns of discrimination and fragmentation. In the longer term a significant part of the complexity will be eliminated when the provisions of all agreements have been fully implemented. Even then however differences may remain in the pattern of product exclusions in the different agreements, there may be significant gaps in the coverage of regional trade by the various agreements, and the region's markets will continue to be divided by the different rules of origin in the different agreements unless steps have been taken to harmonize rules of origin in the meantime.

Taking steps towards the adoption of a common approach to rules of origin could be one of the most difficult but also one of the most important contributions to avoiding the long-term fragmentation of regional markets by PTAs. This would require reaching consensus first on which of the two main competing approaches to rules of origin should be preferred, and then reaching a further consensus on how the preferred approach to rules of origin should be applied across industries in the different PTAs across the region.

Finding ways to link the services provisions of the region, and to harmonize the different approaches to the relation between services and investment provisions, is likely to involve especially difficult challenges.

The diversity in the coverage and content of "trade-plus" provisions in Asia-Pacific PTAs suggests that a "variable geometry" approach to these provisions may be necessary if the FTAs are to be successfully linked. On the other hand insistence by major economies on non-negotiable FTA templates may inhibit region-wide convergence while encouraging convergence within separate "hub and spoke" configurations.

APEC's programme to develop agreed "model provisions" for RTAs/FTAs can make a substantial contribution towards convergence among the FTAs in the region, especially if agreement can be reached on the full range of provisions, and if APEC economies demonstrate a willingness to put the "model provisions" into practice. The most valuable "model provision", but also the provision on which agreement is likely to be most difficult to reach, would be a model provision on rules of origin that specifies in as much detail as possible the approach to be taken to rules of origin in Asia-Pacific PTAs.

Notes

1. A comparison of the Singapore-Korea and ASEAN-Korea FTAs could not be made for this paper, as the text of the latter has not yet been sighted.
2. Modern PTAs typically contain provisions on some or all of the following: investment, standards and conformance, customs procedures, intellectual property, government procurement, competition policy, and electronic commerce. The term "trade-plus" is applied here to these provisions purely for convenience, to distinguish provisions in these areas from measures liberalizing trade in goods and services.
3. GATT Article XXIV and the Enabling Clause contain the WTO rules for provisions on trade in goods in PTAs. GATS Article V contains the corresponding rules for provisions on trade in services. The rules are almost universally agreed to be unsatisfactory, and the possibility of amending them was included as an agenda item in the DDA negotiations. The prospect of securing meaningful change in the rules has however generally been assessed as minimal or zero, even before the DDA negotiations were suspended.
4. There is no formal definition of "developing country" in the WTO. Developing country status is thus a matter of self-selection. Among Asia-Pacific economies Singapore, Hong Kong, Chinese Taipei, Korea and Mexico typically present themselves as developing economies in the WTO context, even though the latter two are OECD members and the first two named have per capita incomes exceeding those of many OECD members.
5. In the case of the ASEAN Free Trade Area (AFTA) a target of 0 to 5 per cent was initially set for tariff reductions. The target was later amended to 0 per cent.
6. WTO efforts on rules of origin have been limited to non-preferential rules of origin. A combined WTO/World Customs Organisation programme, mandated

by the Uruguay Round, to establish an agreed set of non-preferential rules of origin, is many years behind schedule. There has been no move to establish multilateral rules on preferential rules of origin.

7. The way that value added is defined often differs between agreements, and has significant implications. The level (e.g. 4-digit or 6-digit) at which CTC rules are specified can also vary, and also has significant implications.

8. This issue does not arise in the GATS itself, because there is no WTO agreement on investment.

9. There is no Enabling Clause for trade in services.

8

ASEAN Perspective on Promoting Regional and Global Freer Trade

Chia Siow Yue and Hadi Soesastro

I. INTRODUCTION

ASEAN provides a "reality check" for regionalism in East Asia and the wider Asia-Pacific region. It can suggest the kind of regional cooperation that can be promoted and the extent to which regional integration can be deepened.

Two points need to be made at the outset. The first is that the ASEAN region consists of a diverse set of countries, some of which have gained independence and sovereignty only within the previous generation. There are major gaps in their economic capabilities, and some have begun to open up economic and political systems only in the last decade. And yet, they have come together and committed themselves to the creation of an ASEAN Community. The second is that ASEAN has been engaged in efforts to promote cooperation and community building with other nations in the wider regional context of East Asia and the Asia-Pacific region, both bilaterally through regular exchanges with Dialogue Partners and regionally in the ASEAN Plus Three (APT), the ASEAN Regional Forum (ARF), the

Asia Pacific Economic Cooperation (APEC) process, and even inter-regionally with Europe through the Asia Europe Meeting (ASEM) and Latin America through the Forum for East Asia Latin America Cooperation (FEALAC). These interactions have an impact on ASEAN cooperation, and have also resulted in dynamic developments in the wider region.

I.1. ASEAN Style of Regionalism

In Asia, ASEAN is the first attempt at regional community building. ASEAN is an ongoing experiment in community building. It began in 1967 as a regional cooperation arrangement to promote welfare and peace in Southeast Asia. In that sense, it was based on some vision of regional order and regional community. Building this regional community began with some modesty. The regional arrangement sought to promote cooperation in the economic and social fields. This was understandable. The region had just opened up a new page in its history. Having gained independence and having experienced continued internal turmoil for about two decades, and more importantly, having ended political animosities, the five original members of ASEAN embarked on the path of community building by taking steps to learn more about each other and to learn to live together in harmony and peace.

It took these countries almost a decade to bring their leaders together for the first Summit meeting. That happened in 1976 in Bali. From then on, several concrete cooperation programmes were introduced. They included the ASEAN Industrial Projects (AIP), the ASEAN Preferential Trading Arrangement (PTA), ASEAN Industrial Joint Venture (AIJV), and ASEAN Industrial Cooperation (AICO), to name some of the more important programmes. ASEAN members began to learn how to cooperate and work together to achieve some common objectives. They were prepared to pool their resources, but they were unprepared to share their markets. Therefore, there were continuing tensions between "resource pooling" and "market sharing" in implementing and upgrading the cooperation programmes. As a result, not much progress was achieved in the field of economic cooperation.

ASEAN's founding fathers did not envision the economic integration of the region. In their view, that was a remote possibility, perhaps even an impossibility. However, gradually regional economies became more integrated. It was the remarkable economic growth of regional countries and gradual economic reform and opening up that greatly increased their economic interactions. This was not a direct result of ASEAN economic cooperation programmes. Rather, the region saw the working of "market-driven" integration.

This market-driven integration was not independent of developments in the political field and the intensification of ASEAN external relations. As the region turned into an ocean of stability and peace, thanks to the establishment of the regional forum, national governments were able to concentrate on national economic development. In the two decades until the middle of the 1990s, the region was growing at an average rate of 7 per cent or more. This made the region even more attractive for trade relations with and investment from other parts of the world. The wave of Japanese foreign direct investment (FDI) following the Plaza Accord in 1985 further deepened the development of regional production networks.

ASEAN has had established dialogues with its main trading partners since the late 1970s. These dialogues helped shape trade, aid and investment policies of ASEAN's main dialogue partners in enhancing cooperation with ASEAN. In turn they also contributed to ASEAN's increased diplomatic clout in the international arena.

Increased political cooperation among ASEAN members was a manifestation of the growing need to coordinate their views and policies in regard to international and regional strategic and political developments. The fall of Saigon changed the region's political map, but the wave of "boat people" from Vietnam and the subsequent invasion of Cambodia by Vietnamese forces created potential sources of instability for Southeast Asia. ASEAN's determination to help resolve the conflict in Indochina provided strong glue for ASEAN's cohesion. ASEAN's efforts were supported by the international community. Its international standing was at its height and signified ASEAN's success.

It was felt, however, that the region needed to step up its economic cooperation to be able to effectively respond to economic globalization. There was much talk about the need to take "bold" decisions in the economic field. Eventually these led to the decision in 1992 to establish the ASEAN Free Trade Area (AFTA). Its boldness was the agreement to promote regional economic integration through resource pooling *and* market sharing. The ASEAN leaders produced a new kind of community building, namely one that stresses more on openness to each other, economically, socially as well as politically. ASEAN, it was argued, should have reached a state of maturity that allows them to be more open to each other. Due to growing interdependence, developments in one member country are likely to have a greater effect on the neighbours and the region as a whole. Thus came about the calls for "enhanced interaction" that allows for greater openness to comments and suggestions from fellow members on internal developments.

Another major move was the expansion of membership to finally complete the "One Southeast Asia" project. It was remarkable that in the middle of the 1990s ASEAN accepted the membership of Vietnam, its erstwhile enemy. A few years later, Laos and Myanmar were also brought in. Cambodia's membership was delayed because of its internal developments. By the late 1990s, all Southeast Asian countries had become members of ASEAN, realizing the founding fathers' dream. The broadening of ASEAN has become a challenge to ASEAN's deepening. The new members have to take part in AFTA, but they are each given a longer time to implement the trade liberalization programme. In reality, a two-tier ASEAN has emerged. This should not be a problem so long as they share a common goal.

ASEAN Vision 2020 was formulated to provide such a common goal. Its implementation was guided by the Hanoi Plan of Action (HPA). At the mid-term review of the HPA, it was felt that ASEAN members must have stronger commitments to realize the ASEAN Vision 2020. This led to the proposal to deepen ASEAN economic integration towards an ASEAN Economic Community (AEC). By the time Indonesia hosted the Summit in Bali in 2003, ASEAN members agreed to create an ASEAN Community by 2020. As stated in the so-called Bali Concord II, the ASEAN Community consists of an ASEAN Economic Community, an ASEAN Security Community, and an ASEAN Social and Cultural Community. At the following Summit in Vientiane, leaders endorsed a Vientiane Action Programme (VAP) to guide the process of community building in ASEAN for the next five years.

It has taken ASEAN nearly forty years to come to the point where its members agree to form a Community (with a capital C) and not simply a community (with a lowercase c). They have about fifteen more years to realize this vision. This remains a big challenge for ASEAN. It can be argued that this next phase in the integration process will be much more difficult.

The ASEAN model of community building, when contrasted to other experiences, is seen as having a distinct characteristic, namely its loose and open-ended process and its reliance on minimal institutional arrangements. These, plus the principle of consensus and the sanctity of national sovereignty, have characterized the so-called ASEAN way. However, the ASEAN way has undergone a modification. ASEAN's mode of operation has evolved from one that was based on full consensus to one that allows for the emergence of the coalition of the willing. Several members also believe that the sanctity of national sovereignty can no longer be used as a protection against irresponsible actions. A new ASEAN way may be necessary to realize the ASEAN Community.

The experiment will continue. To some extent the ASEAN experience and experiment have inspired community building in the wider region.

I.2. ASEAN and Regionalism in Asia Today

Regionalism has become a "booming" industry in Asia. There are many initiatives to form regional cooperation processes. They can be found at the inter-governmental level as well as at the non-governmental level, and they involve different subsets of countries in the region.

These initiatives have different objectives and manifestations: they may be aimed at strengthening functional cooperation in a variety of areas, developing regional mechanisms and institutions, promoting regional economic integration, as well as establishing a regional community.

It is important to again review the main principles for organizing the region that have emerged from the many discussions involving a wide range of regional stakeholders. They were clearly spelled out in the early years (1980s and 1990s), but in later years they have become blurred.

The first principle is "open regionalism". Regionalism in Asia should not be an inward-looking and discriminatory type of arrangement. When ASEAN formed AFTA, this principle appeared to have been violated. However, ASEAN never meant to create an inward-oriented regional market (an "internal ASEAN" market). ASEAN's trade is predominantly with non-ASEAN countries. Its main objective was to create a competitive regional economy that becomes attractive to global investors that will use it as a production and export platform for global markets. The principle of "open regionalism" in action in ASEAN is manifested in the reduction of MFN tariffs in parallel to or in some instances faster than the AFTA (CEPT) preferential tariffs.

APEC's liberalization agenda is also based on this principle. Liberalization, i.e., removal of trade barriers, is undertaken unilaterally by each APEC economy but in a concerted manner. This modality is known as "concerted unilateral liberalization". There are views questioning the efficacy of this modality. However, APEC is a non-binding process. As such, this modality is the only feasible one. If this process has not delivered on the expectations, this could well be due to the weak "peer" process (pressure) that should drive trade liberalization.

There are two views on the future direction of APEC economic cooperation. Those that are unhappy with the results so far have demanded a radical change towards a formal Free Trade Area of the Asia-Pacific (FTAAP). The status quo group argues that the FTAAP is contrary to the principle of "open regionalism" — and the political feasibility of the FTAAP proposal is highly problematic because the region is so diverse. It could well be that because a region-wide FTA is almost impossible, countries have resorted to subregional and even bilateral arrangements. These have proliferated lately, especially in Asia and the Asia-Pacific region.

The second principle is that regional community building is much more than trade liberalization. It is a comprehensive undertaking and at least must include the following aspects: liberalization, facilitation, and development cooperation. In APEC these aspects have been translated into the TILF (trade and investment liberalization and facilitation) agenda and the ECOTECH (economic and technical cooperation) agenda. In the past few years two other agenda items have been added, namely human security and governance.

The focus, however, remains largely on trade liberalization. APEC's progress is measured in terms of progress in its trade liberalization agenda. This is so because the goals of APEC community building have been narrowly defined as "achieving free and open trade and investment in the region by 2010 for the developed economies and 2020 for the developing economies" (Bogor Goals).

In ASEAN, the focus of economic cooperation is in the realization of the ASEAN Free Trade Area (AFTA) at the latest by 2015 (for some CLMV countries [Cambodia, Laos, Myanmar and Vietnam] and certain agricultural commodities), while the goals and process towards an ASEAN Economic Community (AEC) by 2020 remain ill-defined.[1]

It is reality that FTAs have become to be seen as the main manifestation of regional economic cooperation. They are being broadened to include other aspects, such as investment, competition policy, and a number of behind-border issues. These more comprehensive agreements are called "new age" agreements, EPAs (economic partnership agreements) or CEC (comprehensive economic cooperation) agreements.

They involve hard-nosed negotiations among participating economies as they revolve around exchanges of concessions. The whole atmosphere of "confidence and community building" is being reduced to a game of bargaining. The other aspects of cooperation have been overshadowed by this exercise in bargaining. This is not the idea of Asian community building that is characterized by sharing, solidarity, and mutual support.

East Asia community building, proclaimed to be different from that of APEC because it does not involve such countries as the United States, is in danger of falling into the same trap as other regional initiatives. It lacks innovative ideas to go beyond forming an FTA in developing its institutional identity.

ASEAN is pretty much in the forefront in developing comprehensive FTAs with a number of countries: China, Japan, Korea, India, and Australia and New Zealand. It is also exploring similar arrangements with the EU (European Union) and EFTA (European Free Trade Area) . There is also the Enterprise for the ASEAN Initiative which will consist of bilateral FTAs between the United States and selected ASEAN countries.

In addition, many Asian countries are forming bilateral FTAs with other countries inside and outside the region, causing problems of managing an Asian "noodle bowl".

In theory, ASEAN could play a significant role in maintaining coherence and consistency in all these initiatives because it is placed in the centre stage. This is the main challenge for ASEAN as well as for the region as a whole, but ASEAN still lacks a clear and firm strategy to perform this critical role.[2]

I.3. Consolidating Individual ASEAN Countries' Approaches

Members of ASEAN do not as yet have a single, common approach or perspective on how to develop their role in the development of regionalism in the wider region.

Singapore is perhaps the strongest advocate and practitioner of FTAs in ASEAN, followed by Thailand and Malaysia (see Table 8.1). At the same time, Singapore is also the most trade-dependent and most open economy

TABLE 8.1
FTA Status of ASEAN Countries, at end 2006

Country	Proposed	Framework Agreement signed/under negotiation	Under negotiation	Concluded and signed	Under implementation	Total
Brunei Darussalam	3	2	2	1	3	11
Cambodia	2	2	1	1	2	8
Indonesia	5	3	2	2	2	14
Lao PDR	2	2	1	1	4	10
Malaysia	5	3	5	2	3	18
Myanmar	2	3	1	1	2	9
Philippines	4	2	1	2	2	11
Singapore	5	2	9	1	12	29
Thailand	6	6	4	1	6	23
Vietnam	2	2	2	1	2	9

Source: Compiled from www.aric.adb.org.

in ASEAN and in the global economy; it has removed all MFN applied tariffs under the WTO and is a strong supporter of trade and investment liberalization under the WTO, APEC and ASEAN. Singapore is a living example of the benefits of an open economy and the ability to undertake structural reforms to meet the challenges of globalization. The strong government interest in bilateral FTAs in recent years has been spurred by the slow and uncertain progress in global and regional trade and investment liberalization under WTO, APEC and ASEAN.

The Singapore government views FTAs as building blocks towards global and APEC freer trade. Formation of bilateral FTAs among like-minded partners is seen as a way to avoid the problem in which the pace of trade liberalization is held back unnecessarily. It may also trigger other FTAs with its strategic partners like the case of Japan-Singapore EPA leading to the Japan-ASEAN initiative and the U.S.-Singapore FTA leading to the U.S. Enterprise for ASEAN Initiative. Singapore entered into several FTAs with APEC countries (New Zealand, Australia, Japan, United States and South Korea in force, and Canada, Mexico, Chile under negotiation). Bilateral FTAs enable Singapore to widen and deepen the scope of economic cooperation to achieve targeted results, hence the features of FTA plus and WTO plus. The network of FTAs is also aimed at developing an integrated manufacturing centre in the region; nurturing a knowledge-based economy; and driving the services hub. FTAs improved market access and Singapore's attractions for foreign investors.

In negotiating bilateral FTAs, Singapore is committed to "high quality", going beyond the provisions of GATT Article XXIV and GATS Article V. Negotiations have generally been smooth not only because Singapore has no sensitive agricultural sector; it also does not protect its manufacturing and most of its services sectors, is prepared to open its economy to foreign investors and protect intellectual property rights, and is prepared to undertake continuing domestic reforms to further open up its economy.

In the case of Indonesia, FTAs in the form of RTAs, such as AFTA, are largely seen as a means to strengthen the region's position in the global economy as well as a part of regional community building. FTAs only figure in Indonesia's international economic strategy insofar as they help strengthen Indonesia's unilateral trade liberalization.

As of the beginning of 2006, besides AFTA, Indonesia is involved in only one FTA, namely with China, but through the China-ASEAN FTA. It is involved in ASEAN's FTA negotiations with Korea, India, and Australia-

New Zealand CER. It is negotiating a bilateral FTA with Japan, aimed at concluding an agreement in 2007, to be placed within the larger ASEAN-Japan framework agreement.

All these ASEAN-centred FTAs are seen by Indonesia as an extension of AFTA, to be strengthened by efforts to deepen integration in ASEAN towards an ASEAN Economic Community (AEC). For Indonesia, the rationale for forming these FTAs is the same as joining AFTA.

There have been talks and studies undertaken on Indonesia's bilateral FTAs with a number of developing countries (Chile, South Africa, Iran, Pakistan and Bangladesh) and with the United States and EFTA. FTAs with the developing countries are likely to be insignificant and shallow. No major attention and efforts are given to come to an agreement to begin negotiating them. An Indonesia-U.S. FTA is in the agenda, but the two sides are far from agreeing on starting the negotiations. Recently, Indonesia de-emphasized its efforts towards a bilateral FTA with the United States. Instead it puts serious efforts in strengthening its TIFA (trade and investment framework agreement) with the United States.

Indonesia is a laggard and late-comer in the FTA game, but it is also not pursuing it proactively. How, for instance, will Indonesia play a role in pursuing an East Asia FTA (EAFTA)? There is not yet much talk in Indonesia about EAFTA. If other members of the ASEAN Plus Three are eager to develop EAFTA, Indonesia will go along. But Indonesia will not proactively promote EAFTA.

In the Indonesian policy community, the belief is that at the present moment, the region can only go so far as forming bilateral FTAs between ASEAN with each of the Plus Three partners, China, Japan, and Korea. The main preoccupation here is to have three separate and good agreements. The Indonesian business community is more sympathetic to an EAFTA and other FTAs, largely because of a concern that if Indonesia is not taking part in them, Indonesian exporters will be placed at a disadvantageous position vis-à-vis those in neighbouring countries.

Only in the academic circles in Indonesia is there talk about ASEAN's important role in setting the agenda in the wider East Asian region to ensure that the three separate agreements have some consistency and coherence so that eventually they could be amalgamated into a single East Asia FTA.

Not much thought has been given so far whether India, Australia and New Zealand, who are participants in the EAS (East Asia Summit) and with whom ASEAN also is negotiating FTAs, will also be included in an EAFTA. More recently, in August 2006, Japan has proposed a CEPEA (Comprehensive Economic Partnership Arrangement in East Asia) comprising of ASEAN Plus Six (China, Japan, Korea, India, Australia and New Zealand) However, it is desirable that the agreements with these countries would follow the same template.

Indonesia is unlikely to provide leadership in forming an East Asia FTA. However, if one were to be formed, Indonesia will make sure that it will preserve the basic "outward orientation" as is the case of AFTA, be an efficient agreement by minimizing distortions and unnecessary transactions cost (for example, caused by the "noodle bowl" syndrome), and one that has built-in mechanisms to reduce gaps amongst its participants.

II. THE ASEAN MODEL REVISITED

The ASEAN economic integration model is very different from that of NAFTA or EU. ASEAN was created in 1967 for political and security reasons and its founding fathers did not have economic integration in mind. The first efforts at economic cooperation, not integration, began in 1976 with a preferential trading scheme followed by industrial cooperation schemes. The first serious effort at economic integration was the decision in 1992 to form AFTA. It was established in response to external "threats" of globalization, the emergence of NAFTA and the EU Single Market, and the rise of China.

II.1. ASEAN Economic Integration in the 1990s

The agreement establishing AFTA consisted of only a few pages, unlike the NAFTA document of over 1,000 pages. It was more a political declaration of intent rather than a legal document and detailed roadmap of economic integration. Rules of origin had to be worked out and negotiated much later. There were no safeguard measures and no dispute settlement mechanism. AFTA covered only trade in goods, and had to be complemented by the ASEAN Framework Agreement on Services (AFAS) in 1995, and by the ASEAN Investment Area (AIA) in 1998. In 1997 ASEAN produced the ASEAN Vision 2020, with the aim to forge closer economic integration and narrowing the development gap between older and newer members. Each major step taken on ASEAN economic integration was taken in response to external threats and developments.

Critics point to the slow progress in ASEAN economic integration despite the numerous initiatives.[3] Many factors were cited as responsible — lack of political will; individual ASEAN economies were more oriented and dependent for trade and investment on North America, Western Europe, Japan and the Asian NIEs than on each other; lack of economic complementarity as ASEAN economies produce similar primary products and labour-intensive manufactures and compete in the same export markets and for the same foreign investors; the wide development gap and industrial and technological competence among ASEAN members; and different commitments to an open economy.

ASEAN did not report AFTA to WTO under GATT Article XXIV but under the Enabling Clause for Developing Countries. As conceived in 1992, AFTA did not cover "substantially all trade" and did not plan to bring tariffs down to zero within ten years.

The McKinsey study (2003) found that the many ASEAN initiatives have had limited impacts. For example: (i) intra-ASEAN trade share has not grown with implementation of AFTA; (ii) in 2000 less than 5 per cent of intra-ASEAN trade made use of the AFTA tariff preferences;[4] (iii) wide divergences exist in consumer prices of common household products in the region; (iv) economic complementarity, such as in the electronics sector, has not been well leveraged; and (v) progress with removal of non-tariff barriers has been slow, particularly with regard to harmonization of standards, implementation of mutual recognition agreements, and streamlining of customs procedures.

II.2. Towards an ASEAN Economic Community

The AEC is to be a single market and production base with a free flow of goods, services, investments, capital and skilled labour. The AEC was motivated by deep concerns over intensified competition for markets and investments from the economic rise of China and India. In 2003 China received US$53.3 billion in FDI compared with ASEAN's US$19 billion. An integrated ASEAN with a market of over 500 million people should help retain the region's attractiveness as an FDI destination, and as a viable alternative to China for MNCs cautious of putting all their eggs in the China basket. As momentum for East Asian integration gathers steam, speeding up ASEAN regional integration takes on a renewed urgency. ASEAN economic ministers on 15 May 2006 proposed to advance the AEC completion date to 2015 (instead of 2020). It is argued that, to remain in the driver's seat, ASEAN must be competitive and have certain leverages, otherwise focus will be more on China and India.

As laid out in the Vientiane Action Programme (VAP) for 2006–2010, activities to realize the AEC focus on four components: (i) intensify current economic initiatives and accelerating the integration of eleven priority sectors; (ii) remove, as far as possible, barriers to the free flow of goods, services, skilled labour, and a freer flow of capital by 2010; (iii) develop measures to attract investments, liberalize and facilitate trade in goods, promote regional trade in services, upgrade the competitiveness of ASEAN small and medium enterprises (SMEs), and strengthen the ASEAN dispute settlement system; and (iv) pursue strong external economic relations through free trade areas and comprehensive economic partnerships.

Prior to the Bali Concord that establishes the AEC, two proposals were put forward for the AEC in 2003. The first proposal by ISEAS[5] envisages the AEC as an "FTA plus" arrangement that covers a zero-tariff ASEAN FTA and some elements of a common market (free movement of capital and skilled labour). It argues that, given the different degrees of openness and stages of economic development among ASEAN countries, forming a customs union would be extremely difficult to achieve by the 2020 deadline. The proposal envisages the AEC to have the following characteristics — free movement of goods, services, investments and capital, including zero-tariff FTA and elimination of all non-tariff measures (NTMs); an attractive regional production platform that would be a magnet for FDI; free movement of skilled labour and creative talent; harmonization of customs procedures and minimization of customs requirements; harmonization of standards that are consistent with international standards; and a well-developed institutional and legal infrastructure to facilitate the economic integration of ASEAN.

The second proposal by ASEAN-ISIS[6] adopts a "common market minus" approach, that is, creation of a fully integrated market (common market) by 2020 but taking into account areas where members reserve deeper integration for a larger stage. A common market has complete free flows of trade, including internal trade (as in a customs union) as well as free mobility of labour and capital. Full mobility of labour involves the right to reside and seek employment in all member countries, and mutual recognition of professional and technical qualifications. Full capital mobility requires an absence of exchange controls and full rights of establishment for firms in all countries. Credible removal of tariffs may require policy harmonization or common policies in taxes, wages and prices. It may require common rules governing competition and monopoly as well as environmental regulations.

The High Level Task Force (HLTF)[7] on Economic Integration recommended that: the AEC should be: (i) the end goal of economic integration as outlined in the ASEAN Vision 2020; (ii) characterized as a single market and production base, with free flow of goods, services, investment and skilled labour, and freer flow of capital by 2020; and (iii) approached on a progressive basis with clear timelines by strengthening existing initiatives and building new initiatives to enhance economic integration. It is unclear what is meant by "a single market", since it does not include a common external trade policy or customs union.

Strengthening of Current Initiatives[8]

- *Rules of origin.* By end-2004, finalize the improvement to the CEPT Scheme Rules of Origin — by making it more transparent, predictable and standardized and adopting substantial transformation as alternative criteria for conferring origin status.
- *Non-tariff measures.* Ensure transparency of NTMs and eliminate those that are barriers to trade — Establish the ASEAN Database of NTMs by mid-2004; set clear criteria to identify measures that are classified as barriers to trade by mid-2005; set a clear and definitive work programme for the removal of the barriers by 2005; adopt the WTO agreements on Technical Barriers to Trade, Sanitary and Phytosanitary and Import Licensing Procedures, and develop implementation guidelines appropriate for ASEAN by end-2004.
- *Customs.* Ensure full implementation of the Green Lane system for CEPT products at entry points of all member countries by 2004; adopt WTO agreement on Customs Valuation and develop implementation guidelines appropriate for ASEAN by end-2004; adopt service commitment by ASEAN customs authorities; and adopt the Single Window approach including the electronic processing of trade documents at national and regional level.

- *Standards.* Accelerate the completion and implementation of the Mutual Recognition Agreements (MRAs) for the five identified priority sectors (electrical and electronic equipment, cosmetics, pharmaceuticals, telecommunications equipment, and prepared foodstuff) within 2004/ 05, and other sectors with significant potential for trade; set specific targets for the harmonization of standards and technical regulations to trade focusing on sectors with significant trade value and those with potential for trade in the future; develop ASEAN technical regulations, where possible, for national applications.
- *Trade in services.* Set clear targets and schedules of services liberalization for each sector and each round towards achieving free flow of trade in services and AEM to provide specific mandate in every round of service negotiations, with end-date to achieve free flow of trade in services earlier than 2020; accelerate services liberalization in specific sectors earlier than end-date by countries which are ready, through application of ASEAN-X formula;[9] complete MRAs for qualifications in major professional services by 2008 to facilitate free movement of professional/skilled labour/talents in ASEAN; promote the use of ASEAN professional services through establishment of "professional exchange" by 2008; recognize the AEM as the coordinator for services liberalization across all sectors; and each country to be represented by senior officials who are authorized to negotiate on behalf of the government. (At the AEM in September 2005, it was agreed to push forward the end-date for liberalization of all services sectors to 2015, with flexibility allowed for some sub-sectors. Senior officials were tasked to map out a roadmap to open up services sectors in all modes of supply.)
- *Investment.* Speed up the opening of sectors currently in the sensitive list to TEL, using the ASEAN-X formula, beginning 2004; encourage and promote companies to relocate within ASEAN and where appropriate, special incentives should be given; institute a mechanism to monitor the specific activities and timelines undertaken by each country vis-à-vis their submitted planned actions/activities on annual basis; establish a network of ASEAN free trade zones so that companies could structure their manufacturing processes across different ASEAN countries to take advantage of their comparative strengths and in the process increase intra-ASEAN trade and investment, and special marketing efforts should be undertaken for ASEAN-based companies;

and undertake more effective joint ASEAN facilitation and promotion measures and develop new sources of inward FDI, particularly from potential countries such as China, India and Republic of Korea.

- *Intellectual property rights.* ASEAN IPR cooperation beyond trademarks and patents by including cooperation in copyrights information exchange and enforcement by 2004.
- *Capital mobility.* To facilitate trade and investment flows, expedite the implementation of the Roadmap for Integration of ASEAN in Finance.

New Initiatives[10]

- *Priority integration sectors.* Fast tracking of trade and investment liberalization in specific sectors may help build capacity and constituency for further liberalization. ASEAN identified eleven sectors (later increased to twelve) for accelerated tariff elimination and trade and facilitation measures. Beginning in 2004, a roadmap is developed for each priority sector and implemented with the active involvement of the private sector. Possible measures proposed for the goods sectors — zero internal tariffs, immediate removal of barriers to trade, faster customs clearance and simplified customs procedures, accelerated development of MRAs and harmonization of product standards and technical regulations. Integration of services sectors include accelerated liberalization of these priority sectors by 2010, accelerated development of MRAs, and promote joint ventures and cooperation including in third-country markets. Facilitate mobility of business people and tourists through visa exemption for intra-ASEAN travel by ASEAN nationals by 2005; harmonizing the procedures for issuing visas to international travellers in ASEAN by 2004; and developing ASEAN agreement to facilitate movement of business persons and skilled labour and talents by 2005.
- *Institutional strengthening.* Streamline the decision-making process and ensure effective implementation of ASEAN economic initiatives. These include: (i) decision-making process by economic bodies to be made by consensus, and when there is no consensus; (ii) by end-2004, establish an effective dispute resolution system; and (iii) enhance the capability of the ASEAN Secretariat to conduct research and analytical studies related to trade, investment and finance.
- *Development and technical cooperation.* Address the development divide and accelerate the economic integration of CLMV.

II.3. Progress in Trade and Investment Liberalization

Trade in Goods Liberalization

AFTA originally had a timeframe of fifteen years, from 1993, to reduce tariffs to the 0–5 per cent target. ASEAN has progressively advanced AFTA's completion date and moved the tariff target to zero. The completion date was first advanced to 2003 and, in response to the 1997–98 financial crisis, was advanced further to 1 January 2002. As latecomers, the completion dates for CLMV were set at 2006 for Vietnam, 2008 for Laos and Myanmar, and 2010 for Cambodia. The zero-tariff target is to be achieved by 2010 for ASEAN-6 and 2015 for CLMV. Under the AEC, the eleven priority sectors have been identified for accelerated integration[11] cover about 4,000 tariff lines or about 40 per cent of the total tariff lines in ASEAN. As compared with AFTA deadlines of 2010 for ASEAN-6 and 2015 for CLMV, tariffs will be eliminated on 85 per cent of the products in the priority sectors by 2007 and 2012 respectively.

For ASEAN-6, by January 2005, 99 per cent of all products in the CEPT[12] Inclusion List have their tariffs reduced to the 0–5 per cent target, 64.2 per cent have achieved zero tariffs, all CEPT products have been transferred into the Inclusion List, and the average tariff brought down to 1.87 per cent as compared to 12.76 per cent in 1993. However, intra-ASEAN share of ASEAN's total exports remained stagnant, with 22.5 per cent in 2004 as compared with 21.1 per cent in 1993. For CLMV, 87.2 per cent of the products have been moved into the CEPT Inclusion List, and tariffs on 71.05 per cent have been brought down to the 0–5 per cent level.

As tariffs come tumbling down in AFTA, more emphasis is being placed on trade facilitation, especially customs barriers, electronic processing of trade documents, harmonization of product standards and technical regulations, and MRAs, including for test reports and certification.

Trade in Services Liberalization

Services trade liberalization under AFAS has been very slow and efforts are being made to accelerate it. Two flexibilities were introduced in 2003. First is the faster liberalization for modes 1 and 2 (cross-border supply and consumption abroad), and slower liberalization for modes 3 and 4 (commercial presence and presence of natural persons). Second, an "ASEAN minus X" formula allows two or more ASEAN countries to proceed first, with other members joining at a later date. MRAs are being negotiated to facilitate movement of experts, professional and skilled workers in ASEAN in engineering, architectural and accounting services, as well as nursing and medical practitioners. There are also measures to facilitate intra-ASEAN travel for ASEAN nationals and movement of business people, experts, professionals and talents.

Investment Liberalization

The AIA aims at making ASEAN a competitive and liberal investment area. It would enable investors to leverage on the various complementarities of the ASEAN region to improve business efficiency and lower costs, adopt regional business strategies and establish network operations. Originally confined to the manufacturing sector, investments under the AIA were later opened also to agriculture, mining, forestry and fishery sectors and services incidental to these sectors. ASEAN members are committed to gradually eliminate investment barriers, liberalize investment rules and policies, and grant national treatment to ASEAN investors by 2010 and to all other foreign investors by 2020. The end-dates for phasing out the temporary exclusion lists in manufacturing were set at January 2003 for ASEAN-6 and Myanmar, and January 2010 for CLV countries; for the other designated sectors, they are January 2010 for ASEAN-6 and Cambodia, 2013 for Vietnam, and 2016 for Laos and Myanmar.

III. ASEAN PLUS AGREEMENTS AS BUILDING BLOCKS?

ASEAN is currently negotiating ASEAN Plus One agreements with China, Japan, Australia–New Zealand, India and South Korea. They are all known as comprehensive agreements as they encompass trade in goods, trade in services, investment, trade facilitation, intellectual property, competition policy, government procurement, and wide-ranging areas of economic and functional cooperation. They are all initiated by ASEAN's trading partners and make ASEAN a de facto hub in East Asia. There is also the ASEAN Plus Three framework and the proposal for an East Asia FTA.

III.1. ASEAN Plus Agreements

The ASEAN Plus and bilateral FTA initiatives proliferated in the post-1997 period. Before that, there was only ASEAN and AFTA. There are a number of driving forces.

- *1997–98 Asian financial crisis.* The Crisis demonstrated the close economic and financial interdependence among Southeast and Northeast Asian economies. There was tremendous disappointment with the role of the IMF and the Washington consensus. The ASEAN Plus Three monetary and financial cooperation helps maintain regional economic stability and resilience. The Crisis also provided the forum for formal dialogue between Southeast Asia and Northeast Asia and to the emerging idea of an East Asian economic bloc.
- *Defensive reactions.* The strong interest in regional and bilateral FTAs was a defensive reaction to the competition from globalization, the slow progress in the WTO, and growing regionalism in the Americas and in Europe. The emergence of these continental blocs could impinge on ASEAN competitiveness in export markets and in attracting foreign investments.
- *Responding to the economic rise of China and overtures from major trading partners.* The economic rise of China and its WTO accession is changing the global and regional trade and investment landscape. There is a growing desire and need to strengthen economic relations with China, the emerging economic powerhouse in Asia. In 2001, at the ASEAN-China Summit, China proposed the establishment of an ASEAN-China FTA within ten years. This triggered a domino effect on Japan, South Korea, India, and Australia–New Zealand. Japan reacted to the China challenge to its dominant position in Southeast Asia. With Japan and China seeking FTAs with ASEAN, South Korea could not afford to be left behind. India saw the opportunities with ASEAN to expand its "Look East" policy. Australia and New Zealand CER (Closer Economic Partnership) have been pushing for closer economic relations with ASEAN for some years but did not succeed until political relations thawed. U.S. President Bush, during the APEC Summit in October 2002, announced the Enterprise for ASEAN Initiative, which will entail a series of bilateral FTAs with individual ASEAN countries. The latest "domino" is the proposed ASEAN-EU initiative,[13] seen as the EU response to being sidelined by ongoing ASEAN negotiations with China, Japan, South Korea, India and the United States.

ASEAN-China Framework Agreement and Comprehensive Economic Cooperation

Economic relations between ASEAN countries and China developed only after the end of the Cold War, although historically China has had long trade and people relations with Southeast Asia. China first proposed an FTA with ASEAN in November 2000 as part of a process of confidence building. It seeks to allay ASEAN concerns over the China challenge in export markets and in attracting foreign investment, as well as to access ASEAN's sizeable regional market and energy and raw material resources. For ASEAN, it will force the group as a whole to have a constructive engagement with China. ASEAN also views China as a rapidly growing market for its products and services (including tourism), and as a new engine of growth. The deal was made attractive for ASEAN with the Early Harvest Programme and with a special and preferential treatment and flexibility offered by China for CLMV. The China proposal will also bring ASEAN back to centre-stage. Thus ASEAN did not hesitate to accept China's offer.

The Framework Agreement on ASEAN-China Comprehensive Economic Cooperation (CEC) was signed in November 2002. Many of its components remain to be negotiated.

- An *Early Harvest Programme* (EHP) of tariff reduction and elimination, primarily in agricultural goods, was implemented on 1 January 2004 for three years. There is an Exclusion List and different time frames between ASEAN-6 and CLMV. The Philippines delayed its participation in the EHP.
- The *Agreement on Trade in Goods* was implemented in June 2005. It provides for tariff reduction and elimination along two tracks. For products on the normal track, tariff reductions would be completed by 2010 for ASEAN-6 and China, and by 2015 for CLMV. For products on the sensitive track, the tariff reduction schedule is determined by mutual agreement. The rules of origin are based on 40 per cent value added. Countries are committed to abide by provisions of WTO disciplines on NTM, TBT, SPS, subsidies and countervailing measures, anti-dumping measures and IPR, GATT Article XIX and WTO Agreement on Safeguards.
- Each ASEAN state agrees to recognize China as a full market economy.[14]
- The Agreement on Dispute Settlement Mechanism has also been signed, while negotiations on services and investment are ongoing.

ASEAN-Japan Framework Agreement and Comprehensive Economic Partnership

In recent decades, Japan has been a major trade and investment partner of Southeast Asia and its leading official development aid (ODA) donor. Japanese Prime Minister Koizumi proposed an economic partnership agreement with ASEAN in January 2002, during his visit to Singapore for the signing of the Japan-Singapore economic partnership agreement, and soon after China's FTA proposal to ASEAN. Japan was concerned over China's growing influence in Southeast Asia, and a formalized relationship would help consolidate its economic relations with ASEAN. In turn, ASEAN recognizes Japan as the second largest economy in the world and its role as the regional engine of growth in recent decades. The formalized partnership will anchor Japanese economic interests in ASEAN and balance the rise of China. For the less developed ASEAN economies, Japan is also the largest donor of technical and development assistance.

In November 2002, ASEAN and Japan signed the Joint Declaration to develop a framework agreement and provide for separate bilateral agreements with individual ASEAN economies. The Framework Agreement for Comprehensive Economic Partnership was signed at the ASEAN-Japan Summit in October 2003.[15] The Framework laid out the following principles — comprehensive coverage of countries and of sectors; special and differential treatment for ASEAN states, reflecting their lower economic development levels, and greater flexibility for CLMV; flexibility for sensitive sectors of ASEAN and Japan; early implementation of cooperation in areas which could provide more immediate benefits, such as technical assistance and capacity building to ASEAN, especially for CLMV; trade and investment promotion and facilitation; trade and investment policy dialogue; business sector dialogue; mobility of business people; trade data compilation and exchange; facilitation and cooperation programmes covering a wide field.

The ASEAN-wide comprehensive economic partnership (CEP) including FTA should be realized by 2012 for ASEAN-6 and 2017 for CLMV. Japan has insisted that the ASEAN-wide agreement should be a "single undertaking". It will take account of the achievements of bilateral negotiations and the further progress of the ASEAN integration process. Schedules of liberalization concessions between Japan and individual ASEAN countries in the bilateral agreements would not be renegotiated in the ASEAN-wide CEP, and the bilateral schedules of liberalization concessions would be annexed to the ASEAN-Japan CEP Agreement.

Negotiations on ASEAN-Japan FTA launched in early 2005 stalled and resumed in April 2006.[16] The biggest obstacle to negotiations with ASEAN is Japan's resistance to liberalization of agricultural and labour markets.[17] It wants to maintain its high import tariffs for farm products, including the politically sensitive rice, to shield weak and uncompetitive domestic farmers from cheap imports. This has resulted in Japan lagging behind China in the race to clinch FTAs with trading partners. Both sides agreed to incorporate common factors found in Japan's bilateral FTAs with ASEAN economies into the ASEAN-wide FTA. Then they will take up matters that need work in a ASEAN-wide format. The FTA talks are aimed to conclude in March 2007. Japan has decided to focus on the FTA and tariff reduction and elimination.[18] Japan's strategy is to negotiate with the more advanced ASEAN economies first. Bilateral agreements with Singapore and Malaysia have been signed in November 2002 and 2005 respectively, while negotiations with Philippines, Thailand and Vietnam are ongoing. ASEAN countries that have not concluded bilateral agreements with Japan will negotiate concessions bilaterally. The ASEAN-wide CEP will essentially be an umbrella agreement for the separate bilateral FTAs, in contrast to the approach adopted with the ASEAN-China initiative.

ASEAN-Korea Comprehensive Economic Cooperation

At the ASEAN-Korea Summit in October 2003, Korean President Roh proposed a comprehensive partnership with the possibility of establishing a free trade area (AKFTA). At the Summit in November 2004, a joint ASEAN-Korea Declaration on Comprehensive Cooperation Partnership agreed that (i) negotiations for the AKFTA commence in 2005 and be concluded within two years, (ii) that ASEAN-6 and Korea eliminate tariffs for 80 per cent of all products by 2009, as a key milestone in the realization of the AKFTA, which will have similar features of other ASEAN FTAs in its comprehensiveness and provision for flexibility for CLMV.

The Framework Agreement on Comprehensive Economic Cooperation was signed on 13 December 2005 and came into force on 1 July 2006.

- Korea and ASEAN-6 will start cutting tariffs from July 2006 and the CLMV at a later date. Korea and ASEAN-6 will eliminate tariffs on 90 per cent of their products by 2010, with flexibility until 2012 for a certain number of products. Korea and each ASEAN country may choose up to forty items that could be excluded from tariff reductions. Talks hit a snag over tariffs on food products for ASEAN and automobiles, steel and mobile phones for Korea. Thailand, the world's top rice exporter did not sign the agreement, partly over its dispute with Korea regarding barriers on certain agricultural products under its sensitive items, including rice.[19] Korea wants to put rice on its protected list but Thailand has objected, and so the Thais have asked for more time to sign. Thailand decided to step aside rather than hold the rest of ASEAN back. Tariffs on 97 per cent of about 4,000 categories of goods will be cut by 2010, with the rest by 2016.

- Negotiations on liberalization of trade in services and investments would only start rather than conclude by end-2006 as originally anticipated.
- ASEAN has agreed to treat goods produced at the Kaesong Industrial Complex in North Korea as made-in-South Korea.[20]

ASEAN-India Comprehensive Economic Cooperation

A cornerstone of India's "Look East" policy, born partly of a desire to catch up with China's high profile in the region, was closer and rapid economic integration with ASEAN. Indian Prime Minister Vajpayee offered ASEAN a trade pact during the ASEAN-India Summit in November 2002, one year after China's offer to ASEAN. Subsequent Indian Prime Minister Manmohan Singh's vision of a pan-Asian community is considered to be a natural extension of the FTA that India has with ASEAN. To leverage this "arc of advantage" (ASEAN plus China, Japan, Korea and India), an FTA with ASEAN is expected to get operational in 2007. Strategically, India cannot afford to be left behind by not signing an FTA with ASEAN, as India has been trying hard to be a member of some major Asian trading bloc.

A Framework Agreement for a Comprehensive Economic Partnership was signed in October 2003 and entered into force on 1 July 2004. It envisaged that tariff concessions should cover at least 80 per cent of the trade between ASEAN and India. Tariff reductions were set to start by 1 January 2006 and be concluded by ASEAN-5 (excluding Philippines) and India by December 2011, and Philippines and CLMV by 2016. The number of products listed in the sensitive track should be subject to maximum ceiling to be mutually agreed; products listed in sensitive track should have their respective MFN applied tariff rates progressively reduced/eliminated within timeframes to be mutually agreed. The negotiations to establish the ASEAN-India FTA (AIFTA) have not progressed well.

- The implementation date of the ASEAN-India FTA was postponed from 1 January 2006 to 1 January 2007 and the Early Harvest Programme has been dropped.
- Considerable differences exist over ROOs. ASEAN rejected India's proposal of twin criteria for determining the ROOs, namely the 40 per cent domestic value added plus change in tariff heading. Eventually both sides agreed to at least 35 per cent domestic value added plus change in tariff heading.
- Negotiations also ran into difficulties over India's resistance to tariff cuts on a range of products. ASEAN is one of the most efficient global producers of rice, palm oil, plantation crops (like coffee, tea) and spices (like pepper). India has high agricultural tariffs in the range of 70–100 per cent. Many of the Indian producers are small and marginal farmers. India is also worried about imports of manufactures from Thailand. Initially India presented an exclusion list of 1,414 products (including textiles, rice, vegetable oil, and petroleum products) that represented 44 per cent of ASEAN's total exports to India, of which vegetable oil and petroleum products accounted for 27 per cent of ASEAN total exports to India in 2004. Malaysia is concerned that if palm oil, tea, pepper and textiles are on India's negative list, this would affect 80 per cent of its total exports to India. As a result of ASEAN protests, the Indian negative list has been pruned from 1,414 to 850. However, Sonia Gandhi has written to Indian Prime Minister Singh cautioning him over the issue of farm imports in FTAs. To protect Indian farmers, the Indian government proposed to impose tariff-rated quotas for the import of palm oil from Malaysia and Indonesia; tea, coffee and pepper from Vietnam. But ASEAN negotiators so far are not willing to accommodate.
- India also wants to balance tariff concessions on goods with market access to ASEAN's services sectors where India has recognized global comparative advantage. Many ASEAN countries are not very keen to give India this advantage.

Synthesis and Assessment

Collectively, ASEAN has a population of about 550 million, and a combined nominal GNP of US$630 billion (2003 figures). However, it does not yet have an integrated market. But even an integrated ASEAN has a much smaller nominal GNP than either NAFTA or EU. Hence ASEAN has to be outward looking and has readily accepted proposals for FTAs from its major trading partners, while some ASEAN countries are negotiating bilateral FTAs. Table 8.2 shows the comparative sizes of ASEAN and its FTA partners. By population size, ASEAN Plus Three has 2 billion people, ASEAN-China has 1.8 billion people and ASEAN-India has 1.6 billion people, while ASEAN-CER (Australia and New Zealand) adds minimally to the ASEAN population size. A better determinant of market size is GNP. ASEAN-U.S. has the largest GNP (US$10.7 trillion in 2002), followed by ASEAN Plus Three (US$6.5 trillion), ASEAN-Japan (US$4.8 trillion) and ASEAN-China (US$1.8 trillion). While the United States, Japan, and China have larger economies than the collective ASEAN-10, the economies of India, South Korea and CER are smaller. Another indicator of market size is the volume of trade. The largest is ASEAN-U.S., followed by ASEAN Plus Three. The trade volume of Japan is comparable to ASEAN, but the trade volume of South Korea, CER and India are considerably smaller.

The various comprehensive economic partnership/cooperation initiatives have been dubbed as "FTA-plus" and "WTO-plus", all with a FTA core.

• A domino effect is evident. China's proposal of an agreement with ASEAN, was rapidly followed by similar offers of comprehensive economic partnership/cooperation from Japan, Korea, India, and Australia–New Zealand, with the latest being the EU. Japan chose both an ASEAN-wide framework umbrella and bilateral FTA agreements with individual ASEAN countries. Japan had a bilateral agreement with Singapore prior to the ASEAN-wide initiative, but followed up with bilateral negotiations with Malaysia, Indonesia, Thailand, Philippines and Vietnam. Likewise, Korea and India have bilateral agreements with Singapore before embarking on the ASEAN-wide agreements. China embarked on a bilateral agreement with Thailand after initiating the ASEAN-wide agreement. At this stage of the game, it is unclear what the relationship is between the ASEAN-wide agreements and the bilateral agreements, in particular relating to ROOs

TABLE 8.2
ASEAN's FTA Partners

	Population 2003 (million)	GNP size 2003 (US$ billion)	GNP per capita 2003 (US$)	Exports 2003 (US$ billion)	Imports 2003 (US$ billion)	Total trade 2003 (US$ billion)
ASEAN-10	537.2	641	1,193	451.0	386.4	838.1
China	1,288.4	1,417	1,100	438.4	412.8	851.2
ASEAN-China	1,825.6	2,058	1,127	889.4	799.2	1,689.3
ASEAN's % share	29.4	31.1		50.7	48.3	49.6
Japan	127.2	4,390	34,510	471.9	383.0	854.9
ASEAN-Japan	664.4	5,031	7,572	922.9	769.4	1,693.0
ASEAN's % share	80.9	12.7		48.9	50.2	49.5
South Korea	47.9	576	12,020	194.3	178.8	373.1
ASEAN-Korea	585.1	1,217	2,080	645.3	565.2	1,211.2
ASEAN's % share	91.8	52.7		69.9	68.4	69.2
China-Japan-Korea	1,463.5	6,383	4,361	1,104.6	974.6	2,079.2
ASEAN+3	2,000.7	7,024	3,511	1,555.6	1,361.0	2,917.3
ASEAN's % share	26.9	9.1		29.0	28.4	28.7
Australia-NZ CER	23.9	495	20,711	86.9	107.2	194.1
ASEAN-CER	561.1	1,136	2,025	537.9	493.6	1,032.2
ASEAN's % share	95.7	56.4		83.9	78.3	81.2
India	1,064.4	568	530	54.7	69.7	124.5
ASEAN-India	1,601.6	1,209	755	505.7	456.1	962.6
ASEAN's % share	33.5	53.0		89.2	84.7	87.1
United States	291.0	10,946	37,610	724.0	1,305.6	2,029.6
ASEAN-US	828.2	11,587	13,991	1,175.0	1,692.0	2,867.7
ASEAN's % share	64.9	5.5		38.4	22.8	29.2

Source: From Chia (2005).

and sensitive lists. In contrast, the United States under the Enterprise for ASEAN Initiative is engaged only in bilateral agreements, with an agreement with Singapore preceding the EAI announcement and now with several negotiations ongoing.

- The scope of the partnership/cooperation agreements extends beyond trade liberalization in goods to include liberalization of trade in services and investment; trade and investment facilitation; government procurement; intellectual property protection; competition policy. They also include economic and technical cooperation over broad areas — cooperation in the development of agriculture, industry, fishery, forestry, energy; human resources; infrastructure; small and medium enterprises; science and technology, information and communications technology; and labour and environment. Additionally, they include special and differential treatment, flexibility, and capacity building for the less developed CLMV.

- Framework agreements were reached prior to negotiations on the various components of the comprehensive partnership/cooperation in trade in goods, trade in services, investment, and dispute settlement mechanism. Only the ASEAN-China agreement has implemented an Early Harvest Programme, while the ASEAN-India agreement abandoned such an intention. The trade in goods agreement is usually negotiated and implemented first, while agreements on services and investment are ongoing.

- There are varying implementation and end-dates for tariff reduction/ elimination in trade in goods:
  - AFTA: Implemented in January 1993. End-date of 2010 for ASEAN-6 and 2015 for CLMV.
  - ASEAN-China: Implemented in June 2005. End-date of 2010 for ASEAN-6 and China and 2015 for CLMV.
  - ASEAN-Japan: End-date of 2012 for ASEAN-6 and Japan, and 2017 for CLMV.
  - ASEAN-Korea: Implemented in July 2006. End-date of 2010 for ASEAN-6 and Korea. No end-date indicated for CLMV.
  - ASEAN-India: Implementation date January 2007. End-date of 2011 for ASEAN-5 and India, and 2016 for Philippines and CLMV.

- There are also varying ROOs, creating a "spaghetti bowl" effect:
  - AFTA: 40 per cent value added, amended to include change in tariff heading and product specific as well.

- – ASEAN-China: 40 per cent value added
- – ASEAN-Japan: depends on bilateral negotiations, some of which are still ongoing.
- – ASEAN-Korea: product specific
- – ASEAN-India: 35 per cent value added plus change in tariff heading.
- • The ASEAN Plus and bilateral FTAs have not been able to resolve the sensitive issues that have bugged the WTO negotiations. Some regional and bilateral agreements may have breached the WTO GATT Article XXIV on "substantially all trade" and GATS on "substantial sectoral coverage". Agricultural products are on the sensitive and exclusion lists of several countries, as are textiles and some other labour-intensive products and a range of service sectors.

The various ASEAN Plus agreements have improved ASEAN's market access, improved the scope for scale economies, and improved the attraction for foreign investors. ASEAN also enjoys the political and economic benefits of a "hub". With each agreement signed and implemented, more trade and investment and institutional and procedural barriers have come down and economic efficiency improved. The increased competition from imports and foreign suppliers and investors have also put pressure on ASEAN countries to undertake domestic structural and institutional reforms so as to improve competitiveness. At the same time, the proliferation of ASEAN Plus agreements as well as bilateral FTAs, have given rise to concerns over the "spaghetti bowl" effect and the severe demands on scarce negotiating resources, as well as to concerns that the centrifugal forces may undermine ASEAN economic integration and solidarity.

III.2. ASEAN Plus Three and the East Asia FTA

ASEAN Plus Three (ASEAN, China, Japan, Korea) cooperation started as an initiative for monetary and financial cooperation in the wake of the Asian financial crisis. The grouping adopted the Chiang Mai Initiative in 2000, aimed at fostering regional financial stability and resilience and building on the earlier similar agreements among ASEAN economies. The first component comprises a network of bilateral swap and repurchase facilities to assist beleaguered central banks facing liquidity crunches. The second component is a regional monitoring and surveillance of macroeconomic and financial fundamentals and policies of member economies to pre-empt another currency attack. The third component is the development of the Asian Bond Market.

There was an informal Summit of ASEAN Plus Three in December 1997, at the sidelines of the Second ASEAN Informal Summit. Since then, there has been the 2001 Report of the East Asia Vision Group (EAVG) and the 2002 Report of the East Asia Study Group (EASG). The EASG report was adopted at the ASEAN Plus Three Summit in 2002. It contains short-term, and medium and long-term measures towards an East Asian community.

- Short-term measures: All the recommended measures will be implemented by the tenth anniversary of ASEAN Plus Three cooperation in 2007. Four short-term measures have already been implemented — comprehensive human resources development programme for East Asia; network of East Asia Think Tanks (NEAT); East Asia Forum; and East Asia Business Council.
- Medium and long-term measures: These include a high level conference on investment and SMEs; convening of the East Asia Summit; experts group to study the feasibility of an East Asia FTA; regional financial facility; regional marine environmental cooperation; framework for energy policies and strategies and action plans.

The first East Asia Summit was convened in Kuala Lumpur on 14 December 2005. It saw the signing of the KL Declaration that established the EAS as a forum for dialogue on broad strategic, political and economic issues of common interest to promote peace, stability and economic prosperity. Three issues arise from the EAS. First is the scope of its membership. The inaugural meeting comprises ASEAN Plus Three plus Australia, New Zealand and India, with Russia as an invited observer. However, there are rumblings that other major powers do not want to be excluded. Recent statements in June 2006 by the ASEAN Secretary General, the Indonesian Defence Minister and the Malaysian Deputy Prime Minister indicate that the EAS will not be exclusive. At the same time, there is concern that membership expansion would dilute ASEAN Plus Three confidence building and cooperation. Second is the objective of the EAS. Some observers are concerned that it will become another "talk shop", while others hope it would become an Asian G8 type of meeting. Third is ASEAN's concern that it remains in the driver's seat of EAS in shaping the future of East Asia amid superpower rivalry.

The expert group to study the feasibility of an East Asia FTA was appointed in 2005 and submitted its report to the ASEAN Plus Three governments in mid-2006.

Rationale for and Challenges of EAFTA

The 2001 EAVG Report recommended that East Asia becomes a regional community with collective efforts for peace, prosperity and progress and establish EAFTA ahead of the APEC Bogor Goals. As with the formation of any other regional grouping or bilateral FTAs, there are political and economic rationales.

- *Political objective.* A primary objective of the East Asian community and EAFTA is to reduce political and military conflicts through economic cooperation and integration. That has been the experience of ASEAN leading to a period of peace and stability in Southeast Asia. No comparable grouping currently exists in Northeast Asia. A large East Asian grouping would also increase the East Asian "voice" in international organizations and fora, in equal partnership with the Western Hemisphere and Europe.
- *Economies of scale and scope.* Modelling studies have shown that the larger EAFTA will result in more economic benefits than smaller FTAs. EAFTA, with the removal of barriers to trade and investment and freer flows of capital and labour, will facilitate the regional production networks and supply chains, and incentivize individual countries to undertake reforms and restructure their economies to better meet the challenges of globalization and regionalism in the Americas and Europe.
- *Overcoming the spaghetti bowl.* EAFTA would lead to harmonization and standardization of ROOs, product and technical standards and conformance requirements, thus overcoming the "spaghetti bowl" effect from the proliferation of multi-layered and overlapping FTAs. This "spaghetti bowl" adds to business costs and detracts from FDI.

However, realizing the EAFTA faces a number of concerns and challenges:

- *Development gaps.* EAFTA will comprise a wide mix of economies at different levels of economic development and industrial and technological competence. Complementarities and diversies offer prospects of specialization and efficient regional production. Membership in EAFTA provide the smaller and less developed East

Asian economies to be part of mainstream East Asia and enjoy the spillover effects of dynamism and growth. But it also raises concerns of marginalization of the less efficient economies and producers and suppliers. Hence governments would be reluctant to open up their farm sectors, labour-intensive industries, and SMEs which would be expected to result in adverse effects on employment, poverty incidence and income distribution, without adequate safeguards and financial and technical assistance for capacity building.

- *Common destiny.* Countries in East Asia need to be convinced that there is a common destiny and that the political and economic gains of economic cooperation and integration outweigh the costs from dilution of national sovereignty necessary for the creation of common institutions and common rules and disciplines. Countries in northeast Asia are also still plagued by the historical baggage and mistrust.
- *External orientation.* Some East Asian countries have strong external political, security, economic and technology links with non-members, particularly with the United States and EU. Hence EAFTA cannot afford to be inward-looking and must be outward-looking and inclusive. East Asian regionalism should complement and not substitute for multilateralism.
- *Membership of East Asia.* At the minimum, an East Asia FTA is pragmatically defined as ASEAN Plus Three. However, there are alternative views. Japan's Trade and Industry Minister Nikai proposed a CEPEA, comprising the sixteen countries that participated in the East Asia Summit in December 2005 (ASEAN-10, China, Japan and Korea, plus India, Australia and New Zealand). Indian Prime Minister Singh called for a pan-Asian FTA combining all the EAS members as a way forward towards an Asian Economic Community as an "arc of advantage".
- *EAFTA design.* EAFTA should be WTO-plus. In the areas of trade in goods and services, coverage should be comprehensive, conforming to GATT Article XXIV on "substantially all trade" and GATS Article V on "substantial sectoral coverage". Sensitive and exclusion lists should be kept to a minimum and be time-bound. Rules of origin should be intended to prevent trade diversion and not be restrictive and protective. For most rules and disciplines, it is better to conform to the international standards agreed on in the WTO. Special and differential treatment and flexibility should be accorded the least

developed economies, together with financial and technical assistance for capacity building.

Possible Roadmaps to EAFTA

The proliferation of ASEAN Plus and bilateral FTAs in East Asia opens up a number of options to reach the region-wide EAFTA.

- *Merge the Southeast Asian and a Northeast Asian agreements.* ASEAN has already an agreement among the ten Southeast Asian countries and the economic integration programmes are well advanced. But there is no parallel trilateral or bilateral agreement among China, Japan and Korea, and these could be difficult to work out, particularly in the present political climate. A merger of Southeast Asia and Northeast Asia would, on the surface, be highly disadvantageous to ASEAN, since the three northeast economies have an economic weight of 90 per cent and ASEAN only 10 per cent.
- *Consolidate the various ASEAN Plus One FTAs.* Since ASEAN is already negotiating FTAs with China, Japan, South Korea (also Australia–New Zealand and India), these ASEAN Plus One agreements when realized, could serve as the basic framework for EAFTA. On the plus side, these agreements would have agreed common frameworks and liberalization schedules over large areas, reducing possible areas of dissent and dispute to a minimum. On the negative side, there is no common template in the ASEAN Plus One agreements under negotiation, resulting in a spaghetti bowl that would be difficult to unravel and forced into a convergence.
- *Deepen ASEAN Plus Three.* An EAFTA could be achieved using the existing ASEAN Plus Three framework. It was within the ASEAN Plus Three framework that EAVG and EASG recommended the formation of an EAFTA as a mid-term and long-term measure and the ASEAN Plus Three Economic Ministers in 2004 created the Joint Expert Group of Feasibility Study on EAFTA. An issue would be whether ASEAN would be negotiating the FTA as a group or as ten separate economies. It would be difficult to arrive at a consensus, given the diversity of the thirteen economies. The issue of agriculture between Southeast Asia and Northeast Asia, particularly rice, would also be difficult to resolve.

IV. AN ALTERNATIVE APPROACH: THE P4?

The Trans-Pacific Strategic Economic Partnership (SEP or P4 for short) is the first trans-Pacific plurilateral FTA involving the four small like-minded economies of Brunei, Chile, New Zealand and Singapore. It could incorporate the Bogor deadlines of 2010 for developed economies and 2020 for developing economies.

An initial proposal for P5, incorporating Chile, New Zealand, Singapore as well as the United States and Australia failed to materialize.[21] The P3 (Chile, New Zealand, Singapore) was first launched in October 2002 during the APEC Leaders Meeting in Los Cabos and negotiations began almost immediately.[22] Brunei joined half-way through the negotiations and has been granted specific flexibilities. Chile, New Zealand and Singapore signed the agreement on 18 July 2005 and Brunei on 2 August 2005. The Agreement entered into force on 1 January 2006.

P4 has an open accession clause to encourage other APEC members to join the grouping. The criterion for accession is acceptance of the terms and conditions of the Agreement without renegotiation. It is reported in the media that APEC members that have expressed an interest in accession include Malaysia, Thailand, Mexico and Peru.

The P4 are relatively small Pacific economies, having a combined GDP of only US$280 million. But these are among the most open economies in the Pacific. The rationales are political, strategic and economic. On the economic front, it promotes trade and investment liberalization among the four countries, although these economies are already very open and (except for Brunei) are engaged in a growing number of sub-regional and bilateral FTAs, so the value added could not be very much. However, it was billed as providing a "demonstration effect" to push APEC forward and hence has strategic benefits. Chile and Singapore position themselves as "strategic platforms" for foreign investors in their respective Latin American and East Asian regions. The strategic value to New Zealand and Brunei is not obvious. Given the physical spread of the P4 members, increased trade is crucially dependent on compressing distance by improving air and maritime transportation linkages.

The P4 Agreement has similar comprehensive coverage as the ASEAN Plus One agreements. It covers trade in goods, rules of origin, trade remedies, SPS measures, technical barriers to trade, trade in services, government procurement, customs procedures, intellectual property, temporary entry of persons, competition, institutional provisions and dispute settlement. What is probably unique is the "big bang" approach to trade in goods liberalization — Singapore has achieved MFN zero tariffs; for New Zealand, all tariffs would be eliminated with immediate effect; for Chile, tariffs on 89.3 per cent would be eliminated immediately, 9.57 per cent within three years and the remaining 1.13 per cent in six years. There are breakthroughs in agricultural trade liberalization, particularly as Chile and New Zealand are both southern hemisphere countries with similar climates and seasons and compete in a range of agricultural exports. Rules of origin took into consideration outward processing as an integral part of modern manufacturing processes. Customs facilitation procedures include self-certification for the claiming of preferential tariffs; risk management; and advance rulings. For services trade liberalization, P4 adopts the more liberalizing negative list approach, that is, all sectors are open except for those measures/sectors that have been expressly reserved. There is also a chapter for cooperation in five fields, that is, economic, education, primary industry, cultural, and science, research and technology. The Labour Cooperation MOU will enable the countries to work closely together on labour and human resource issues and provide opportunities to share views and experiences. The Environment Cooperation Agreement will enable the countries to work closely together on environment issues and provide opportunities to share views and experience.

Could the P4 be the building block to an APEC-wide FTA? P4 is a very high quality FTA, perhaps too high in view of the realities of political and economic sensitivities that characterize many less open APEC economies. The "demonstration effect" of P4 would be stronger, if some major economies such as the United States and Australia have been among the founding members. For countries that have the political will to liberalize their economies, joining P4 would be the right path to take.

V. CHALLENGES FOR ASEAN AND APEC

V.1. A Key Role for ASEAN?

ASEAN has definitely left a footprint in regional community building in East Asia and the Asia-Pacific because ASEAN has played a critical role in the development of cooperation processes in the wider region.

ASEAN's critical role has been due to two factors. First, its experience as the "first mover" in the region influenced the modality of other regional processes in which it is involved. Second, ASEAN's dialogue process with major countries, which established the regular (annual) Post-Ministerial Conference (PMC), provided the inspiration for a wider regional process.

When the idea of an Asia-Pacific cooperation process began to take hold, ASEAN proposed that the ASEAN PMC process be the basis for it. A proposal for an Asia Pacific Forum (APF) was adopted by ASEAN Foreign Ministers but was not endorsed by some ASEAN members. The initiative was then taken by Australia, and the first Ministerial Meeting of APEC was held in Canberra in 1989. Recognizing the fact that ASEAN had first come up with the initiative and the critical role ASEAN's participation has in any Asia-Pacific process, an agreement was made that any other APEC meeting must be held in an ASEAN country. ASEAN has since become the co-pilot in the APEC community building process.

The APEC process is characterized by the important role of the chair in shaping the agenda. The one year cycle of APEC's chairmanship has its positive and negative aspects. However, the main problem with APEC is its loose and open-ended nature and its minimal institutionalization. APEC was ahead of ASEAN in setting a clear target for its process when in 1994 leaders endorsed the Bogor Goals of "free and open trade and investment in the region" by 2010 for developed countries and 2020 for developing countries. APEC undertook its mid-term review towards the Bogor Goals in 2005 and the widespread view is that the process will not be able to deliver on the leaders' commitment. APEC is in the process of some soul searching now. The APEC Business Advisory Council (ABAC) proposed that APEC abandoned its voluntary nature and move towards the creation of a Free Trade Area of the Asia-Pacific (FTAAP). At the APEC Summit in Chile in 2004, leaders rejected this proposal as being infeasible.

The other Asia-Pacific process, the ASEAN Regional Forum (ARF), appears to have stagnated as well. Formed in the middle of the 1990s to promote cooperation in the political and security fields, in parallel to APEC's economic cooperation process, the ARF was to become an important pillar of the Asia-Pacific regional architecture. In terms of defining the process, the ARF should be less open-ended as it has formulated the three phases of confidence building, preventive diplomacy, and conflict resolution. However, the process lacks the mechanism to move from the first phase to the next, largely because it also is a very loose process. It has been questioned whether ARF's stagnation could be overcome by ASEAN's willingness to release its driver's seat in the process. The ARF is by design ASEAN-driven. This resulted from a recognition that the process would not have taken off at all if it is not driven by ASEAN. The proposal for a co-chairmanship has been aired, but there has been no decision on this.

In addition to APEC and ARF, ASEAN is involved in, and in fact also the initiator of other processes: ASEM, FEALAC, and most importantly the ASEAN Plus Three (ASEAN+3) and the East Asia Summit.

There have been regular meetings of ASEM and FEALAC, but these two processes failed to produce concrete programmes or measures that can confidently be seen as creating bridges to connect East Asia with Europe and Latin America, respectively.

In comparison much more is going on in the ASEAN Plus Three process. A great deal has been written lately about this process. However, the region fails to develop a strategic plan for the ASEAN Plus Three process. This is in part the failure of ASEAN, which is in the driver's seat, to do so. Instead, governments agreed on holding an East Asian Summit without having clearly visualized and articulated a strategic plan. It is really strange to have two parallel tracks involving the same countries and with no clearly distinct agenda. This resulted in an agreement, largely as an after-thought, to expand the membership of the East Asian Summit to include India, Australia, and New Zealand, the three countries with which ASEAN also has agreed to form a Free Trade Area.

The original proposal by the East Asian Vision Group (EAVG) that was endorsed by the East Asian Study Group (EASG) was to transform the ASEAN Plus Three process to an East Asian Summit process. This was to happen after a lot of preparations and a consolidation of the ASEAN-driven ASEAN Plus Three process. It was unfortunate that the East Asian Summit was prematurely placed on the region's agenda in 2005. Had a strategic plan for East Asia been properly worked out, it would have been concluded that the transformation of the ASEAN Plus Three process to an East Asian process is the most critical element for East Asian community building.

At this stage, ASEAN's main task is to consolidate its role in the region's community building processes. It must have a strategic plan to develop a new vehicle that would ensure that it as well as the Plus Three members would feel comfortable to travel in. As things stand today, ASEAN is in the driver's seat of a defective vehicle.

It is in this new vehicle that a better "roadmap" can be travelled in. But the passengers must also behave, and the driver must be fit.

China, Korea and Japan should not continue to quarrel and must come to settlement of their historical burden. Governments must, once and for all, stand up above the public and not to allow the relationship (China-Japan and Korea-Japan) be used for domestic political purposes. ASEAN too must agree on a modality that ensures the effective functioning of its international diplomacy and not allow the organization to be held hostage to one of its members, whose regime remains illegitimate.

ASEAN also needs to deepen economic integration amongst its ten members. This is a major undertaking in view of the big differences in levels of economic development and economic openness. When AFTA was agreed in 1992, ASEAN only had the six members. When joining ASEAN the new members had to accede to the AFTA agreement. They were each given longer time frame. A two-tier ASEAN was created.

In 1997, ASEAN-6 and the new members charted a new direction, the ASEAN Vision 2020, with the aim to forge closer economic integration and narrowing the gap in the level of development amongst its members. The vision is to "create a stable, prosperous and highly competitive ASEAN Economic Region in which there is a free flow of goods, services and investments, a freer flow of capital, equitable economic development and reduced poverty and socio-economic disparities."

In 2003, at the Summit in Bali, ASEAN leaders agreed to establish an ASEAN Economic Community (AEC) by 2020. The AEC is one of three pillars (the other two being the ASEAN Security Community and the ASEAN Socio-cultural Community) that make up the ASEAN Community. In line with the ASEAN Vision 2020, it is envisaged that the AEC will be a single market and production base with free flow of goods, services, investments, capital, and skilled labor. The AEC remains vaguely defined. The AEC has been conceptualized as a "FTA-Plus" arrangement that covers a zero-tariff ASEAN free trade area and some elements of a common market. ASEAN officials opted for a pragmatic approach, essentially moving on a sectoral basis. Eleven priority sectors have been selected for fast-track integration. The eleven sectors are: wood-based products, automotives, rubber-based products, textiles and apparels, agro-based products, fisheries, electronics, e-ASEAN, healthcare, air travel, and tourism. A roadmap is being drawn for each sector. What remains missing is the overall roadmap towards achieving AEC, although ASEAN has produced an internal document, Roadmap for ASEAN Integration, prior to the decision to move towards an AEC.

At the same time that ASEAN undertakes its AEC project, it has been wooed into FTAs with a number of trading partners. Two immediate issues confront ASEAN. First, would these FTAs be completed before ASEAN realizes the AEC? In terms of the plan (intention), ASEAN-Korea FTA will be completed in 2009, ASEAN-China in 2010, ASEAN-India in 2011, and ASEAN-Japan in 2012, all with some built-in "flexibility", allowing for some countries or some sectors to be realized later. However, the AEC is scheduled for completion by 2020. This means that ASEAN members must try to accelerate the implementation of their AEC initiatives. At least the fast-track sectors should be fully liberalized by 2010. ASEAN could also adopt an approach which clearly defines the minimum measures to be taken for the region to become a single market and production base, namely so-called "core" elements of the AEC, and all members should agree to implement them by 2010.

The second issue regards the need for ASEAN to develop a common framework for its extra regional cooperation, particularly in forming FTAs. A common framework would make it easier for the various FTAs or PTAs to become building blocks for or to be amalgamated into wider regional arrangements. More importantly, in so doing ASEAN can become a "hub" to drive the process in East Asia through the ASEAN Plus One agreements. In addition, a common framework can help reduce tensions between ASEAN members.

Finally, for ASEAN to become a production base, it also needs to minimize business transaction costs by having similar rules and schedules of tariff reduction to ensure use of most efficient supplier. Most important in this regard is the ROO, which constitute one of the elements of a common framework. Restrictive ROO constrains sourcing of inputs. New ROO can also change sourcing decisions away from use of inputs from existing partners. In essence, a common ROO can facilitate the spread of full cumulation and the development of regional production networks. In its FTA with the United States, Singapore has introduced two new approaches in calculating ROO that takes into account regional production networks. The first is the principle of outward processing that recognizes manufacturing chains and outsourcing. The second is the so-called Integrated Sourcing Initiative (ISI), allowing parts and components produced in Singapore's neighbouring countries as coming from Singapore, but this is limited to certain non-sensitive items only (IT components and medical devices).

Beyond trade in goods, a common framework also needs to be developed for services and investment, and perhaps also competition policy and intellectual property rights. Many of these elements form an integral part of the AEC project.

The many technical issues identified above should not overshadow the main task faced by the ASEAN countries, namely to develop the political will and the capacity to drive the process. If ASEAN fails to do so, potentially only China is in the position to be the main driver for the East Asian integration process. The region, the United States, and the world may not be ready for this.

V.2. Challenges for APEC

A reform process is already under way in APEC. This reform appears to have been driven by two concerns. First, that the most important agreement among APEC leaders thus far, namely to achieve the so-called Bogor Goals, will not be realized as scheduled. The first target date for its realization by the developed members of APEC is 2010, which is fast approaching. Second, that the APEC process has been losing steam and that APEC no longer captures the imagination of governments and peoples in the region.

If so, the objective of the reform is also twofold. First, it is to ensure that APEC can deliver on its own pledge. Second, it is to maintain APEC's relevance and attractiveness to its stakeholders.

But what will guide the reform?

APEC's pledge to achieve free and open trade and investment in the region remains ill defined. Therefore it will not be easy to translate this commitment into a clear and operational agenda. This could be the reason why the Bogor Goals no longer create the excitement they once did. APEC will be regarded by its stakeholders as relevant and attractive if its agenda is seen as relevant and attractive.

But what will be required to successfully modify and improve the organization's agenda?

APEC needs to make changes in its agenda-setting mechanism and procedures. Setting APEC's agenda also requires sufficient appreciation of its implementation. Institutional structure and capacity will determine what agenda can or cannot be successfully implemented by APEC. The past sixteen years should provide sufficient information about the weaknesses of APEC's institutional structure and capacity.

APEC's reform should be "agenda-driven". The reform is essentially about changing the mechanism and procedures to setting the organization's agenda that can be implemented. This should begin with a renewal of APEC's agenda.

APEC has developed an agenda that will assist its members in achieving the Bogor Goals. On the basis of its mid-term stock take, it has designed a roadmap for future work, the Busan Roadmap to Bogor Goals. The Roadmap is meant to "fix" APEC's agenda, which now should have the following key components:

(a) continuing work of the WTO;
(b) more ambitious and effective CAPs and IAPs with strengthened implementation and review processes;
(c) a more intensive focus on trade and investment facilitation and improving the business environment behind the border;
(d) more focused and action-oriented cooperation on ECOTECH and a strategic approach to capacity building; and
(e) a comprehensive workplan on RTAs/FTAs.

Should APEC reopen the debate on how the Bogor Goals relate to APEC's objective of building a regional community? Some have felt that the Bogor Goals are too ambitious but at the same time too narrow. They are too ambitious if "free and open trade and investment in the region" means a removal of all barriers to trade and investment by the target dates. But APEC has not defined this, and so long as this is left open, the process remains flawed.

ABAC has also made suggestions on APEC's reform. ABAC's agenda is straightforward. This group of stakeholders wants to get business done. They feel that the process of removing barriers to trade and investment is too slow. Their suggestions include:

(a) Make the IAP review process more robust and forward-looking and IAPs more specific, transparent and accessible. Focus on what member economies have yet to do to reach the Bogor goals;
(b) Strengthen capacity-building initiatives, especially tailoring them to each economy and building public-private partnerships to this end;

(c) Transform the APEC Secretariat into an OECD-type Secretariat with greater resources and authority;
(d) Enhance ABAC-APEC communication aimed at increasing private sector input, including by establishing a formal feedback mechanism of ABAC recommendations;
(e) Increase APEC coordination on positions in WTO and multilateral fora, including in key areas of agriculture, market access and services liberalization.

ABAC feels that APEC should be able to bind commitments. It is considering whether it should or should not propose the idea of a Free Trade Area of the Asia-Pacific (FTAAP), but it is likely to abandon this when it realizes that it will take a very long time to form an FTAAP.

In a recent policy brief, the Lowy Institute in Australia made the following suggestions:[23]

(a) APEC should abandon any aspirations to intra-APEC trade liberalization and get back to its original purpose, namely to use its economic weight to support global multilateralism and to facilitate economic integration around the Asia-Pacific region;
(b) It should pare back much of its current over-ambitious agenda, possibly transferring some of this activity to new East Asian forums;
(c) It should resist efforts to bureaucratize the annual leaders' meeting;
(d) When the current membership embargo expires in 2007, APEC should declare its membership permanently closed;
(e) The inadequate APEC Secretariat should be reorganized and provided with a more realistic funding base.

These may be some of the real issues that APEC has to confront. The underlying interest here is "to save APEC". This is perhaps a legitimate agenda, but there must be compelling reasons for saving APEC. APEC should reopen a debate on what these compelling reasons are.

The first question to address is why the East Asian members of APEC have the strong urge to organize themselves in an East Asian regional structure, and why is it that the United States has great difficulties sustaining an interest in participating actively in APEC?

The second question is whether an East Asian regional structure will compete with APEC or whether there can be a kind of division of labour between the two regional structures?

In East Asia a strong momentum is building up to seriously explore alternative ways ("regional architectures") that could strengthen East Asia's position in the wider region and globally. For East Asia, APEC's attractiveness is the promise that this forum can actively engage the United States in a community-building process. Community building, to be meaningful, must have a strong strategic underpinning. Is this still present in the Asia-Pacific region?

An East Asian process began in 1997 in the form of ASEAN Plus Three (APT). To some extent this was a reaction to APEC's inability to come to the assistance of crisis-hit countries in East Asia. Why could this assistance not be mobilized in time and in a meaningful way? Is it because as an organization APEC was ill-prepared to do so, as it has no mechanisms to deal with financial crises? Or is it because the United States, the largest economy in APEC, was not sufficiently focused on assisting fellow members of APEC, their partners in Asia Pacific community building? Is this because the notion of community building is too vague? Why, on the other hand, was the United States capable of making maximum use of APEC to mobilize support in its fight against global terrorism following 11 September?

East Asia then began with the search for its own regional mechanisms. An Asian Monetary Fund (AMF) failed to materialize; instead, it has come up with the setting up of a network of bilateral swap arrangements, known as the Chiang Mai Initiative (CMI). This CMI is a poor substitute for an AMF-type regional financing facility, but it has become an important cornerstone of community building in East Asia.

The East Asia Summit as it came into being was an accident, in terms of the timing of convening it as well as expanding its membership beyond APT to include Australia, India, and New Zealand. The agenda of EAS is likely to overlap with that of APT and also of APEC. EAS is not based on the concept of geography. Instead, it is rather fuzzy. Senior Minister Goh Chok Tong of Singapore recently suggests that an EAS should be "an architecture of variable geometry and flexible boundaries", and as such can accommodate the United States in some fashion yet to be designed.[24] Many members of EAS feel that in one way or other the United States must be drawn into this East Asian process. But isn't this recreating APEC?

If EAS succeeds to engage the United States, it could well be that APEC loses its appeal to both East Asia and the United States. A new regional architecture will emerge. It can have a competitive edge vis-à-vis APEC.

First, its membership is smaller but includes the important Asia-Pacific countries, with India as a bonus. Second, it can set an agenda that will not repeat the mistakes of APEC.

Is there hope for APEC to come up with an agenda that makes it compellingly attractive? Let us do a quick assessment of current APEC's organs that produce the organization's agenda.

Main Organs

- *Leaders Meeting (Summit)*. This is perhaps the single most important event in the public's eyes. How should the leaders influence APEC's agenda? (a) Should they be the start of "top-down" processes to promoting regional cooperation by issuing "instructions" to ministers?; (b) Should they, instead, be at the end of "bottom-up" processes to promoting regional cooperation by "signing off" recommendations by ministers, advised by the SOM, that will shop around from amongst the Working Groups?; (c) Can the top-down and bottom-up processes be combined?; or (d) Should the "Leaders Track" be decoupled" altogether from APEC's "Track One" to be the region's G-8 for dialogue on strategic and critical regional and global issues. The modality that will be opted for will determine how all other APEC organs should function.
- *Ministerial Meeting*. Since the Leaders Meeting has gained prominence, the Ministerial Meeting appears to have been "out-competed" by the Summit.
- *Sectoral Ministers Meeting*. Many of these Ministerial Meetings end up being "social clubs".
- *SOM and its Committees*. They are the real "working horses" of APEC, but they are either running without a cart or they cannot move because each horse wants to go in a different direction.
- *Working Groups*. Some may be "the living dead" in APEC. There are many important, interesting, and relevant subjects to be addressed and tackled, but the right format is yet to be found.
- *Secretariat*. If it is to function only as APEC's "P.O. Box", it cannot become APEC's kitchen. Without a proper kitchen, APEC cannot open an attractive restaurant that can cater to the tastes of its potential clientele from the rather wide and diverse neighbourhood.

Broad Agenda

The APEC Restaurant must have an attractive menu offering a variety of dishes, but they should not be overwhelming.

- *Liberalization.* The focus should be on regional efforts to strengthen the multilateral trading system. APEC's own liberalization agenda should be strengthened, but "No Champion, No Go". Unfortunately potential champions are currently more interested in "quick-yielding" bilaterals. Should the liberalization agenda be seen as the "appetizers?"
- *Facilitation.* The Lowy Institute sees this as APEC's "hidden strength". It may indeed be APEC's "main course".
- *ECOTECH.* This is definitely the sweetener. It is the dessert that will complete the meal. A bad dessert will spoil the entire meal. In this sense, ECOTECH is at the heart of APEC.[25] Today, much of the ECOTECH projects should be put out for fire sale. This may finally be realized by APEC officials. A decision was made in 2005 to restructure the SOM Steering Committee on Economic and Technical Cooperation (ECOTECH). But this SOM Steering Committee cannot be turned into the kitchen.

How should this agenda be operationalized and be advertised to the wider public? The main course (facilitation) cannot be attractive on its own. Facilitation measures are meticulous efforts and do not capture the public's imagination. Thus, it should be the entire meal (the Set Menu) that makes it an attractive proposition.

Implementing this will definitely require further reforms. The reforms will be guided by this agenda. This is "agenda-driven" reform at work. APEC's mode of operation should be task-oriented. Working Groups, for instance, must have a clear sunset clause.

A Hanoi Action Plan that is concise and focused can guide this process. This can complement the Busan Roadmap, and together they can produce a more balanced agenda for APEC.[26]

Beyond the reform, it may well be that after all, APEC itself should be an "agenda-driven" process. For some time to come, it cannot be a process that is driven by leaders or by institutions. But leadership is still important for the process. This underlines the notion of "issue specific" (or agenda-driven) leadership that should characterize APEC.

ASEAN should promote this "agenda driven" process for APEC. It is consistent with ASEAN's approach. The involvement of other countries in APEC will help make sure that on the basis of this approach, APEC can have a dynamic (progressive), realistic (implementable), and an interesting (relevant) agenda.

Notes

1. At the 2006 Summit in Cebu, ASEAN leaders agreed to accelerate the realization of the AEC to 2015. An ASEAN Economic Community Blueprint has been drafted to clarify the goals of the AEC and to indicate the roadmap to realizing it.
2. The draft AEC blueprint has a section on developing a coherent external economic policy.
3. See, for example, Simon Tay, Jesus Estanislao and Hadi Soesastro, eds. *Reinventing ASEAN* (Singapore: Institute of Southeast Asian Studies, 2003).
4. Possible explanations include declining margin of preference as MFN rates have also come down; lack of private sector awareness; lack of clarity in the application of rules of origin; problems with customs authorities; and lack of dispute settlement mechanism. Problems with rules of origin have led to a revision that incorporates change in tariff headings and product specific rules.
5. ISEAS Concept Paper on the ASEAN Economic Community.
6. ASEAN-ISIS Report on Towards an ASEAN Economic Community.
7. Recommendations of the High-Level Task Force on ASEAN Economic Integration, annex to the Bali Concord II, 7 October 2003.
8. This section contains recommendations by the HLTF.
9. ASEAN may also use the 2+x approach where 2 member countries that are ready to integrate certain sectors can go ahead first. However this approach could be problematic as it does not require a consensus among all member countries (unlike the ASEAN minus X principle). The other concern is that the bilateral nature of this process could lead to a fait accompli where the third "plus X" country may be bound by whatever has already been agreed by the first 2 countries.
10. This section contains recommendations by the HLTF.
11. These are agro-based products, air travel, automobile products, e-ASEAN, electronics, fisheries, healthcare, rubber-based products, textiles and apparel, tourism, and wood-based products. In 2006, a twelfth priority sector, logistics, was added.
12. The Common Effective Preferential Tariff is the main instrument to implement AFTA.

13. Officials from ASEAN and EU have held three rounds of talks. Myanmar's poor human rights record might be a problem. The ASEAN-EU Vision Group has been given the mandate to study and submit recommendations on the future of ASEAN-EU economic relations including possibility of an ASEAN-EU FTA.

14. ASEAN will not apply Sections 15 and 16 of the Protocol of Accession of the PRC to the WTO and Paragraph 242 of the Report of the Working Party on the Accession of China to WTO.

15. The objectives of the Framework cover: strengthen economic integration through the creation of a comprehensive economic partnership (CEP); enhance the competitiveness of ASEAN and Japan in the world market through strengthened partnership and linkages; progressively liberalize and facilitate trade in goods and services as well as create a transparent and liberal investment regime; explore new areas and develop appropriate measures for further cooperation and economic integration; facilitate the more effective economic integration of CLMV and bridge the development gap among ASEAN members.

16. A stumbling block was Japan's proposed plan to remove trade barriers on more than 90 per cent of goods between the two sides. However, ASEAN proposed a 100 per cent tariff cut in all of the goods from the grouping to Japan, while seeking some exceptions in goods from Japan. ASEAN which has been in FTA talks with China, South Korea, Australia and New Zealand have created tariff-cutting frameworks in their respective negotiations. In those frameworks, the parties can unilaterally declare a limited number of items to be excluded from trade liberalization so that politically sensitive goods would be immune to drastic tariff reductions. But Japan does not want to adopt this practice and instead is seeking to discuss tariff elimination of each item by exchanging requests and offers.

17. Japan's prototype FTA/EPA was with Singapore and had negligible agricultural content. Agreement with Mexico allowed some access for Mexican pork in Japan but the agriculture issue will have to confronted more directly with the Philippines, Thailand, Indonesia and Korea.

18. In March 2006, the Japanese government decided to expedite FTA negotiation process by changing its policy of giving priority to conclude EPA over an FTA, noting that an EPA negotiation is more time-consuming as it is more comprehensive and include investment, intellectual property and dispute settlement issues. Japan was prompted to speed up the process, after China signed a deal with ASEAN, while Korea reached a basic agreement.

19. Negotiations have also been stalled by Thailand's political crisis, as the current government has no mandate to make decisions after the 2 April snap polls were annulled.

20. The Kaesong Industrial Complex is jointly run by South and North Korea. It

has figured highly in all of South Korea's FTA negotiations since the complex went into operation in 2004. South Korea wants to help North Korea open to the world and expand inter-Korean cooperation. But the matter causes problems because it conflicts with WTO regulations on tariff exemptions on goods produced in third countries. The 9 October 2006 North Korean nuclear test has occasioned a change in South Korea's policy towards the North and this would affect the Kaesong Industrial Complex.

21. It was reported that the United States preferred the bilateral track with Chile and Singapore and Australia preferred the multilateral track.

22. Negotiating problems centred on agriculture, services and investment. In particular, Chile faced resistance from large-scale agricultural landowners in the south, while New Zealand had technical and political problems finalizing its "negative list" on services.

23. Malcolm Cook and Allan Gyngell, "How to save APEC?", *Policy Briefs*, Lowy Institute for International Policy, 14 October 2005.

24. Goh Chok Tong, "Towards an East Asian Renaissance", Address at the opening session of the Fourth Asia-Pacific Roundtable organized by the Global Foundation, the World Bank and the Institute of Southeast Asian Studies, Singapore, 6 February 2006.

25. See Andrew Elek and Hadi Soesastro, "Ecotech at the heart of APEC: Capacity-building in the Asia Pacific", in *Asia Pacific Economic Cooperation (APEC): Challenges and tasks for the twenty-first century*, edited by Ippei Yamazawa (London: Routledge, 2000), pp. 218–54.

26. See Neantro Saavedra-Rivano, "Options for APEC Reform", paper presented at the International Conference "APEC Reforms and Evolving Trends: New Ideas for Materializing Busan Roadmap and Making Hanoi Plan" organized by the Vietnamese Academy of Social Sciences (VASS), Ha Noi, 27–28 April 2006.

References

ASEAN Secretariat website. McKinsey & Co, *ASEAN Competitiveness Study* (March 2003).

ASEAN Secretariat website. Documents and press releases of ASEAN Plus One and ASEAN Plus Three meetings.

Chia, Siow Yue. "Current Developments of FTAs in East Asia". Draft paper for the Joint Expert Group on the Feasibility Study of the East Asia Free Trade Area, 2005*a*.

———. "Regional Trading Arrangements and the Multilateral Trading System". Background paper prepared for the International Trade Center, 2005*b*.

Cook. Malcom and Allan Gyngell. "How to save APEC?". *Policy Briefs*, Lowy Institute for International Policy, 14 October 2005.

Elek, Andrew and Hadi Soesastro, "Ecotech at the heart of APEC: capacity-building in the Asia Pacific". In *Asia Pacific Economic Cooperation (APEC): Challenges and tasks for the twenty-first century*, edited by Ippei Yamazawa, pp. 218–54. London: Routledge, 2000.

Goh Chok Tong. "Towards an East Asian Renaissance". Address at the opening session of the Fourth Asia-Pacific Roundtable organized by the Global Foundation, the World Bank and the Institute of Southeast Asian Studies, Singapore, 6 February 2006.

Hew, Denis, ed. *Roadmap to an ASEAN Economic Community*. Singapore: Institute of Southeast Asian Studies, 2005.

Tay, Simon, Jesus Estanislao and Hadi Soeasastro, eds. *Reinventing ASEAN*. Singapore: Institute of Southeast Asian Studies, 2001.

The Contributors

Vinod K. Aggarwal is a Professor of Political Science at Haas School of Business, serving as the Chairman of the Political Economy of Industrial Societies Program from 1991 to 1994. He is also the Director of the Berkeley Asia Pacific Economic Cooperation Study Centre at the University of Berkeley California and is a lifetime member of the Council of Foreign Relations. He has previously been a Professor at the Graduate Institute of International Studies, Geneva and has been a Research Fellow at the Brookings Institution, the East West Center and the Woodrow Wilson International Center for Scholars. A consultant to various multinational corporations, Professor Aggarwal is also a consultant to the Mexican Government, U.S. Department of Commerce, WTO, OECD and the World Bank. Having contributed papers to various publications and authoring several books, Professor Aggarwal's most recent publication covers bilateral trade agreements in the Asia-Pacific. He is a graduate of the University of Michigan and received his M.A. and Ph.D. in international political economy from Stanford University.

C. Fred Bergsten has been director of the Institute for International Economics since its creation in 1981. He was assistant secretary for international affairs of the U.S. Treasury during 1977–81. He also functioned as undersecretary for monetary affairs during 1980–81, representing the United States on the G-5 Deputies and in preparing G-7 summits. During 1969–71, starting at age 27, he co-ordinated U.S. foreign economic policy in the White House as assistant for international economic affairs to Dr Henry Kissinger at the National Security Council. Dr Bergsten has been a senior fellow at the Brookings Institution (1972–76), Carnegie Endowment for International Peace (1981), and the Council on Foreign Relations (1967–68). He was chairman of the Eminent Persons Group of the Asia Pacific Economic Cooperation (APEC) forum from 1993 to 1995, authoring its three reports that recommended "free and open trade in the region by 2010 and 2020" as adopted at the APEC summits in 1993 and 1994. He was a member of the two leading commissions on reform of the international monetary system: the Independent Task Force on The Future International Financial Architecture, sponsored by the Council on Foreign Relations (1999), and the International Financial Institutions Advisory Commission created by Congress (2000, on which he led the dissenting minority). He received his M.A., M.A.LD, and Ph.D. degrees from the Fletcher School of Law and Diplomacy and a B.A. magna cum laude and honorary Doctor of Humane Letters from Central Methodist College.

Chia Siow Yue is a Research Associate with several international and regional organizations including Singapore Institute of International Affairs. Formerly professor of economics at the National University of Singapore and retired as Director of the Institute of Southeast Asian Studies in October 2002, she also serves as Regional Coordinator of the East Asian Development Network since 1998. With a Ph.D. in Economics from McGill University, she has published extensively, with over 150 books and journal and professional articles. She specializes in international trade, regional cooperation and international political economy.

Charles E. Morrison has been president of the East West Center since 1 August 1998. In September 2005, he was elected international chair of the Pacific Economic Cooperation Council (PECC). He is a founding member of the U.S. Asia Pacific Council, the U.S. National Committee for Pacific Economic Cooperation and a member of the U.S. Committee for Security Cooperation in Asia Pacific. He is a past chair of the U.S. National Consortium of APEC Study Centres. A former director of the Centre's Program on International Economics and Politics, he is a former U.S. Senate aide and a research adviser to binational Japan-U.S. commissions. He holds a Ph.D. in international relations from Johns Hopkins School of Advanced International Studies.

Robert Scollay is Associate Professor and Director of APEC Study Centre at the University of Auckland and is an active member of Pacific Economic Cooperation Council's trade network. He has also spent time as a visiting scholar at the Institute for International Economics, UNCTAD in Geneva, Institute of Southeast Asian Studies in Singapore, Bocconi University, Milan and Universidad del Pacifico in Lima. Specializing in issues relating to regional trade agreements and regional integration in the Asia Pacific region, Professor Scollay has done consulting for the World Bank, UNCTAD, Inter-American Development Bank, Commonwealth Secretariat and the Pacific Islands Forum. He was educated at Victoria and Auckland Universities in New Zealand and at Cambridge University in England.

Sheng Bin is a Professor at APEC Study Centre, Nankai University, China and has been Senior Researcher at the Institute of International Economics since November 2003. He was formerly a visiting scholar at the Copenhagen Business School in Denmark and Helsinki Business Polytechnic and Seinajoki Polytechnic in Finland. He specializes in international trade and political economics and has published many books and articles including *Political Economy of APEC Development* (Tianjin, 2005) and *WTO and Multilateral Agreement of Investment* (Tianjin, 2003). In 2004, Professor Sheng was awarded the Research Award by the HuoYingdong Education Foundation. He has a Ph.D in Economics from Nankai University.

Hadi Soesastro is the Executive Director and Senior Economist at the Center for Strategic and International Studies in Jakarta and a member of the National Economic Council and is on the international advisory boards of various international institutions including The Asia Society in New York and the Pacific Economic Cooperation Council. He has lectured at national universities and at Columbia University, New York and is also an Adjunct Professor at the Research School of Pacific Asian Studies. He has edited and authored numerous publications and has been actively contributing to "track two" activities with PECC, CSCAP and CAEC. He earned his Ph.D. from the Rand Graduate School in California.

Sherry M. Stephenson is the Acting Director of the Department of Trade, Tourism and Competitiveness at the Organization of American States (OAS) and is an active member of the Pacific Economic Cooperation Council's trade network. She previously served as Adviser to the Ministry of Trade, Government of Indonesia in Jakarta and has held positions within the GATT Secretariat in Geneva and with the Trade Directorate, OECD in Paris. Also having done consulting work for the World Bank, Asian Development Bank, APEC and several national governments, Dr Stephenson has taught at George Mason University and has published many reports on trade policy particularly on services and standards. She has an M.A. in Economics from New York University and a Ph.D. from the University of Geneva, Switzerland.

Shujiro Urata is Professor of Economics at Graduate School of Asia-Pacific Studies, Waseda University, Research Fellow at Japan Center for Economic Research, and Faculty Fellow at Research Institute of Economy, Trade and Industry in Tokyo. He specializes in international economics and economics of development. He has held a number of research and advisory positions including senior adviser to the Government of Indonesia, consultant to the World Bank, OECD, the Asian Development Bank, and the Government of Japan. He has also published and edited a number of books on international economic issues in English and Japanese, including *Winning in Asia, Japanese Style: Market and Nonmarket Strategies for Success* (Palgrave, 2002), *Competitiveness, FDI and Technological Activity in East Asia* (Edward Elgar, 2003). He is a graduate of Keio University, and holds M.A. and Ph.D in economics from Stanford University.

Index